DJ and wri̶ ̶ ̶ ̶ ̶ ̶ ̶ ̶ ̶ ̶ ̶ g debut at the Hacienda in 1986. He pl̶ ̶ ̶ ̶ ̶ ̶ ̶ ̶ ̶ almost five hundred times, ꞌuding on the final night of the club in 1997. Laurent Garnier, Brown, Tim Burgess, Justin Robertson, and the Chemical ꞌrothers were regular visitors to Haslam's ground-breaking ꞌJing events at the Hacienda, and all have credited Haslam as n inspiration.

is journalism has appeared in *NME*, the *Guardian* and ny more. His first book, *Manchester, England*, a cultural ꞌraphy of Manchester, was published in 1999. On World k Day in 2003 *Manchester, England* was declared one of ̶e ten books that best represent England (alongside books by ꞌremy Paxman, Zadie Smith and George Monbiot). His latest ꞌok, *Life After Dark: A History of British Nightclubs & lusic Venues*, was published in 2015.

Sonic Youth
Slept On My Floor

Music, Manchester, and More

A memoir

Dave Haslam

CONSTABLE

CONSTABLE

First published in Great Britain in 2018 by Constable
This paperback edition published in 2019 by Constable

1 3 5 7 9 10 8 6 4 2

A CIP catalogue record for this book is available from the British Library.

ISBN: 978-1-47212-751-8

Typeset in Sabon by SX Composing DTP, Rayleigh, Essex
Printed and bound in Great Britain by Clays Ltd, Elcograf S.p.A

Papers used by Constable are from well-managed forests
and other responsible sources.

Constable
An imprint of
Little, Brown Book Group
Carmelite House
50 Victoria Embankment
London EC4Y 0DZ

An Hachette UK Company
www.hachette.co.uk

www.littlebrown.co.uk

To my parents, with love and gratitude.

Contents

'Fear not for the future, weep not for the past'

Percy Bysshe Shelley, poet

'Be normal/Be unusual'

Pete Shelley, poet

1

A Bag Of Cassettes

A former Poet Laureate, Andrew Motion, wrote that what he enjoys most in a biography is information about ordinary matters, such as haircuts. I have all the encouragement I need. Already I'm thinking about one particular haircut, and the circumstances surrounding it.

It was the mid-1980s. I was in my early twenties, with a deep desire to meet interesting people, especially musicians, artists, writers. I'd been bewitched by the world of great music and electrifying ideas since my early teens.

I had started a fanzine called *Debris*. From the late 1970s to the mid-1980s, there were hundreds of fanzines: small, independent magazines, usually photocopied on A4 or A5, in which writers – often just one person, an enthusiast and an early adopter, or a small crew – would evangelise about music that wasn't widely appreciated.

I had a little gang of mates, but I didn't know anyone in 'the media'; there was never an option to write for a 'proper magazine'. I didn't know who to phone. I carried with me a plastic bag full of cassettes, and a heart full of dreams.

I was floundering a little, but I expected one day not to be. I was under the impression that somehow, as you got older, things became easier; you'd feel comfortable in your skin, untroubled by anxiety. I expected to find a map of where to find happiness. Ask me now, and I'll tell you: there is no map. But I always had music through the good times and the bad. I understand this from Maya Angelou: 'Music was my refuge. I could crawl into the space between the notes and curl my back to loneliness.'

In 1985, I was a regular customer at the Haçienda, a club in Manchester that had been opened by Factory Records and New Order three years earlier and featured mostly, but not only, live music. In the early years, some gigs were busy and there was sometimes a queue, but many events, including a 'Club Zoo' night featuring a secret Teardrop Explodes appearance, were attended by just a few dozen people.

I was queuing outside the club once – it was a night Cabaret Voltaire were playing – and I saw *NME* journalist Paul Morley walk to the front of the queue. He had a confident stride, a long coat and a lovely, striking girl on his arm. It was Claudia Brücken from the group Propaganda; I think Paul and Claudia were engaged to be married at the time.

Prior to the opening of the Haçienda, the prevailing look of British nightclubs and discotheques included swirly-patterned, cigarette-singed and drink-sodden carpets, and a desperate and usually not very well-executed attempt at glitz involving yards of chrome and maybe a few plastic palm trees.

Factory called on the services of Ben Kelly, who had designed the facade of the Seditionaries shop for Vivienne Westwood and Malcolm McLaren. His Haçienda design made a feature of the ex-warehouse's look. There were no carpets and no attempt at glitz.

Inspiration for the Haçienda came from the look and concept of New York venues like Danceteria and the Mudd Club. Tony Wilson, the co-founder of Factory Records, explained the club would be a 'videotech' and two large screens were installed either side of the stage. The video operator in the early days was Claude Bessy. Claude spliced, cut up and compiled idiosyncratic film montages, all on slightly wobbly VHS. These were projected onto the screens. He favoured shots of dancing girls, Nazi rallies and air disasters, and clips from films by the likes of Luis Buñuel and Kenneth Anger. It was the least MTV-ish video selection imaginable.

I'd be in the Haçienda to see the bands but also often to sell the fanzine. I took a pile of them out most nights. I'd walk around venues badgering the crowd at gigs by the likes of Orange Juice, the Fall and the Smiths, and start by trying to sell them to the queue. A few people would regularly volunteer to help me. There were a couple of girls who used to sell loads of them: Carol Morley, who went on to become an award-winning filmmaker, and Janet, who became a sex therapist.

Andrew Berry ran a hairdressing salon called Swing on week-days in the basement of the Haçienda. His haircutting business wasn't a nine-to-five operation; he would close Swing for the day, on a whim, or turn up three hours late. You wouldn't expect to make an appointment. Friends of Andrew's such as Johnny Marr would drop by for a haircut. Genesis P-Orridge from the group Psychic TV was a visitor. Multiple conversations would ensue. You willingly gave up half your day if you wanted a haircut at Swing.

A guy called Neil worked alongside Andrew, and two girls were employed too: Tracey and Heather. Swing would advertise in *Debris*, but Andrew's adverts were curious. He wanted me to put in a big photo of Charles Manson with 'Hair by Swing' as the strapline. I wasn't 100 per cent sure Charlie Manson was the right person to represent Andrew's salon. It wasn't just that he was a nutcase and a murderer but also Manson's hair was a mess. Andrew backed down and said he'd come up with a new idea. The next day, he gave me a picture of William Shatner playing Captain Kirk, which he had doctored by drawing a swastika on Shatner's face. As a piece of PR I wasn't convinced that this was an improvement, but I needed that £40 for the full-page ad.

Andrew and his Swing contingent weren't the only people I knew who worked at the Haçienda in the early days. Susan Ferguson, my housemate and best mate, worked behind the bar. I knew Sue because we'd been to school together in Birmingham and then both moved up to study at the University of Manchester in 1980. She got a job at the Haçienda two years before I got a regular DJ job there. She was far more sociable than me, had a fantastic smile, and lots of people would take a shine to her. We had a hundred mutual interests and we looked after each other.

The first time I met Mark E. Smith, I was introduced to him as a friend of Sue Ferguson's and it was the same when I met Terry Hall. She particularly enjoyed the shifts she worked alongside Glen and Brendan in the Haçienda's cocktail bar – the Gay Traitor, as it was called. I'd be bored some evenings and get the bus into town and take Sue a snack or a gift.

4

I remember one time being stopped at the door and having to explain my mission to one of the doormen. 'It's Dave from *Debris*,' I explained. 'I've come to bring a banana to one of your staff.' I showed him the banana. He let me in.

In addition to cutting hair, Andrew was also a DJ. He used to DJ at the Haçienda, usually under the name Marc Berry; he'd be employed to play records before and after bands, and I'd go stand with him in the DJ box to watch the bands. Overlooking the dancefloor, and with a great view of the stage, the DJ box was only accessible from a corridor running from the back of the balcony down to the main bar. Next door was another wooden box, where the lighting boys sat, and that's also where the videos were operated from. The door into the DJ box was similar to the kind you might find in a stable; the top half could be opened (inwards) but you could lock the bottom half of the door. (The DJ box will be the site of several episodes later in this book, including one featuring a naked girl and another featuring a man with a gun.)

Andrew had three things I didn't have: a girlfriend, a successful business and a busy social life. Some evenings he was too busy or simply couldn't be bothered to do his DJing, so he'd call me and I'd fill in for him. It was never discussed with the Haçienda management. I enjoyed the challenge of finding the right selection of music to help build up expectation before a live set, and then choosing something to play immediately the band had finished in the hope that, instead of leaving, some of the audience would stay, have a drink, improve the bartake and maybe even get on the dancefloor.

The Haçienda was ahead of its time. It was on the outskirts of town and, like most pioneering ideas, on the edge of culture.

Being on the edge of culture wasn't much help commercially. On plenty of occasions, taxi drivers would respond to my request to go to the Haçienda with 'The where? The Hassy-what?' That it wasn't in the public eye made no difference to me – in fact, I liked that it was semi-secret. The notion of having a high profile wasn't imaginable or even interesting.

Tony Wilson was probably the one person who imagined, and chased, the idea of the club having historical significance. A graduate of Cambridge University and a presenter on Granada TV, he was a strong-willed visionary and an amazing propagandist for all things Factory and Manchester. He had numerous qualities and quirks. He was fond of saying that Shaun Ryder was as great a poet as W. B. Yeats (Tony studied Yeats in his third year at Cambridge). One of his favourite words was 'praxis', which he especially enjoyed using in front of audiences who weren't likely to understand it. He was always far more interested in the big picture rather than the detail. Instead of worrying exactly what music the DJs were playing, he'd be paying more attention to nurturing the 'aura' and feeding the mythology.

The prevailing ethos of Factory, as I understood it, was to be different and not to chase dollars. I assumed this from the moment I first bought records released by the label and first walked through the doors of the club, way before I became a DJ there. There was no point doing the Haçienda if it was the same as everywhere (or even anywhere) else. DJs were appointed who relished adventuring beyond the obvious. Once we were given the chance, we were left to our own devices.

I only ever had one conversation with Tony Wilson about the music I was playing. One Thursday, he knocked on the door of the DJ box with a record in his hand. He had just come back from London and a record company had given him a promo pre-release of a twelve-inch single, which he was dutifully delivering to me as one of his DJs. After taking it out of the brown manila mailer he was carrying it in, he looked at the record, looked at me, and said, 'Do we play reggae, Dave?'

'No, Tony, not really,' I said.

'Thought not,' he said, gave me the record anyway, and then moseyed on downstairs towards the bar.

The owners and management would no more tell the Haçienda DJs what to play than tell Bez what to wear or Bernard from New Order what he should sing about. We never had meetings about the music the DJs should play; we just got on with it, we did what we felt was right.

We just trusted our instincts. *Debris* wasn't part of a grand plan and it was the same when it came to choosing what music to play when I was behind the decks at the Haçienda. Afterwards, I might rationalise why I did things in a certain way. That's when I learned what Tony meant by praxis.

Among Tony's ambitions for the club was for it to make a significant contribution to Manchester, and not just to its music scene, but to its sense of identity and self-worth too. He explained that one of its aims was 'to restore a sense of place'. It was always about more than music; it was about ideas, art, fashion, cities, communities, life.

In due course, Tony's ambitions would be achieved. In the last four years of the 1980s, the Haçienda helped to power the astonishing surge in Manchester's music scene. The city's transformation was so conspicuous that Manchester was redefined and dubbed 'Madchester'.

In the late 1980s, I watched from the DJ box as the Haçienda grew in intensity, the music evolved and electronic dance music exploded. The club became internationally known, bands like the Stone Roses and Happy Mondays became hit makers. In July 1990, *Newsweek* devoted a front-cover feature to Madchester and the Haçienda. Manchester is a 'dank industrial center, 185 miles north of London, once known for high unemployment and sandwiches made of French fries and butter,' the magazine explained, before announcing in ultra-excitable tones that a new movement had broken loose in the city. It quoted Danny Kelly, deputy editor of *NME*, declaring, 'This is the most important music since punk.' Activities at the Haçienda were also discussed in British broadsheet and tabloid newspapers, the influential French arts/music magazine *Les Inrockuptibles* (*Les Inrocks*) and the *Chicago Tribune* (which reported from 'England's music capital' on 'the abundance of mild hallucinogens' in the club).

But back in 1985, to anyone sitting in Swing or even queuing waiting for a Cabaret Voltaire gig, there was no awareness of history being made. I was working one day a week at a clothes stall called Identity in Affleck's Palace. I was a fanzine editor living off a diet of John Peel, the *NME* and sandwiches made of French fries and butter. Far from chasing blue plaques or a place in the history books, in the mid-1980s the attitude among most of my friends was let's get up in the morning (or the afternoon) and do something that makes us feel alive. Like getting my head shaved.

I was living on Great Western Street in Moss Side, just around the corner from an all-night club called the Reno. There, one of the most played albums was an electro hip-hop compilation called *Crew Cuts*, and certain tracks from it were played else-where too to the extent that it was inescapable as 1984 slid into 1985. The vinyl included Nuance 'Take A Chance' and Malcolm X 'No Sell Out'. The front cover featured a photo of two shaved scalps. The time was right to take all my hair off.

Apart from the first seven or eight years of my life, when my hair fell straight and benefited from a parting, until 1985 it had always been bushy. It was softer than an afro, but wiry and light brown. As with other things, this hair ran in the family, specifically my mother's family, but where exactly these curls came from was a bit of a mystery. My mother came from a family of Methodists, and she could trace her family line a few generations back to West Bromwich in the West Midlands. Her great-grandfather was a baker on the High Street and a director of West Bromwich Albion FC in the 1890s.

I guess the softness of the curls could have been the result of some Jewish ancestry; I've heard people talk of a 'Jew-fro'. It's also possible that there is some Caribbean connection somewhere buried in the family. Occasionally there would be a family discussion about all this and my mother would look at my curly hair, shake her similarly curly head of hair, and tell me, using a phrase you stopped hearing in the 1980s, that I'd inherited 'a touch of the tar brush'.

My head of soft curls was never fashionable, in any scene, in any sense, in any era, ever. Through my curly teenage years, the only person who shared my haircut was Art Garfunkel. He had a higher forehead, but I remember seeing Art Garfunkel in Nicolas Roeg's film *Bad Timing* and that was my hair he was wearing.

So, late one morning in Swing, Andrew and Neil stood behind me, supportive and excited. They were adamant I was doing the right thing. I guess they were thinking this; if we can persuade him to put a photo of William Shatner defaced with a swastika in his fanzine then we can persuade him to have all his hair shaved off.

It was shorn, totally, down to the scalp. A big moment: the years of the curls were over. They shaved the sides down to the scalp first, and then we stopped for a discussion about that week's *NME*. I'd gone from Art Garfunkel to Travis Bickle of *Taxi Driver* in less than ten minutes.

Andrew and Neil completed the job. I took to the new look well and when the hair had grown a millimetre or two, I liked the feel of it when I, or someone else, stroked it. It worked well with my clothes too. I didn't wear jeans much. I wore black trousers and a jacket, usually dating from the 1940s or 1950s and bought second-hand from Oxfam or the Salvation Army. With my head shaved, in my more deluded moments, I thought I had the look of the Russian poet Vladimir Mayakovsky. I developed an obsession with him that lasted for at least three weeks, long enough for me to include a full-page photo of him in an early issue of *Debris*.

Some people grow up admiring Jim Morrison and basing their look on him. Guys dress like Liam Gallagher (and walk like Liam Gallagher). I had some offbeat role models. I make no apology. It's how I was; full of fanciful ideas.

I was idealistic. I had marched carrying a 'Rock Against Racism' placard in the late 1970s and danced to 'Free Nelson Mandela'. In the mid-1980s I wore a 'Coal Not Dole' sticker on my coat and organised two benefit gigs for striking miners. I liked hanging out with other people with fanciful ideas or, better still, people who wanted to change the world. Boys with earrings who liked Tarkovsky films or were in a band, or both. Girl poets on 'Reclaim the Night' marches who looked like Siouxsie Sioux or Patti Smith, who had a girl-crush on Anna Karina, maybe, or Valerie Solanas, or both.

Years after I no longer had Art Garfunkel's haircut, I was mistaken for Fatboy Slim a few times. In 1998, I got semi-mobbed at the first Creamfields when I was walking across the field carrying my record box. I also had a few months of looking a little bit like Neil Tennant. I once got a postcard from someone who was in a band in the early 1990s – he always wanted to be famous and he never was – on which he wrote, 'Hey Dave, I knew you would get on *Top of the Pops* before me.' I've never found out who he had mixed me up with: Neil Tennant or Fatboy Slim. Maybe someone else. Whatever was going on, it wasn't me on *Top of the Pops*, not that I ever told him that. Sometimes I think it's OK to pretend to be someone you're not.

In *The Falling*, one of Carol Morley's films, one of the characters declares; 'We are all three people. The person we think we are. The person other people see. And the person we really are.' That might be right, but these things are fluid. If we are three people, all these identities change, grow, develop or regress. There's a relationship between who I am now and the twenty-three-year-old me. Perhaps one day I'll work out exactly what it is.

Self-knowledge, though, is hard to attain. On some level you can get it as wrong as a clubber at Creamfields. You can mistake yourself for someone else. Thirty years later I was talking to Tracey Donnelly about my trips to Swing. I told her that I felt a bit reserved, shy, when I was there, a bit out of my depth. 'No, definitely not shy,' said Tracey. 'I was always a bit in awe of you as I knew you were clever and you were confident. I think we were all kind of different and eccentric maybe in our own way. It was as if we were all part of a gang . . .'

Certainly, we're not always the best judge of who we are; we delude ourselves with wishful thinking (or, as Wittgenstein said, 'Nothing is so difficult as not deceiving oneself.'). We persuade ourselves that we're doing stuff right, or we go the other way and do ourselves down, not seeing our own qualities. And, as a result, a part of us never blossoms.

We're all likely to be guilty of wrong perceptions. The person we have down as aloof and standoffish is insecure. The person who laughs a lot turns out to be lonely a lot. But then it's hard to be sure of people's perceptions of you either; it's not something you can control.

In any case, who we are is not fixed for life. So many encounters and events have an impact on us, disturb us, energise us or knock us into a new phase – great holidays, bad drugs, new neighbours, the death of a parent, birth of a child, watching the trauma of 9/11 unfold on the television – but, in addition, you can also will yourself into a new version. For example, you can teach yourself to swerve situations that might bring you down. In social situations, we make small adjustments, learning to adapt behaviour to improve relationships. Reflecting this, T. S. Eliot talks of preparing 'a face to meet the faces that we meet'. These temporary changes we can make permanent. Our identities are fragile, which gives us opportunities to reinvent ourselves, to change, perhaps even to 'create' ourselves.

John Taylor of Duran Duran is one endearing and instructive

example of how to make the changes we feel we need to make. When I interviewed him, I was very taken with one particular part of John's life story: the way he reinvented himself to find himself. This was when he was in his mid-teens, known by his birthname Nigel, wearing spectacles and massively into music. He swapped his spectacles for contact lenses and began to call himself John. It was a process to becoming someone else; not a fake version, but a step on the route to becoming a person he wanted be.

I now wonder if the severe haircut Andrew gave me that day in 1985 was my version of Nigel becoming John, part of some sort of reinvention to help me push on towards a new start or a new chapter, a re-creation, a transformation. I also now wonder if it was related to the news I was absorbing at the time, that my mother was ill. Head shaving is a tradition of mourning in some cultures. It could have been something to do with anxiety, me feeling some kind of pre-grief.

My mother had breast cancer and, after a brief respite when it looked like the cancer had disappeared, her health deteriorated rapidly. She was bedridden by October 1985. She was uncomfortable, ill, and she was never going to get better. My dad, like so many men of his generation, didn't cook or launder but he was doing his best looking after the house. They were both churchgoers and they seemed to take comfort from their beliefs and their network of friends from the church. People stopped by; guests, well-wishers, my mother's best friends. They would gather in her bedroom and my dad would make cups of tea.

I'd go down on the train from Manchester to Birmingham New Street or take the coach to Digbeth Coach Station. During one of the last visits to the family home before she moved to a hospice, I watched my dad doing his best for her while my mum made every attempt to catch my eye, smiling at me through her pain. She spent all day and night in her bedroom. Ten years or so earlier, my grandfather had moved in with us in the last months of his life, and we'd installed a TV in the room. Next to the TV, there was a silver carriage clock. The clock was tarnished on one side, and had stopped. It hadn't been rewound, repaired or replaced. I remember watching the clock all through this visit and wishing it would miraculously start ticking again.

During my visits home, I didn't really take it all in. Perhaps it's always like this when someone close to you is dying; part of your brain shuts down, some form of denial kicks in, your imagination can't comprehend a world without them. None of us in the family were facing up to what was going on. None of us were saying the unsayable until close to the end, when my mother had been in the hospice a week and my uncle said, 'She's going to die, isn't she?' And she did, one Saturday morning, in December 1985.

Do you ever process such an experience? I've had to deal with deaths and a traumatic relationship break-up, but I know somewhere there's a part of me that has never accepted the reality of what happened; part of me thinks, it's a mistake, I can press rewind, relive the moments and somehow create a happy ending. Words help, time helps, but there's a legacy to these traumas, a persistent heartache that never leaves you.

I didn't give myself enough time or space to consider what my mother's death meant to me, or to my father, my brother, my sister. I was immersed in my own small world. I worked at

Identity on Fridays. I'd be going to see films at a cinema called the Aaben in Hulme and gigs in town.

Debris had become a kind of mission. Mostly I was trying to uncover music, films and books that were worth celebrating and sharing, but also I realised that there are huge parts of our lives that are under-documented. So, I also wrote about what I thought of as 'real-life stuff'. I interviewed the woman who ran the launderette on Moss Lane East and a newsagent on Princess Road. Over the period of a month, I visited a trio of seventy-year-old barbers who had been working in the city centre for decades, and I wrote up short interviews with each of them.

I devoted space in *Debris* to my enthusiasms, even the esoteric ones. I liked the idea that an interview with a newsagent would appear alongside an appreciation of Tarkovsky, an interview with Sonic Youth, a discussion of the merits of the cheese on toast at the Alesia café on Newton Street and a story from an old barber about the time he cut Matt Busby's hair in 1947. These things all add up, don't they? To something bigger? Maybe something significant?

At twenty-three, I had no ambition in the sense of wanting to make a ton of money or own a house or a big car. I had a vague hope that maybe one day I would walk to the front of the queue at the Haçienda with a striking girl on my arm and get my name ticked off the guest list. My only definite plan was to write about what I wanted to write about, and to make sure a barber took his clippers to my hair once a fortnight.

So, in one way I wanted nothing much: I was happy adventuring in music and the world of ideas. But on another level, I wanted everything. In 1985 I believed if you read lots, went to see as many arthouse films as you could, listened to John Peel and spent your days and nights listening to music, thinking and writing, you could eventually make sense of the world. I really thought that. I really did.

2

You Ain't Seen Nothing Yet

I have an older sister who initiated a Thursday evening ritual of gathering the family around the TV to watch *Top of the Pops*. During the chart rundown, we would cheer our favourites and boo the others. You didn't have to like everything, you could pick and choose.

In the early years of the 1970s, Motown was everywhere. *The Jackson 5ive* was a kids' TV cartoon series featuring various adventures of the Jackson 5. You'd go to the fair and you'd ride the dodgems or you'd be whirled around on the waltzers while the Motown sound spilled from tinny fairground speakers. At the football, you'd be listening to Motown blaring out before the game. Summer afternoons in the park, someone close by would have a transistor radio and it would be playing the Supremes, the Four Tops, 'Tears of a Clown'.

As I got older, I still appreciated Motown, but I was also being drawn to music that was in your face, sheen-free, rougher, frazzled. On the cusp of becoming a teenager, I discovered Black

Sabbath. I'm trying to think why even the best Motown wasn't enough for me any more. Maybe it was connected with the way the body rules the mind when testosterone starts pulsing through a young man and I was looking for a soundtrack to all that. If you'd asked me in 1974, I'd probably have told you my favourite records were 'Paranoid', 'Whole Lotta Love' and 'Silver Machine'.

Birmingham was very much a heavy-metal town. The pre-dominant youth tribe were the rockers. The 1970s were very tribal and music was the key to everything about identity. Your choice of music dictated what you wore; clothes were a marker, a badge and, sometimes, a provocation.

As well as the heavy-metal kids, the Rastas were also conspicuous on the streets and reggae basslines reverberated around Handsworth and Balsall Heath. Then there was disco; at my youth club, we had an evening out to see *Car Wash*.

I absorbed all these genres, threads and varieties of music, and wanted to hear more. By the time I was sixteen, I was a big fan of the Pop Group. Their music was everything I wanted music to be: punk, be-bop, reggae, incendiary, angular, fizzing with life.

The older generations in my family definitely enjoyed music but no one had an obsession. My father was a solicitor for many years before deciding in the mid-1970s to walk away from the law and train for priesthood. My mother worked at home bringing up us kids; she'd had various jobs before my parents married. She listened to music most of the day, but she was primarily a Radio 3 person who loved Elgar and Tchaikovsky. My parents had met in the mid-1950s – their family homes were just around the corner from each other in Harborne.

I have an older sister and a younger brother, and for some of my childhood, mostly between the ages of five and twelve, my parents fostered too. Social services would phone and a child, or two siblings, would arrive at our door a few hours or a day later. The kids would be temporarily fostered with us for a variety of reasons: sometimes the mother was trying to escape domestic abuse, or she was in hospital or in jail (there weren't many fathers around). Occasionally the kids would be tiny babies, but usually they'd be only just a bit younger than us and we'd treat them just like a brother or sister. We would argue and play football or hide-and-seek with them, and they would come on family holidays – some of them had never been to a beach or the countryside.

In the space of five or six years, around thirty-five foster kids came into our home and our lives for anything between a few days and several months. Very occasionally, a parent visited. A father arrived one Sunday afternoon, and I could tell it was killing him that, whatever nightmare the family was going through, he was unable to care for his child. Just once or twice, we met up with a brother and sister after they'd left us – their whole family was living in a single rented room in Balsall Heath, trying desperately to keep things together. A different brother and sister – maybe five and seven years old – came on holiday with us and on the morning of the first day, their first visit to a beach, there was such a look of enchantment on their faces, overcome by the magic of the waves and the feel of the sand between their toes.

My parents' fostering gave me an insight into the lives of other children, their precarious, volatile home life, their distressing stories. I drew many lessons from the experience of knowing those kids, not least to value my stable family life, but also to never forget the heavy loads some people have to carry. They were among the most significant encounters I ever had.

My parents had become teenagers just as the Second World War ended and then left school during the years of rationing and austerity. Growing up in the 1950s wasn't quite as grey and constrained as some histories have had us believe, and it's arguable that the era had several advantages over our own; not least, secure jobs for life.

Their formative years were less than flexible; unlike my contemporaries, they didn't have the luxury nor the encouragement to pick and choose. Social pressures to conform were strong, and there was little acknowledgement that alternative lifestyles existed, let alone were possible. They got engaged for three years, during which time my father spent a year doing National Service. They saved for a flat, got married; by the time the Beatles and the Rolling Stones emerged my parents were thirty, with three kids under the age of five. They were part of the last of the pre-rock-and-roll generation.

I never asked them, but it's possible they looked on enviously as conventions loosened through the 1960s. The cliché is that the older you get, the more reactionary you become but, politically, my parents moved slightly to the left through the 1970s and into the 1980s. My mother's father was an accountant, and she married a lawyer, so she was not a natural candidate for rebellious political activity, but one Saturday in the early 1980s she took a coach down to Greenham Common and joined a women-only picket of the American airbase there; that day, thousands of women held hands around the six-mile perimeter of the base in protest against nuclear weapons.

My big sister usually led the cheers when Slade, Bowie and Rod Stewart and the Faces were on *Top of the Pops*. Most of her youth club peers were folkies; they started off liking Ralph McTell and then moved on to Neil Young (my younger brother is now also a massive Neil Young fan and follows him everywhere).

When I started secondary school, the older lads were into all sorts of rock, including Bachman–Turner Overdrive, Pink Floyd and, some of them, even Wishbone Ash. I was at King Edward's, a direct-grant, all-boys' school. In the sixth form, there were several joint activities – such as drama productions, and the end of year disco – with the adjacent girls' school, and some subjects, such as Economics, were taught to mixed classes.

The alumni at King Edward's were a rum selection: Enoch Powell, who was a fool and an embarrassment; J. R. R. Tolkien, who wrote *The Hobbit* and *The Lord of the Rings*; and Kenneth Tynan. My father's older sister had moved in the same school-age circles as Tynan, so his was a name I heard a lot in our house.

Ken Tynan had left King Edward's in 1945 and went on to become a theatre critic, feted for his role supporting ground-breaking drama, although he became much better known for supposedly being the first person to say 'fuck' on British television, during a live broadcast in 1965. In issue eighteen of *Debris*, I conducted an interview with his widow, Kathleen (Ken died in 1980). It appeared alongside interviews with Neneh Cherry and A Guy Called Gerald. We talked a little about the theatre, but mostly Kathleen and I discussed hedonism, pornography and adultery.

When I first read *NME*, which was probably around 1974, the 1960s generation was in charge, and they were adamant that the phenomena that had emerged during the previous decade – the Beatles, Carnaby Street, Woodstock – were the touchstones of all that could be good about rock and roll and popular culture. I was indignant that the sixties generation expected us younger kids to worship at the altar of their idols. I loved Jimi Hendrix, but I didn't want to be told I'd missed the boat and that some kind of golden age was over.

When the Sex Pistols first arrived, I didn't really get what or who they were. I came to understand them retrospectively, but to me they seemed like some sort of hype or fashion thing. I didn't think any of the music I heard by them was better than 'Paranoid'. The other new thing in 1976, the Ramones, had a simpler appeal; less threat than the Pistols, and more readily comprehensible to a fourteen-year-old.

By 1977, waves of music were washing over me and I was devouring books. I'd realised there were ways of seeing beyond the obvious, conspicuous stuff. I was aware that separate from conventional attitudes, and away from the school curriculum or the mainstream, there was an alternative world, maybe several, where you might find marginal and oppositional creative activity, underground newspapers, books, music, films.

Access was problematic. You couldn't easily get to see films you wanted to see, let alone stream them. Books were different; you could go and look in a library or a bookshop (I was a fan of second-hand bookshops), but even then some things were impossible to find. You'd hear about underground newspapers or comics, an amazing Robert Crumb cartoon, say, but all things Crumb-related would be somehow out of reach.

Now, the internet makes available to us films of all sorts, music from everywhere, books, photographs and information galore, but back in the late 1970s, the existence of some films and books was just a rumour. You'd have to imagine what *A Clockwork Orange* or *Scorpio Rising* were like. (Forty years later, I saw *Scorpio Rising* in a cinema in Paris and realised it was way beyond what I'd ever have been able to comprehend or imagine aged fourteen.) I was far from alone in feeling like I was denied access to alternative, cultural happenings. Pete Wylie was an habitué of the venue Eric's in Liverpool and the Probe record shop, mixing with a switched-on crowd, but he told me they were still asking each other, 'Have you seen *Eraserhead*? Do you know anyone who's seen *Eraserhead*? How can we see *Eraserhead*?'

I was fascinated by the idea of what was off the radar. I'd be sitting watching TV shows like *Are You Being Served?* or *It Ain't Half Hot Mum*, thinking there must be more to life than this. Thanks to my big sister and her friends, I had heard enough music to understand *Top of the Pops* wasn't the whole story and the world wasn't all Showaddywaddy. By extension, I decided that not all the realities and ideas out there were reflected on news programmes like *News at Ten* or *Nationwide*.

The mainstream acted as a kind of surface noise drowning out or at least distorting things that were difficult or taboo. There was shadowy stuff going on in Ireland, including collusion between the security services and loyalist paramilitaries, for example. Uncomfortable truths were being suppressed; the BBC bowed to government pressure and declined to show the Peter Watkins film *The War Game*. Secrets and lies were powering the Cold War and the nuclear arms race, and in the first half of the 1970s, the Watergate scandal illustrated how endemic deceit and cover-up were among the governing classes.

I looked for clues, and followed the rumours of where and what the counter culture might be; trying to decipher curious graffiti on walls, following outlandishly dressed young men and women, catching late-night films on TV like *Belle du Jour*, or seeing a BBC2 *Arena* show about the Chelsea Hotel in New York, its history and inhabitants.

In the search for weird ideas and cultural stimulation, you were blessed if there was an arthouse cinema a bus ride away – somewhere like the Arts Lab, housed in a former brewery on Holt Street, just outside Birmingham city centre. The venue offered an ambitious film programme that had a cineaste rather than commercial appeal, and, in addition, a magazine was produced that included listings and essays on forthcoming films. This was invaluable; a chance to see and learn more about the likes of *Lenny*, *Midnight Cowboy*, *Ashes and Diamonds* and *Les Quatre Cents Coups*. And, to spot in the listings, yes, at last: *Eraserhead*.

At fourteen, I'd already started going into town to see films and gigs, sometimes alone, sometimes with friends. I was in love with live music and, generally, when I was fourteen or fifteen I didn't mind much how I spent my £2 entrance money. In 1977, I went to see the new-wave doo-wop band Darts, whose singer Den Hegarty had a thing for clambering on the speaker stacks at the side of the stage (by far the highlight of the set). I saw the Stranglers and Steel Pulse at the Mayfair Suite, Dr Feelgood at the Odeon, Eddie and the Hot Rods at the Town Hall and the Clash at the Top Rank, and started going to a club, Barbarella's on Cumberland Street. One of the first gigs I saw there was Howard Devoto's Magazine in January 1978.

Barbarella's had a different demographic to the Arts Lab, but shared a sense of being an alternative community. A good gig would attract a gathering of like-minded people from across the city who otherwise might not know of each other's existence. Iggy Pop played there in May 1979, on the *New Values* tour. I felt excited and inspired to be among a crowd of weirdo music fans, seven hundred or so of us crammed under a low ceiling in the venue's live room. On that tour Iggy didn't have a great band with him but the gig still had an amazing sense of occasion. I saw Generation X at Barbarella's. They so disappointed me, I took refuge in the disco room next door. The DJ played 'Can You Feel the Force?' by the Real Thing. A realisation dawned: whatever rock bands I would pay to see, I'd still have one foot in the disco.

I was reading the *NME* and occasionally the other two weekly music papers too – *Sounds* and *Melody Maker* – a new generation of bands, and journalists, were making themselves heard. At last, my tribe was emerging: those of us too young for punk but thrilled by new, adventurous music, and less wedded to guitar thrash than punk had been. Like the Pop Group. By 1979 there were spiky, dubby, weirdo bands playing in venues in most towns and cities. I was then seventeen, an age when going to gigs seemed like one of the best things in the world.

A big attraction of post-punk was that much of the music wasn't detached from the wider world of ideas. To me, it was an attractive and educational thing that Joe Strummer of the Clash might be interested in the Spanish Civil War or Howard Devoto's lyrics in Magazine's 'A Song from Under the Floorboards' referenced the work of Russian writer Fyodor Dostoyevsky. Devoto was responsible for me scurrying off to a second-hand bookshop to buy Dostoyevsky's *Notes from Underground* to add to my burgeoning collection of Penguin Modern Classic paperbacks.

I loved diving headlong into anything in the *NME* written by two journalists particularly – Paul Morley and Ian Penman. Not everybody cared for the way they wrote, which could be convoluted at times and awash with theories, ideas and obscure points of reference. Often, I couldn't follow them but it didn't matter. The ambition mattered and the belief that music had a connection to big ideas, deep philosophy, great books and films.

I had an appetite for live music and despite not feeling the love for Generation X, I always felt that live music tasted the best at Barbarella's, even though it was in the middle of a derelict part of the city centre, down some half-lit street. Or maybe it was because of that.

I felt ultra-wary walking through town at night, especially if I was somewhere unfamiliar. In contrast to today's high-octane nightlife industry, towns and cities were virtually empty at night and being deserted made them feel less safe. It wasn't the viciousness, lawlessness and relentless turf wars of the Victorian age with peaky blinders or scuttlers running amok, but incidents of random street violence were high, including malevolent drunks battering weirdos.

In the late 1970s, Jayne Casey was in a band called Big in Japan, alongside Holly Johnson (before he was in Frankie Goes to Hollywood, of course). Her flamboyant crew of unashamed weirdos – which also included Pete Burns (before he was in Dead or Alive) – was often confronted on the street. She once told me, 'We attracted violence, every night, which was good; we hated the world and expected the world to hate us.'

On tour with Big in Japan and in unfamiliar surroundings, though, Jayne learned to be more cautious. 'I used to love Barbarella's. That was the best laid-out club, all the dark corners. But Birmingham at that time was a scary space. People were angry, and the punks got that, didn't they? In Birmingham punks couldn't get into pubs. All the lads would go out after the soundcheck or whatever, and me and Holly would just sit in the dressing room.'

Despite all this, there was a kind of romance to the ritual of walking across town from the 35 bus to Broad Street and on to Barbarella's, through the concrete underpasses, skirting deserted, unlit streets, passing an occasional chippy or a late-night café, turning off Broad Street surrounded by boarded-up workshops and factories, and along Cumberland Street. You'd see a clutch of unfriendly doormen, and then finally you'd be through the doors and arrive in a different world.

Most of our city centres have been transformed in a similar fashion to Birmingham. The boarded-up old industrial buildings around Broad Street have long gone, replaced by hotels, restaurants, a conference centre, a Bannatyne gym and, around Brindley Square and behind the Symphony Hall, blocks of apartments.

In the late 1970s cities like Birmingham, Manchester and Liverpool were pre-gentrification and post-war, post-industrial, post-everything; acres of dereliction. No one lived in luxury apartments in city centres, although lots of people lived in council flats in the inner city (not the same thing). For the dead spaces to live again, someone needed to make something happen there. The music scene became instrumental in this. In the late 1970s, musicians and music fans took advantage of uncontrolled, cheap spaces to create rehearsal rooms, recording studios, record shops and venues. Music lovers nationwide took to visiting empty or dodgy parts of town to find soul clubs or see inspiring bands.

I'd learned that if you knew where to look, you could take a walk along half-deserted streets and find your way to musical bliss. A month after my sixteenth birthday, I wandered through town to Barbarella's, to see Blondie.

3

Joy Division In A Mod Club

I had heard Blondie's 'Rip Her to Shreds' single, and seen the photos, read the reviews and become fascinated by Debbie Harry. I looked around for clues to Debbie Harry's world. The band were from New York, which connected with what I already knew about the Ramones, but then some further digging led me to Patti Smith and the scene at CBGBs. Then I heard 'Marquee Moon' by Television – probably near the end 1977. It was the first twelve-inch single I ever bought. I wasn't buying albums at this point and my vinyl 'collection' consisted of a dozen or so seven-inch singles.

Maybe it's just me, maybe I'm somehow too unsettled, but do we at various points carry this idea around: an obsession with some city somewhere, some other place? A wondrous place that could be home, should be home. New York, Berlin, Paris.

The music of Blondie, Television and Talking Heads opened up in my mind a beguiling version of New York; *Mean Streets* and *Taxi Driver*, Patti Smith, the Velvet Underground, and an abiding interest in Andy Warhol – the Factory and his films, his art and his superstars like Edie Sedgwick.

Debbie Harry and Iggy Pop were pop stars from afar but I was also beginning to pick up on a sense of culture and potential closer to home. John Peel and *NME* were talking about acts recording and releasing their own music. These acts were from all over: Glasgow, London, Manchester, Liverpool. Or if they weren't releasing their own music, they were getting signed to independent labels such as Rough Trade. I heard Peel play '6000 Crazy' by Spizz Energi, a Birmingham band; a Rough Trade release.

I kept my eye on gig listings in *NME*, and looked out for fly-posters on derelict buildings and in underpasses, A4 photocopied pages sellotaped on to lampposts near Barbarella's and information in Inferno, the record shop, and elsewhere.

Another Birmingham band, called Fashion, released 'Steady Eddie Steady' on their own label; they were a three-piece, alternative, arty, ambitious. I went to see them play in an art gallery. The drummer, Mulligan, had a bit of a following among the dressed-up art-school crowd, and there were a couple of dozen very attractive weirdos there. It wasn't exactly the Velvet Underground and Nico live at the Film-maker's Cinematheque, 125 W 41st St, New York, in 1966, but I guess it was as close as Birmingham was going to get.

Becoming aware of things near to home, I began to visit a venue called the Fighting Cocks close to where I lived in Moseley. Almost exactly one year after seeing Blondie at Barbarella's, I went to the Fighting Cocks to see Spizz Energi and another local band, the Prefects. The Fighting Cocks had been built in the mid-1800s, and its function room on the first floor had a separate entrance to the left of the building. It was an undistinguished rectangle of a space with rickety wooden floors and dirty curtains pulled across the windows.

The Prefects had toured with the Clash, and Buzzcocks had given them multiple support slots too. And in October 1977 they played the last night of the Manchester venue, the Electric Circus. In an era of self-financed singles and small labels, the Prefects were probably the biggest post-punk band without a record release. They were recorded, though, for the John Peel show. Peel and his producer John Walters booked bands into the studio to record exclusive sessions for the show, and the Prefects featured a couple of times. When I ventured to the upstairs room at the Fighting Cocks to see them play, it was 10 February 1979. I had just had my seventeenth birthday.

Onstage, the Prefects made a lovely racket and performed in a markedly unshowbiz way. Singer Rob Lloyd was unresplendent in a shirt, a V-neck pullover, an old man's jacket, a pair of plain black trousers and very sensible shoes. He stalked around the stage, looking suspiciously at the audience, and barking his sarky, bitter, pointed lyrics. The Prefects inconveniently split up just a few weeks after I had decided they were one of my favourite bands ever.

I went back to the upstairs room at the Fighting Cocks as often as I could, and saw mainly local acts there, including the Dangerous Girls, Fast Relief, the Pinkies, UB40 – who rehearsed at the Midland Arts Centre in Cannon Hill Park, half a mile down the road – and the Au Pairs. The Au Pairs were a Moseley-based four-piece featuring Paul Foad, an exciting guitarist with an idiosyncratic, choppy guitar action, and a female singer/guitarist, Lesley Woods. I loved them.

31

The Au Pairs were passionate, and intent particularly on questioning traditional and misogynistic views about sexuality and gender. 'Love Song' and 'Domestic Departure' were both very sceptical about the idea that a woman's place was in the home. They had an amazing energy onstage, a visceral appeal that their albums would never quite capture. And they made me think. I liked that; I wanted to know stuff.

Women's liberation, which had gained momentum in the 1960s, was opening minds and changing lives through the 1970s. Feminist voices were strong, particularly in academia and in magazines like *New Society* and, of course, *Spare Rib*. In addition, there was a specially created women's page in the *Guardian*. On the other hand, these apparent advances were more than slightly at odds with prevailing images and widespread attitudes in wider society, from the objectification of women in the world of advertising to the plethora of porn in high-street cinemas. Young women would routinely face harassment and were assumed to be fair game in the street and in the workplace.

Decent songwriters are receptive to what's happening in the world. Post-punk bands, particularly those fronted by women – the Au Pairs, the Raincoats, Poison Girls, Ludus and the Slits – to varying degrees intervened in this battle of ideas.

One particular horror that added intensity to the debates about violence and misogyny was the activity of the so-called Yorkshire Ripper. From 1975 onwards, Leeds and other northern cities were the site of a number of violent sexual assaults including thirteen horrific murders of women. The search for the killer was public, desperate and seemingly never-ending. Sometimes there are big, shared social calamities (such as 9/11) that hang heavy in the air, and trigger clouds of anxiety and upset. The Ripper crimes played out over a number of years, darkening everything and changing the landscape forever.

Everybody was aware of the vulnerability of women on the streets. One of the three songs on the first Au Pairs seven-inch EP in 1979 was 'Kerb Crawler'. There were red-light zones in the bedsit area of Moseley and down in neighbouring Balsall Heath, and a couple of what were then termed 'battered wives homes'; houses that were designed as safe havens for victims of domestic abuse.

In the post-punk period, the small independent label and DIY path to recording and releasing was well trodden. In September 1979, the Au Pairs glued together the sleeve of their first record themselves and sold copies locally, including at the 'alternative' bookshop, Prometheus. Their manager, Martin Culverwell, ran their record label, which was called 021, the area code for Birmingham.

I buttonholed Martin at one of their Birmingham gigs and asked if I could see the Au Pairs soundcheck at an upcoming London show. I'm not sure I even knew what a soundcheck was – I came to realise later that they could be incredibly boring (fifteen minutes of the drummer going 'thump, thump' and ten minutes of the road crew making noises into microphones). But this was all part of my eagerness to see more, to understand more. Martin said, 'Of course,' and I walked home happy I was going to get behind the scenes.

One day in July 1980, having travelled down to London on a National Express coach, I turned up at the YMCA on Tottenham Court Road, on the afternoon of an Au Pairs gig with the Passions, and banged on the door. Eventually someone let me in and I went into the auditorium where

Martin was standing. He didn't recognise me let alone recall our encounter or my request. Over the sound of drummer Pete Hammond thump, thump, thumping, I attempted to tell the whole story; his promise, my journey. There was a pause, Martin looked at me. 'Something, something here now, something,' he shouted.

'What?'

He raised his voice again. 'You're here now, so you're here.'

'Yes, I'm here!' I yelled at him.

'Good,' he said, and quite rightly walked away to do something more important than having a deafening conversation with an anxious young man who had somehow decided that attending an Au Pairs soundcheck would be a dream come true.

Three months later I went to buy the *NME* and Lesley from the Au Pairs was featured on the front cover. This accolade didn't mean the band were selling lots of records or that they were set for mega-stardom, but it struck me as a sign that something small, local, with undeniably prosaic roots could gain cultural significance. Being on the front of the *NME* was the mark of achievement in my eyes. At last, those feelings that everything that was of worth or was exciting – or both – had happened a long time ago or was somewhere out of reach were being challenged.

When I interviewed Lesley nearly thirty years later, she was living in east London. For some reason, it hadn't clicked that Lesley and guitarist Paul Foad were dating when the band began (she told me they had met at a bus stop not far from my house). The spikiness of their relationship was played out onstage and in the songs they co-wrote, in the ferocious energy of 'Love Song', 'Set Up' and 'Come Again'. Lesley and Paul were exploring their identities and their relationship at a time of weapons-grade feminism, mad drugs and post-punk.

In May 1983, the Au Pairs split up and Lesley told me that they had never spoken to each other again. I quoted Walter Pater to her: 'To burn always with this hard, gem-like flame, to maintain this ecstasy, is success in life.'

She laughed, clearly unconvinced.

Ninety per cent of what we talked about was unprintable: who slept with whom, who took what drugs. In the other 10 per cent, there was a story she told me about an encounter with Dexys Midnight Runners – specifically the band's singer Kevin Rowland. She recalled how antagonistic Dexys could be; 'They used to go round in a gang, those boys, I think they liked intimidating people they didn't like the look of. They were like real blokes, real lads.'

One evening, Dexys gatecrashed a party at Lesley's flat, which she shared with another woman. Some jewellery went missing, a diamond ring, and Lesley asked them to leave. When they wouldn't leave, she tried to knock Kevin Rowland off a chair; 'At this point they all started to go for me and my friends then rushed to my defence,' she said. 'I remember the door of the flat got ripped off its hinges. There was a really terrible scene.'

The next day, she tracked down Kevin's number and phoned him; 'I remember saying that there was a ring gone missing and it's very valuable, that one of his guys had taken it and if they didn't give it back they'd have the police and Interpol on their back . . .'

'Interpol?'

'Yes, OK, I don't know where all this bullshit came from! Anyway, he called me back, he sat in a room with me for about three hours talking about violence, I got the ring back. Amazing isn't it?'

When I interviewed Kevin at the Green Room in Manchester, I took the opportunity to ask him about this incident, and told him about Lesley's memory of the event. He laughed. 'It's something like that!' he said. 'She came around to mine. I was shocked, we didn't know those people, they were from the other side of town; Moseley, middle-classy, studenty, CND, different kind of thing to us completely. I was quite surprised, she came around unannounced with some guy.'

'What did she say?'

Kevin adopted a middle-classy, studenty, CND voice; '"What is this Dexys against the world thing, Kevin? What is it?"'

'What did you reply?'

'I said, "I dunno."'

I told Kevin Lesley found it intriguing that he'd metamorphosed from someone that she thought was quite intimidating to someone who would sit down and talk about stuff.

'I don't think I had a lot of choice with her!' he said. 'We did want that separate thing, we didn't want to be like them. We liked the fact that everyone hated us in Birmingham, we wanted that and enjoyed that reputation. It was a little bit silly and she had a point.'

That Green Room interview was one of three I did with Kevin in the three decades after I first saw Dexys play in 1979. Back then, I'd begun adventuring in the world of new bands but I knew almost nothing about them. Someone said that a lad from school was in them, or was going to be in them, playing keyboards.

I saw an A4 poster advertising a Dexys gig at a venue called Romulus, along Hagley Road. I'd never been there, but it seemed too good to miss; plus, the support band were Joy Division. I'd been hoping for a chance to see Joy Division and here they were, playing not far from the No. 1 bus route, which went past the end of our road.

The Joy Division debut album, *Unknown Pleasures*, had been released six or seven weeks earlier. I had heard tracks from the album on John Peel and had bought it. Joy Division rejected punk formulas, but drew on punk energy, reservoirs of personal anguish and restless intellectual adventure. They questioned themselves with more ferocity than punk had questioned society. This is how Tony Wilson explained the shift; 'Punk enabled you to say "Fuck you", but somehow it couldn't go any further. Sooner or later someone was going to want to say "I'm fucked", and that was Joy Division.'

They'd formed a productive alliance with producer Martin Hannett; he slowed Joy Division's music down, and added iciness and Gothic grandeur to the mix. There's space in *Unknown Pleasures*, like something's missing, some silence at the heart of the music, dragging the listener in.

Joy Division hadn't exploded into the big time. The band were playing many unheralded venues (one of their next gigs after Romulus was at a youth centre in Walthamstow). At the beginning of August, they were still some way short of selling the first 10,000 copies of *Unknown Pleasures* that Factory had pressed.

I was confused, more than anything, by my first Joy Division concert. Despite the album reviews and the John Peel coverage, there were only around eighty people there when Joy Division came onstage at Romulus. The sound system wasn't great, or something else was hampering the sound – I wasn't quite sure.

I was expecting the very crisp sound on the album and to be pulled into the echoey spaces. But the band were a slightly chaotic blurred noise and the sound was a bit rushed.

The most powerful part of the performance was how they looked onstage. Joy Division had intensity, all four individuals self-contained in a zone of their own. Drummer Stephen Morris, a little sideways on, not catching anyone's eye, appeared to be focused on some point in the middle distance; Hooky was fronting the audience, his bass low-hanging; Bernard was facing Ian, but not watching him; and Ian inhabited a force field, concentrated, electric.

The most unexpected thing about the whole event was that it appeared to be a mod night of some sort. Romulus was a haunt of the new generation of mods, and early Dexys appealed to that audience. Mods were a big retro thing at the time, with bands including Secret Affair and the Purple Hearts (later in the year, the film *Quadrophenia* tapped into this).

I saw Joy Division three times. All the gigs were, to some degree or other, ramshackle or disconcerting or both, but ever since the Romulus gig I have never been hung up on judging a live performance by how close it is to the sound of a record. If you want to hear the band just like on a record, you're best off staying in and listening at home; during a live show, I want the band to reveal something else, including their imperfections, as musicians and/or as people. This especially seemed true of Joy Division, a group whose motivation and appeal seemed to be bound up with the struggle towards articulacy.

The very next day after the Romulus show, I went to buy the *NME*, and there were Joy Division looking back at me from the front cover (Ian and Bernard photographed on a stone wall by the cenotaph on St Peter's Square in Manchester). As well as an extended interview with the band, the paper also included a review by Adrian Thrills of a gig in London; 'Joy Division were phenomenal,' he wrote. 'They have the spirit and the feeling.'

I can imagine the promoters of the Romulus show were deeply disappointed; for them, it was the kind of publicity that could have added dozens of people to the audience the night before. The management of the youth centre in Walthamstow were probably thinking they'd hit the jackpot.

Any lingering doubts I had about Joy Division after that Romulus show disappeared when they appeared on the TV show *Something Else* in September 1979, released the 'Transmission' single and announced a tour with Buzzcocks. I went to see the tour. It was a Friday night, 27 October 1979, at Manchester Apollo. Stephen Sheen took me. He was at school with me, and once delighted me and probably only about four other people with a rendition of Patrik Fitzgerald's 'Safety-pin Stuck in My Heart' at a school concert.

On one occasion when I interviewed Morrissey we talked about adolescence. I asked him if he thought he made a myth out of the idea that adolescence is something special. 'Well, I think it is special,' he told me. 'It forms your opinions for the rest of your life. I think we shouldn't really underestimate it.'

At seventeen, you're growing into life. At that age, you're especially permeable; ideas and experiences flow straight into your soul. Good or bad experiences; you're taking them all on board for life's journey. I was becoming conscious of the potential pathways music seemed capable of opening up. Through devouring Public Image Ltd, Joy Division and the Pop Group, I was discovering much else besides; I was finding a way to ideas.

On 2 May 1980, I got another chance to see Joy Division. This time they were headlining, with support from A Certain Ratio. The venue was a University of Birmingham building: the refectory on the ground floor of High Hall, one of a handful of student residences grouped around the north and west of a lake in some well-fashioned grounds. It turned out to be the last ever Joy Division show; at the end of May, a day or two before the band were due to fly to America, Ian Curtis committed suicide.

Joy Division opened with a new song for which they hadn't yet agreed a title; it was later named 'Ceremony'. They also played a version of 'Sister Ray' by the Velvets, which they often did as the song could be belted out by the band for ten minutes or more; this was at a time when Ian was often too ill to complete some songs. He twice left the High Hall stage while the band played on and he tried to get himself together. Songs recorded live at the gig were later included on the album *Still*.

I remember being impressed by the support band, A Certain Ratio. I soon got myself a copy of their cassette-only release *The Graveyard and The Ballroom*. In May 2016, a few months after I'd sold all my records to the DJ Seth Troxler, Seth and I went onstage in front of four hundred delegates at the International Music Summit in Ibiza to give our thoughts on the transaction and to play two songs from the collection. I think the audience were expecting some bangin' house classics, but one of Seth's choices was 'Flight' by A Certain Ratio, from that 1979–80 era. The record, played over the high-spec sound system at the conference venue, sounded stunning. Seth and I looked at each other and exchanged a mutual 'wow'.

So many things that have happened to me could be tracked back to those months watching Joy Division, preparing for my A levels and setting my heart on a securing a place at the University of Manchester to study English, but I had no idea of the experiences ahead. Instead, I was left trying to process yet another chaotic Joy Division gig.

The music of Manchester in the post-punk era is now much talked about, but there wasn't a mass movement; far from it. In 1980, thanks to local record labels like Factory, Rabid and New Hormones, and the championing of the scene by Tony Wilson and journalists including Paul Morley, Jon Savage and Mick Middles, Manchester had a more well-developed infrastructure than Birmingham but, nevertheless, my prevailing memory was that fans of Factory bands and the scene around the Beach Club and Pips were a tiny minority. I reckon more people in Manchester cared about Dire Straits than bought records on all those local labels combined. And there weren't long queues to see Biting Tongues at the Beach Club or the Distractions at the Cyprus Tavern.

One particularly rundown building was known as the Squat, which was on Devas Street, almost where Academy 1 is now. Early in the 1970s, the university authorities planned to knock down the building, which had formerly housed the Manchester Royal College of Music, in order to make way for a car park. But students had taken over the building, renaming it the Squat, and arranged gigs there as well as theatre performances and meetings of various student societies. It was demolished in 1982. I saw New Order at the Squat in my third or fourth week as a student at the university.

Susan and I walked up the stairs into a rectangular room with a high, vaulted ceiling; dusty, very few facilities, certainly no cloakroom. It held two hundred people and, by the time the band took to the stage, it was no more than half full (a few people had left as there was uncertainty as to whether New Order would play, and it was midnight before they came on).

It was five months since that last Joy Division gig, and here I was in Manchester and there were New Order. They performed 'Ceremony', lyrics written by Ian, but now performed by Bernard (he took most of the vocals but fell over at one point, either through nerves or excessive Pernod, or both). Hooky sang 'Dreams Never End', and I seem to remember Stephen taking the lead vocal for at least one other song. It wasn't much more than a public rehearsal with a hundred people in attendance.

As well as the three surviving members of Joy Division, there was a girl on keyboards; it was Gillian Gilbert's first gig. Gillian had been in a band called the Inadequates who rehearsed at the same place as Joy Division, T. J. Davidson's on Little Peter Street. Stephen once told me that the Inadequates had chosen a name that was supposed to be ironic, but turned out not to be. He also said that the Inadequates had really posh equipment and Joy Division used to offer to look after it in the hope they could use it. Stephen started dating Gillian, she joined the band, and New Order were complete. They had arrived not just at a new chapter; it was a new beginning.

4

Magic Mushrooms And
Four Barry Whites

I launched *Debris* in December 1983 with a party in Berlin, which sounds glamorous but it was a small basement club at the bottom end of King Street South. Securing Berlin for the launch event wasn't straightforward. It transpired that to book the club I had to meet some fella called Vic at Blueberries, a wine bar on Faulkner Street at the edge of Chinatown. Vic was helpful, although he was keen to avoid paperwork. I asked him if he would give me a receipt for the £15 hire fee and he laughed.

Weekends at Berlin were pretty ordinary but, as at many small clubs in British cities, midweek was an entirely different matter; that's usually when music tribes with esoteric tastes and the new scenes find a home.

I'd been there a number of times on a Tuesday to hear Colin Curtis DJ. I hadn't followed him or his career – I didn't know he'd had an important role to play in the soul scene in the 1970s – I just loved finding the scene his music was a part of.

He was playing jazz at Berlin and I loved the strong look that his crowd had: zoot suits and spats for the guys, and the girls in pencil skirts and fancy millinery.

Andrew Berry played at the *Debris* launch. The club was equipped with two belt-drive Garrard decks, which were pretty much industry standard at the time. In future years DJs would expect Technics decks, vari-speed options (not just 33 rpm or 45 rpm) plus buttons to flange and mess with, but the decks at Berlin were primitive; a penny was sellotaped on top of the cartridge to stop the stylus from flying around.

The first issue of *Debris* was sixteen pages, A4, with a print run of five hundred. I discovered this place called the Manchester Free Press – I thought the name meant they printed things for free but that wasn't the case. They printed lots of radical political things and they believed in the free press; that was it. *Debris* lasted six years. The contents included a large amount of copy about music, but it was also about so much more than music.

I managed to produce three or four issues of the fanzine each year. As well as my columns of type, the adverts and the occasional illustration, it would feature photos I'd cut out from magazines, but sometimes I would commission people to take photos. Steve Wright took a great photo of Mark E. Smith and Ian Tilton also took some photos for me. I'd glue all these columns of type and photographs onto big sheets and they'd be printed, cut and stapled by the so-called Free Press.

Early issues of *Debris* had less than half a dozen advertisers and sold for 40p. I hoped that it would pay for itself, that sales and adverts would cover the print bill. I'd receive orders for copies from a few regular subscribers and people who had heard John Peel talking about it on his night-time show on BBC Radio 1 or read about it in fanzine round-ups in *Jamming* or the *NME*. There were a few stockists, too, including the vegetarian café On the 8th Day and an alternative bookshop on Newton Street called Grass Roots.

Thanks to what I now understood about post-punk, the Prefects, the Au Pairs and Factory Records, I'd learned that culture wasn't the preserve of dead artists, country houses and pop stars from afar. Being talked about by John Peel and the *NME* had cultural significance, live events had energy and potential, music could open doors and ideas, and songs could articulate so much about what was happening in the world or what was happening in your head.

I had unearthed an important revelation about cultural activity: if you want to be involved, you don't need money, just resourcefulness. The step into the world of ideas could be as confusing as Joy Division playing at a mod night in a disco bar, but taking that step was no bigger than the step onto the stage at the Squat or the Fighting Cocks.

I spent very little time prevaricating about doing a fanzine. I just plunged in. It was the spirit of the tribe and the times; the post-punk years. Don't wait for your world on a plate, make it happen, create, form a band, make a fanzine, run a label. Enthuse. Participate. A year before *Debris*, I made my first foray into staging live music by hosting two gigs by a band called the Marine Girls. They were a trio; sisters Jane and Alice Fox, and Tracey Thorn.

I had first met Tracey and her boyfriend Ben Watt in the late autumn of 1981. At that time, I was a second-year English Literature student sharing a house in Smart Street in Longsight with Jack Atkin, who had been my best buddy in the first year. Jack was originally from Hertfordshire, where the Marine Girls were from, and he knew the band. Tracey and Ben came to stay. They had both moved to Hull to study at the university there, met in the first week of their first term and, of course, bonded. A month into their relationship, they journeyed over to Manchester to see a gig by Vic Godard. Vic wore a suit and a cravat; the lounge jazz Club Left thing wasn't really my scene but I admired the way a man who'd been involved in the punk scene had the vision and the balls to swerve the obvious career and wardrobe choices.

The Vic Godard gig was at Rafters, a basement club on Oxford Street. I'd been there a number of times but missed the night Morrissey reviewed a Depeche Mode show there: 'Their sophisticated nonsense succeeds only in emphasising how hilariously unimaginative they really are,' he wrote in *Record Mirror*. As if looking for a killer line to dismiss them, he called them 'four Barry Whites'. I'm not sure what Morrissey was getting at there, but to me if they were four Barry Whites that would make them amazing.

I didn't see Ben and Tracey before the Vic Godard gig as I'd spent the earlier part of the day not with Jack but with other friends. An hour or so before making our way to the gig, this other crew and I had taken magic mushrooms. I'm not sure why I'd thought it would be appropriate to be doing magic mushrooms at a lounge jazz event, but something started to go awry once Mr Godard took to the stage. I began hallucinating and losing my mind. I left Rafters in a state of agitated paranoia and then went back, but then left a final time and ran down the middle of the road towards Oxford Road Station, keeping well away from the streetlights, which were on fire. They were blazing, bending in from the kerb and across the road. I was in danger of being engulfed by a wall of flame, so I jumped on a bus and went home.

Back in the kitchen in Smart Street I washed all the cutlery and dirty dishes that Jack and I had accumulated over the previous few days, and began vacuuming the stairs. Jack, Tracey and Ben arrived after the gig just as I got close to the top step. I stopped what I was doing, said hello to the house guests, made us all tea and toast, and started talking at them. I have no memory of what I was saying, but I do recall them staring at me while the words came out.

Although I was studying and living in Manchester, I would sometimes visit the family home in Birmingham outside term time, and I began working alongside Jim Newell and Chris Armstrong on what we called 'extravaganzas': evenings which included music, and various performances including plays. We staged Harold Pinter's *The Dumb Waiter* and Beckett's *Krapp's Last Tape* at the Hexagon Theatre at the Midland Arts Centre in Cannon Hill Park. Fortunately, our initial meeting didn't dissuade Tracey from joining Jane and Alice on a journey to Birmingham to play two consecutive nights at one of these extravaganzas.

Hanging out with the Marine Girls was a joy. I kept a diary and reported their stay in great detail, from the moment I met them off the coach at Digbeth bus station: 'They arrived about 4-ish with guitars in solid, little, battered brown cases. Tracey is the oldest and most musical and quietest, Jane is by far the most enthusiastic, and Alice is the singer and she was wearing a big flying jacket with fur neck and collars, and leopard skin shoes. When we got home I tried to feed them but they weren't bothered and so we walked up to Boots for throat lozenges.'

The second day, I took the Marine Girls into town. According to my diary 'We spent ages trying to buy a stamp for Tracey. In HMV the man there put their LP on when he saw them, he was very excited and said he was coming to the gig. Then we went buying sweets in the Bull Ring and Alice was excited because she'd been studying the Bull Ring in her geography lessons.'

These Marine Girls gigs, which were more or less my first cultural intervention, were a moderate success, attracting fifty people, maybe fifty-five, each night. Now they're a cult band, especially after it was revealed that Kurt Cobain considered *Beach Party* one of his top-fifty favourite albums of all time.

During their stay, the Marine Girls came out on the town with me, joining two of my friends, Lesley and Libby, at their party at a club called Holy City Zoo. Sharon Duckworth – a friend of mine and Susan's from school – was there with Pete Wylie of the band Wah! Heat. He asked me not to introduce him to the Marine Girls. He said pop groups meeting each other in clubs was 'gross'.

Wylie had become an inspiration to me; he was the first music-paper cover star to give me the time of day. I saw his band play a few times and went over to Liverpool one day and Wylie and Sharon showed me a few places around town. Pete helped initiate my belief that we are not united by postcode so much as by attitude. The places and people he introduced me to were part of a small, very attractive Liverpool scene.

When you grow up in a city or move to another city, the biggest adventure and the most valuable reward is to find your tribe. We search for the places that draw the people we share interests with, or feel comfortable with, or attracted to, or inspired by. Tim Burgess of the Charlatans, in his book about hunting for vinyl in record shops, says a great record shop is like 'a refuge'. The same can be true of a club, an arthouse cinema, a particular pub, a café-bar, a boutique, a bookshop or, as Tracey Donnelly and I found, a hairdressing salon in a nightclub basement.

In Birmingham, in the late 1970s, I'd inhabited Prometheus, the Arts Lab, Inferno, Barbarella's – a bookshop, an arthouse cinema, a record shop and a music venue. In Manchester, by 1982, I'd been frequenting venues like the Beach Club, the Cyprus Tavern and then the Haçienda. The pull of the local alternative bookshop was still strong; Grass Roots replaced Prometheus in my affections. My teenage passion for arthouse films, stimulated by visits to the Arts Lab in Aston, found an outlet at the Aaben in Hulme where I saw *Stalker* and *Repo Man*.

Wylie had his favourite haunts, the various homes of his tribe. He took me to the News From Nowhere bookshop, the Open Eye Gallery, the Armadillo tearooms and Probe Records, and on one of the next visits I met Jayne Casey for the first time. Over the next couple of years, I spent a lot of evenings and nights back in Liverpool, including a couple of nights at Plato's Ballroom (aka Mr Pickwick's) where I saw Dead or Alive play at an event co-hosted by Nathan McGough, who went on to be the manager of Happy Mondays.

Of course, you are more than likely to have plenty in common with people you share a postcode with, but it's not inevitable; you may feel happy where you live or you may feel alienated. When you find your tribe, your kindred spirits, they may be from the other side of town, or another town, a different city.

There was no one more loyal to Manchester than Tony Wilson but the Factory crowd was adventurous and outward-looking. Tony, Factory co-director and New Order's manager Rob Gretton, the bands, the journalists, all appeared connected to things happening worldwide; the label had built links with Ruth Polsky, Arthur Baker and others in New York, which became crucial in developing the idea of a club in Manchester along the lines of Danceteria. Early in 1982, *City Fun* covered the announcement that the Haçienda was opening. Although generally a little cynical (they described it as 'Wilson's folly'), they welcomed its ambition to avoid 'the provincial introversion that plagues every city that is not London'.

City Fun (not to be confused with *City Life*, which was a Manchester listings magazine founded in 1983) was a fanzine that had started in 1977 as an informal collective, but by the time I became a regular reader there had been something of a coup and Liz Naylor and Cath Carroll were among those taking it in a very entertaining, piss-taking, radical lesbian direction. It was part of that alternative world. It had a listings section of forthcoming gigs in the city, but its bigger value was that I found it very stimulating and funny.

Punk wasn't quite the Year Zero it is sometimes portrayed to be. The music had a debt to the likes of the Stooges, for example. Fanzines had some antecedents too. Although I have never been sure about reverence for Carnaby Street and Woodstock, one element of the 1960s that I have since come to appreciate is the underground press; titles like *International Times*, *Oz* and *Friends* (and in Manchester, *Mole Express* and *Grass Eye*).

The underground press in the 1960s had filled an information vacuum. In the mainstream media, there was no useful information about drugs, and no dissenting views on Vietnam or revolutionary views on education. The underground press emerged to pass on this suppressed or ignored information, together with listings and other useful material. The evidence of a connection between fanzines and the underground press became clearer when Liz Naylor told me she had been an avid reader of *Mole Express*.

In the mid-1980s, there was still an information vacuum. One of the undocumented areas of Manchester life was the gay scene, which was then more hidden than it is today and subject to suppression and hostility. In the early part of the decade, *City Fun* devoted several pages to a tour of venues frequented by gay men and lesbians, from the New Union on Canal Street to Dickens on Oldham Street. No mainstream newspaper or magazine at the time would have provided such coverage, certainly not in such an entertaining style.

We were being told lies about the economy, about Reagan arming the contras, about the policing of the miners' strike. In 1980, I'd gone down to London for a CND rally and walked from Victoria Embankment to Hyde Park for speeches by Bruce Kent and Neil Kinnock. There were said to be 80,000 people there, perhaps more. *Debris* included pieces about CND, mental health and prison reform, but I should have got stuck into the political world more.

Questions of sexual/gender relations that had concerned and energised the Au Pairs at the beginning of the 1980s remained potent. The years of terror created by the Yorkshire Ripper came to an end in 1981 when the killer, Peter Sutcliffe, was arrested. But that's not to say that the streets of cities now felt safe. Several of his victims were murdered in Manchester.

At the university and elsewhere in the city, questions of personal safety were coupled with a heightened political consciousness. This fed into the Reclaim the Night movement, women-only protests against sexual violence and for gender equality. The Cornerhouse arts complex in Manchester had its main screen in a building that, in the 1970s, had been a porn cinema; the Reclaim the Night marches regularly mounted a picket there.

In the 1980s, activists on the progressive left tended to be internationalists, with an interest in South America – opposing Pinochet in Chile, supporting the Sandinistas in Nicaragua – as well as campaigning to free Nelson Mandela, boycott Barclays and push for an end to apartheid in South Africa. While I was at university in Manchester, there was a vote passed to name the Students' Union after Steve Biko, the South African civil rights activist killed in police custody in 1977. One issue of *Debris* included a feature on the anti-apartheid movement.

A man called Eddy Shah had a newspaper publishing business specialising in local titles. One of his printing plants was in Warrington where he insisted on employing non-union members at cheaper rates, and began a purge of union workers. The sacking of six workers in 1983 led to a mass picket being mounted at the headquarters of the *Warrington Messenger* by the National Graphical Association. There was one evening at the end of November when four thousand protesters were attacked by police in full riot gear. I had planned to be there. In my diary, I wrote: 'I was supposed to go with Juliet and Sarah to Warrington, but I decided to go to the Haçienda instead.'

I was obsessed with music, that's the truth, and sometimes apart from the idea of enjoying and sharing my latest music passion nothing else seemed to matter. In *Debris*, I included what I liked. I was very definitely conscious of the general post-punk belief that barriers between music genres could be broken. I found space for an article on jazz musician Roland Kirk, the New York act Ut and A Guy Called Gerald.

I wanted my fanzine to be eclectic in its contents, not just about the music it championed, and that's why *Debris* included features on the Russian film director Tarkovsky, an article on fish-and-chip shops and a piece about prison reform, as well as interviews with old barbers and the launderette owner. Putting your head above the parapet – engaging in any kind of cultural intervention – is hard work and requires emotional investment, so if you're going to do something, you may as well do something different. Dare yourself.

Fanzines reflected the attitudes and personalities of the people who made them, which is as it should be. One punk fanzine writer said that when he's writing it's like he's punching the keyboard. You can tell that in his writing: it's loud, gung-ho, combative. Well, that's not me, why should it be? I'm just not a ker-pow kinda guy. Me and my keyboard are going on an emotional journey; we're not fighting.

Sometimes you define yourself by what you don't want to be; I didn't think it was necessary for *Debris* to look like the dozens of fanzines since 1976 that had a punky, cut-up, shambling, scruffy look. I thought that if it looked classic, and legible, then it would demonstrate that I'd taken love and care in the making of it, and people would take love and care in the reading of it.

One of the other features of *Debris* was the inclusion of lists. I did lists of queues and top-ten bus routes, for example. I used to do horoscopes too, which were utterly random and predicted bad times for everyone. Daft stuff; one Wednesday in June a cat will drop from a tall building and kill your best friend. Things like that.

I did most of the writing in *Debris*, but issue 16 (December 1987) included a piece written by Robert Forster of the Go-Betweens. I'd always loved the Go-Betweens and admired the look Robert was sporting in 1987, especially his hair, which was so extremely lustrous. I thought that if Robert had the conviction to sport such a look, he must be some kind of an expert so I asked him if he would write about how to care for your hair.

As well as Robert Forster, other contributors included a future law professor and a future *Guardian* columnist, plus Donald McRae, who has gone on to write several great books, beginning with *Nothing Personal* about prostitution. Gibby Haynes from the Butthole Surfers was another contributor. He wrote a review of his own band's gig at Leeds Polytechnic in 1987. He submitted four handwritten pages of colourful prose (it was probably the best review the band ever had), but in the end I didn't use it in *Debris*, partly because later the same evening I fell out with him over the décor in my flat in Hulme.

As well as taking copies of *Debris* to gigs, with Susan, Carol and everybody helping sell them, and having a handful of stockists, mentions on the John Peel show made a big difference to sales. When he received a copy, Peel would read out my address and within a couple of days I'd have twenty or so letters containing a postal order or a cheque and a request for *Debris* (occasionally there would be two twenty-pence coins sellotaped to a small piece of cardboard). Several subscribers would keep in touch between issues and send me feedback, and

I'd add their letters to my plastic bag of cassettes and notebooks and we'd correspond to the extent that we'd become pen pals.

Aside from covering print costs, the commercial aspect was less important to me than the writing. I'd draft reviews, deliberating for hours, spend a whole evening working on the right 150 words to say about the B-side of a single that would probably sell even fewer copies than my fanzine. In 2009, I got an email from a big cheese at the Sub Pop label asking me about a review of a single called 'Son of a Gun' by the Vaselines I'd written in 1987. I'd been sent the Vaselines record by Stephen Pastel, who had released it on his 53rd & 3rd label. Eugene from the Vaselines had kept the *Debris* review, and was so fond of it that he wanted to make it a feature on the artwork of a retrospective Vaselines boxset. When I dug out the review, I liked it: it was charming, funny and true. However, I had absolutely no recollection of ever writing it.

5

Young Contemporaries

It was nearly eighteen months after the Marine Girls shows that I went over to Hull to interview Ben and Tracey for *Debris*. By this time, the Marine Girls had split up, and Ben and Tracey were second-year students, living together on Salisbury Street. They had solo careers (Tracey had an album called *A Distant Shore*) but, together, they were Everything But the Girl. As well as releasing 'Night and Day', they had recorded, but not yet released, their debut album *Eden*.

I made pages and pages of notes while I listened to *Eden* on pre-release cassette over and over again. I did lots of research, analysed all the songs and formulated various lines of questioning. I wasn't going to just turn up and hope for the best. I've never believed in 'winging it'.

I still overprepare for interviews, and I also have a ritual or two. Often, I'll buy a new A4 or A5 notebook in the run-up to an interview, and maybe a new pen too. Preparation includes finding out as much important and even unimportant stuff as

I can about the interviewee. It calms me to know I have done my research. It also makes sense in terms of the psychology of the encounter; the interviewee will always appreciate the effort, increasing the chance you'll get good responses, something beyond stock answers.

When I am about to interview an actor, I re-watch their film and TV performances, make notes on their biography, look at old interviews. With writers, I'll read as many of their books as I can. When I arranged to interview Nile Rodgers of Chic in front of an audience in November 2011 it was more than thirty years since I had danced to 'Le Freak' in the disco room at Barbarella's. I grabbed the chance to listen again to lots of his music and, as well as scrolling through dozens of websites, my research also included making notes on his autobiography.

About ten minutes into the interview, Nile was talking about his early years as a musician, going out live, performing in various line-ups and backing a vocal group called New York City. Explaining who New York City were, Nile told me they'd had a hit, 'I'm Doing Fine Now', and then paused.

In an instant, my brain flicked through the songs I'd heard and the things I'd read, the megatons of research and preparation, and out popped the words 'Produced by Thom Bell.'

'Yes!' said Nile, 'A Thom Bell production.'

When he clocked that I knew stuff, Nile and I were both suddenly on another level. Nile gives a lot of time to interviewers – in fact, to anyone with whom he comes into contact – but from that moment he had even more sparkle in his eyes. He was extra generous with his insights, and we went on to talk so much and at such length that I had to throw in an unscheduled interval.

Johnny Marr was in the audience, and at the interval followed us offstage and into the dressing room. I thought they had met before – they both played on 'Driving Me Wild' by Bryan Ferry but I guess they had played their guitar parts at different times, probably in different continents. My opening remarks at this auspicious moment? "Nile, this is Johnny Marr," I said. "Johnny, this is Nile." And they talked for ten minutes (mostly about guitars) while I drank some of Nile's Perrier.

I may overprepare for interviews, but I try not to allow all that knowledge to clog up my brain. I need to be loose, ready to respond to an answer and to know when to let the conversation zoom off on a tangent. Also, facts aren't really important. The audience want entertainment and revelation rather than encyclopaedic detail. The Thom Bell fact was the least interesting thing in the interview but it helped create trust and respect between me and Nile. Trust is a big part; without that you can't expect Bernard Sumner to speak from the heart about his memories of Ian Curtis. When I interviewed Terry Hall he trusted me enough to talk about being addicted to Valium when he was a teenager. And I guess all this also explains why, when I teased Nile Rodgers about not sleeping with Madonna, he didn't hit me.

However, diligently reading material about interviewees doesn't always guarantee you'll be on firm ground with your line of questioning. When I interviewed Mark E. Smith at the Green Room in 2011 in front of 250 Fall fans, I asked him about his drug use, a subject he had been relatively candid about in his autobiography, *Renegade*. I said to him; 'I'm intrigued by the story in your book about taking Mandrax in a pub called the Church . . .'

I knew he was a fan of amphetamines and alcohol, and I knew he had taken acid, but using a heavy sedative didn't seem very Mark.

'Mandrax??!' He was incredulous.

'Yes, Mark, it's in your book.'

'Mandrax!' he said, mockingly. 'In a church?'

'The pub, Mark, in Prestwich. Taking Mandrax in the Forresters and the Church.'

When Mark wanted to wind me up, he called me David. 'Where do you find this stuff, David?' he asked.

There followed a few minutes of confusion, during which I looked for the reference in his book, while he shook his head, laughed with the audience and took two swigs from my glass of wine.

'The Church. It's in your book.'

'What are you talking about?'

'Mandrax,' I said. 'Here; page thirty-five.'

'Really?' said Mark, looking at the audience, and then back at me. 'That ghost writer has a lot to answer for.'

For the Tracey and Ben interview I filled a notebook with ideas. I didn't just stick to music, although I made no plans to discuss with them their use (or otherwise) of Valium, Mandrax or any other heavy drug. Nevertheless, there was still so much to talk about in regard to their music, but also beyond their music.

At the time that I journeyed over to Hull from Manchester, I was living in Amberidge Walk in Hulme, a run-down and semi-derelict estate outside the city centre. The most famous architectural feature of Hulme were the Crescents; huge tower blocks built in the early 1970s and named after great architects of the past, such as William Kent and Robert Adam. Streets of Victorian terraced houses had been demolished; many inhabitants, rehoused elsewhere, had resented having to leave their homes and move away from established communities and their families. The flats were soon faced with major problems: damp percolated through the concrete; the dividing walls became home to hordes of cockroaches; the underfloor heating turned out to be expensive and inefficient.

The degeneration of the area was exacerbated by poverty and rising unemployment in the area during the mid-1970s. The council considered, but then delayed, a decision to demolish the new buildings, and, instead, started to move families out to other locations, leaving huge numbers of the flats across Hulme empty. Jeff Noon, in his novel *Vurt*, draws heavily on Hulme in his portrait of the area he calls Bottletown, and tracks what happens after the families leave; 'the young and listless move in'.

The flats became favoured by creatives, students, bands, fashion designers, poets and hundreds of other young people looking for uncontrolled space, cheap rent and somewhere to live close to town. Sue Ferguson lived in one of the Crescents – I'd go over to see her or bands like Big Flame and the Inca Babies or my friend Kate from a band called the Rattlesnakes.

I lived across the bridge from the Crescents, on the side of Hulme around Duxbury Square and Epping Walk. This area of Hulme, mostly three- or four-storey deck-access properties, was behind the university, borderline Moss Side and close to a brewery. My flat on Amberidge Walk was fifty yards from Salmon Cabs on Greenheys Lane. At the back of the taxi office, Mr Salmon had a tiny shop, stocking the essentials for the local neighbourhood up-all-nighters: milk, teabags, chocolate biscuits, cornflakes, Rizlas. Salmon was my cab of choice until about 1993, by which time Mr Salmon had branched out into selling fried chicken. I never bought any chicken, but spent hundreds of pounds riding in Mr Salmon's cabs.

I'd been living in Hulme for a year when the Haçienda opened. The Haçienda was the Hulme side of town, as was the Ritz. On 4 October 1982, Andrew Berry helped stage a night at the Ritz headlined by Blue Rondo à la Turk. His partner in this endeavour was John Kennedy. John was a creative young guy, and a denizen of the small number of gay-friendly venues in town, such as Hero's. I didn't know him until a few months later, when we began to meet up in a café on John Dalton Street and discuss our plans to change the world.

Andrew and John asked their pals the Smiths to support Blue Rondo à la Turk – even though they only had four songs. The Smiths played; it was their first public performance. They were joined onstage by James Maker, in high heels, who did a bit of dancing. The bass player was Dale Hibbert – his one and only show with the band before Andy Rourke joined.

I wasn't there. I was at the Haçienda that night, a Monday. At the Haç, Psychic TV were headlining, with support from William Burroughs. Burroughs sat at a desk onstage and read from various works. We sat on the dancefloor and listened; me and 324 arty people. Burroughs was ancient-looking, with an amazing sonorous voice that cracked and boomed out of the Haçienda speakers. I didn't appreciate Psychic TV – I tried and I failed. In fact, I saw them three times and I don't know why I kept going back. Burroughs didn't stay until the end, but he did stalk once around the club in an overcoat and fedora before exiting.

Maybe I made the wrong choice that night. In retrospect, which event should I have gone to – the Burroughs reading or the debut Smiths gig? I still don't know.

I first saw the Smiths in November 1983, when they headlined the Haçienda. Tracey Thorn got in touch and came over from Hull for the gig, which was a Thursday – my signing-on day. I signed on at 10.15 a.m. at a bleak building on Aytoun Street only four hundred yards from Piccadilly Station, so I went up there afterwards to wait for Tracey to arrive. In the evening, we walked through Hulme to the Haçienda to see the Smiths. The band had distributed £200 worth of flowers to the audience. When Tracey and I made for the exit after the second encore, we had to pick our way through the flowers crushed and broken across the emptying dancefloor.

The next day, Tracey and I visited the Smiths' office on Portland Street. Their manager Joe Moss owned Crazy Face, a clothing company with a store in Stockport and on Chapel Walks in Manchester. Joe employed Liz Taylor to design Smiths T-shirts at the Portland Street offices, and Tracey bought one when we dropped by.

When Tracey came over from Hull for the *Debris* launch party a few weeks later, she stayed on in Manchester and the following evening we walked through Hulme together and went to see the Cocteau Twins at the Haçienda. Our relationship was confusing, complicated; she was with Ben, but she came to stay with me in Hulme. Whatever our relationship was, it didn't last long, but it meant a lot to me then, and still.

During the day of the Smiths gig, Tracey and I walked around the Whitworth Art Gallery, which was then showing the *Young Contemporaries* exhibition. Also during that visit, we browsed for books at Grass Roots, where Tracey bought a book called *Pornography and Silence* by Susan Griffin. On the Cocteau Twins day, we found time to visit the Art History department at the University of Manchester. My friend Jo Labon had recommended a lecture there by Lucy Bland so I took Tracey. Never let it be said that the earnest young fanzine editor and the singer-songwriter student didn't know how to have fun (the lecture was entitled 'The Construction of Femininity').

Thirty years later, we would have exchanged hundreds of texts and a few dozen emails, but this was 1983, even before faxes, so we wrote each other letters. I loved getting Tracey's letters – five or six pages in her very tidy handwriting. I'd read each letter quickly and then reread it slowly, savouring the words. We were eager to share stuff. Have you read this book, what did you think of that TV play, isn't the new Prefab Sprout single brilliant? I recall very clearly being in the launderette under Epping Walk in Hulme with a letter I'd received that day and spending the hour there reading and rereading the letter and drafting and re-drafting a reply.

For my birthday in January 1984, Tracey sent me a beautiful shirt and a volume of James Joyce's poetry. We swapped mix tapes – sixty-minute cassettes of records we'd chosen and taped – a lovely cliché of the time. A great way of sharing and connecting, in theory, but it didn't always work. On one cassette I included 'The Classical' by the Fall and she told me she hated it. Another time, I sent Tracey a seven-inch vinyl copy of 'Hey Joe' and 'Piss Factory' by Patti Smith but, despite being packaged with bubble wrap, the record broke in half in the post.

That January, we spent three days together and decided not to pursue whatever relationship we were moving towards. It rained for all three days and I walked with Tracey to Piccadilly Station and we said goodbye.

In April 1987, when I helped to organise a benefit gig at the Haçienda for Aidsline – an advice and counselling hotline for people needing information and help about issues relating to HIV and AIDS – Tracey and Ben played an acoustic set, the Woodentops performed live, and we also featured Marc Almond as a non-singing special guest (he drew the raffle prize). Since then, of course, Tracey and Ben have continued to have a long and successful career together, including the mega-hits 'I Don't Want to Talk About It' and 'Missing', plus their solo careers. Now, they are married and have three kids.

When Ben's first memoir, *Patient: The True Story of a Rare Illness*, was published in 1997, I went to a reading at Waterstones in Manchester and around the same time I went down to London to see him DJ at Notting Hill Arts Club. In 2003, when Tracey began to consider writing her autobiography, she came up to Manchester and we had our first proper conversation after that walk to the station and three decades of parallel lives.

Back in the early 1980s, I was a long way from understanding my head or my heart. In 2011, when I was interviewing the novelist Jeffrey Eugenides, author of *The Virgin Suicides* and *Middlesex*, we got deep and I confessed that, when I was a young man, I was intellectually clued-up but sexually and emotionally more-or-less illiterate. When we agreed our emotional lives can be incredibly chaotic, especially when we're young, I was thinking mostly, but not only, of those times with Tracey. Those times when feelings arrive and you don't know where they've come from or where they're taking you.

When my daughter was fifteen years old, we were talking through things one day and she shook her head at the latest situation she was in. 'Boys don't have feelings,' she said. I told her she was wrong; boys do have feelings but they're confused by them and don't have words for them.

6

When Morrissey
Came To Tea

The second issue of *Debris* wasn't going to write itself, so I made plans, wrote some ideas on scraps of paper and knocked on doors. Within a couple of weeks of the launch party, I'd arranged for Morrissey to come to my flat in Hulme. The day after Boxing Day, 1983. That was the day Morrissey came for tea and I cooked him cauliflower cheese. Sometimes stuff happens and it's only later you realise it was one of the highlights of your life.

I was always wandering in and out of the Crazy Face offices where the Smiths' management was based, saying hello to Liz Taylor and nosing about. Most of the visitors were people in the rag trade; it was through Joe that I met Leo Stanley, who ran the clothes shop Identity in Affleck's Palace. You could always tell if Joe Moss was in as the office cassette player would be belting out the likes of Chuck Berry or John Lee Hooker.

When I first started this stalking stuff, the Smiths had just released 'Hand in Glove'. By November 1983, I was popping in once or twice a week. I asked Liz if she would ask Joe to ask whether Morrissey would grant me an interview, and word came back via Liz that he was happy to oblige.

I panicked a little because I didn't know where to go to do the interview. It was scheduled for when Joe was having a day off, so we couldn't meet at the management's office. I didn't know much about Morrissey and there was no internet to go on to search and research. I'd heard two singles and their B-sides and some other stuff on the radio; I'd seen the Smiths play; I knew Morrissey was a vegetarian, and I knew he was celibate (or, at least, he said he was); from what I'd seen and heard, I concluded he was a delicate soul and I decided that maybe we'd not meet in the pub. He didn't give me the impression of a man who wanted to be out in public sinking pints all evening.

Another major reason for avoiding the pub was that I needed somewhere quiet. It was only the second interview I'd ever done. I had a tape machine that recorded onto cassettes, it was bulky, and you had to press 'play' and 'record' at the same time, plus you also had to make sure that neither you nor the interviewee was too far away from the built-in and not very clever microphone.

With all these issues worrying me, I decided that the best rendezvous point for me and Morrissey was my horrible little flat in Amberidge Walk in Hulme. I'd be there on my own and we'd not be disturbed. So I asked Joe if he thought Morrissey would mind coming round to my place. Joe said it wouldn't be a problem, and Liz said, 'I'll pick him up in the car and come over.'

I was twenty-one and Morrissey was twenty-four. I suspect Joe had told Morrissey I was enthusiastic and harmless, and encouraged Morrissey to accept my request for an interview. Ian Curtis had once said, 'Fanzines are the future of the world.' Morrissey was another true believer in the importance and potential of fanzines in that era, and in the local scene.

Morrissey was a fan of *City Fun* fanzine, as was Linder Sterling, Morrissey's close friend from the band Ludus (her work for *City Fun* included the front-cover design of issue 8). Liz Naylor and Cath Carroll, the main characters piloting the fanzine in 1982, were also in a band together, the Gay Animals, and they managed Ludus for a time. *City Fun* printed the first ever Smiths review, from their gig at Manhattan Sound in January 1983. A few months later, Morrissey, using the pseudonym Burt Macho, wrote an eight-hundred-word feature for *City Fun* about Sandie Shaw. If you followed only the mainstream media, you'd never have known all this stuff was happening.

Thinking ahead to my evening with Morrissey, I wondered if I should cook him his tea, because we'd agreed he'd come round at seven o'clock and I wanted to be hospitable. Liz Taylor said, 'Yes, I think he'd like that,' and we talked about what I might cook. These were the days before Quorn or ready-meal veggie versions of meat dishes, and I didn't do dinner parties, so I had a very limited repertoire in any case, meat or non-meat. Liz told me Morrissey liked eggs, but I was much less of a fan. So I decided to make a massive bowl of cauliflower cheese.

Morrissey arrived wearing a dark grey pullover, brown shoes and what appeared to be the same jeans he wore on *Top of the Pops* during the week of the Haçienda gig (or maybe he had a whole stock of 32–34 jeans that sagged off his backside). I spent some time getting the cheese sauce just right while he browsed my bookshelves and cast his eye over a pile of magazines next to the TV. I put on some music.

It turned out that Morrissey's mum had already cooked him something, so he wasn't hungry. He told me to go ahead and feed myself and Liz, though, and then sat there and watched us eat cauliflower cheese with some carrots and a slice of white bread. A New Order track started playing, and he asked who it was. I told him I thought he might have known it was New Order. 'Oh,' he said and melodramatically raised his eyebrows.

After the food, I pressed 'play' and 'record' simultaneously and we talked. He told me he'd had 'a very monotonous teenage existence'. We talked about how he'd fallen in love with music. He recalled buying 'Come and Stay With Me' by Marianne Faithfull (the first record he ever bought, purchased from the Paul Marsh record shop on Alexandra Road). 'In the history of my life,' he said, 'the high points were always buying particular records. And hearing records and being immersed in them, and really believing that these people understood how I felt about certain situations.'

I asked him about the Haçienda show from a few weeks earlier, and the fact that Joe and the Smiths had spent £200 on flowers. He linked the flowers to CND and the nuclear debate. I remember several years earlier being struck by the power of a photo of a young woman at an anti-Vietnam War demo in Washington confronting armed soldiers by holding up a flower. It was a strong image, so I knew what Morrissey was getting at. He was very specific, though, and had a more contemporary anti-war movement on his mind. 'At the time I introduced the flowers, the daffodil had become like the Greenham women's symbol,' he said. 'I wanted to introduce something on that level that could speak politically. But people never actually saw it that way.'

We talked about some of his songs being 'genderless' (he said, 'We're dominated by very cemented and boring ideas about what is sexual; this completely revealed sexuality'). Cath Carroll rang up for Morrissey and he said he'd call her back. The conversation spiralled off into a discussion about 'the cult of the beautiful', the François Kevorkian remix of 'This Charming Man' and Morrissey's frustration that 'you can say something flippantly which will be written in blood in the music press and it sounds as though you're deadly serious'.

We finished the interview and I said, 'So, shall we go to the pub?' and, contrary to my preconceptions, he was up for it. He called Cath from my phone and we arranged to meet at a pub near where I lived, called the Grants Arms, on Royce Road (near the PSV Club). We got into Liz's car and drove along Boundary Lane and over Princess Road.

Morrissey was telling me about living in Hulme before all the terraced housing came down. As we arrived at the Grants, he waved his left arm in the general direction of the Aaben cinema and told me he'd grown up over there. When Hulme was cleared, his childhood home on Queen's Square was demolished (by that point, the Morrissey household had moved to Stretford). However, St Wilfrid's, his first school, survived. We probably had time for a proper wander around that area, but I didn't think to ask him. He did say he'd dig out some photos of when he was a young lad for me to reproduce in *Debris*, but he never did and I never reminded him about this promise.

We ordered bottles of lager and sat there cringing at whatever people put on the jukebox. Liz (Taylor) was still with us, and then Cath and the other Liz (Naylor) arrived. I still threw questions at him, and we chatted for another hour or so. We returned to talking about the François Kevorkian remix, which Rough Trade distributed even though Morrissey hated it, and he consequently told fans not to buy it. Morrissey was annoyed with Rough Trade, and looking back I guess it was one of the first of several incidents that caused him and the band to fall out of love with the label. At the time, though, everyone was convinced that the only way for a band to keep their vision pure was to sign to an independent. He said he hadn't wanted to sign to a major record label because 'it just seemed like going back to school'.

I took off on some long exposition of the status of the artist in a capitalist society, saying that all relationships, including those between a band and a label and between a band and an audience, are no more and no less than one based on money. 'You're a commodity, Morrissey. Our connection is really a transaction. And don't you think the whole idea of "artistic integrity" is a fallacy?'

He said, 'I don't know.'

He had with him proof copies of the 'What Difference Does It Make?' sleeve which featured Terence Stamp as the cover star. Cath and Liz quizzed Morrissey about the cover. The two young women seemed to me so very sussed and worldly-wise. I have no idea if that's how they felt themselves to be – they may have simply been fuelled by a mix of half-buried angst and Pilsner lager, as I was – but I was in awe of them. They seemed steely, strong, but not unfriendly.

It was a lovely first encounter with Morrissey and very funny. Morrissey and I really did get on. I'd never met anyone like him before. He wasn't flippant but, on the other hand, he was far from earnest. There was a coyness about him, a playfulness that was very attractive. I called the interview 'Up the Garden Path with Morrissey'.

Even though it was relatively early on in his career with the Smiths, Morrissey was fully formed, ready. Maybe if I had met the long-haired New York Dolls fan Steven Patrick Morrissey from Stretford in 1976 I might have met a pre-Morrissey version of the man I'd just interviewed. Certainly, by December 1983 he had created himself, he had constructed Morrissey; it was if he'd prepared himself for these encounters all his life.

In every encounter there's a degree of performance; perhaps it's just that when you meet some people you are more conscious of a performance. Morrissey was a curious, intelligent character with an enchanting way with words, and when I say 'a character', I mean a character: a creation.

In one of my favourite books, *The Lonely City* by Olivia Laing, the author describes Andy Warhol being ambivalent about human contact, making a tactical withdrawal from physical relationships, and adding layers of self-protection. The description matched a lot of what I saw in Morrissey. In the case of Andy Warhol, Laing says that his persona – what she calls his 'simulacrum' – was something 'that he could both shelter behind and send into the world at large'. Warhol, however, found speaking a challenge, to the point of appearing inarticulate, whereas Morrissey was erudite, charming and talkative.

My diary for 1984 gives me the full rundown of all the encounters with Morrissey that year. On my birthday, 10 January, in addition to a package of presents from Tracey, I also received a postcard from Morrissey. A day or two after he'd been round to my flat, the Smiths had jetted over to New York. The postcard depicted a New York street scene on one side, and on the other Morrissey had written, 'Hello Dave, At the Danceteria I fell off the stage. I am critically maimed. Does this interest you? Morrissey'.

Two weeks after the postcard, I phoned Morrissey. 'What Difference Does It Make?' had just come out and the band were scheduled to do a couple of TV shows that week. I was at home watching a drama series on TV called *The Jewel in the Crown*. It was boring me, so I turned off the telly and called up the singer from the Smiths. My diary entry reads; 'I was bored so I rang Morrissey and we talked about snow, *Debris*, his move to London, the tour, *Top of the Pops* on Thursday, *The Tube* on Friday, the Shangri-Las etc.' I have no idea what that 'etc' might have been. From snow to the Shangri-Las, what else was left for us to discuss?

Two days later, around eight o'clock in the evening, just after that week's *Top of the Pops*, which I had sat and watched, the phone rang. It was Morrissey calling. 'What did you think, Dave?' He wanted to get my feedback on the TV performance. I guess I could have asked him why he performed wearing a hearing aid. Or suggested he should have undone the last button on his shirt at the end to give us a real treat. But I said, 'It was magnificent.'

Although the early months of 1984 were full of Morrissey and the Smiths, not every diary entry at that time sings loudly of happy times hanging with Morrissey, the Smiths or any other fledgling cultural icons. Other entries from around that time include: 'Susan and I went to the Archway where I'd arranged to meet Andrew and Neil from Swing but we didn't get in and they weren't there anyway.'

At the end of January, Joe and Liz organised a coach trip over to a Smiths' show in Sheffield. Susan and I went to Amigos to eat before getting to the rendezvous point outside Manhattan Sound. The coach then picked up Andrew Berry and several other people at the Haçienda and stopped in Marple to pick up the remainder of the crew.

The Smiths played to over a thousand people that night at City Hall in Sheffield. Their set lasted barely three-quarters of an hour but we sat for ages in a hotel bar afterwards – for sure, it was one of those occasions when no one wanted the night to end. Eventually the coach driver persuaded us that it was home time, and we all journeyed back across Snake Pass in the dark, back to Manchester.

By the time the first Smiths album was released in February 1984, I'd heard most of the songs, on the singles, via radio sessions for Kid Jensen and John Peel, and from live gigs. I realised how deep and schooled in music they were, yet they transcended all their influences (although I can hear a touch of the Shangri-Las in some of their songs – the melodrama of 'I Know It's Over' and 'Last Night I Dreamt That Somebody Loved Me', for example).

The Smiths, on their first tour post 'This Charming Man', were met with genuine excitement, even hysteria, at the gigs. They were soon playing to devoted audiences, which, though insanely boisterous, seemed to embody Morrissey's hopes in 'I Know It's Over' to be gentle and kind; this would turn out to be in contrast to some of the audiences that I later saw

Morrissey perform in front of, which seemed to have a much higher proportion of laddish males than attended Smiths gigs in 1983 and 1984.

I loved how the Smiths connected with their audience and I enjoyed watching their emergence. One reason for my delight was the way they challenged the mainstream version of what great pop music was. To me, they seemed like the antithesis of the likes of Duran Duran. As in every era, episodes of *Top of the Pop*s featured a mix of music and you'd occasionally get a real gem, perhaps two, but generally in the early 1980s, the producers and the presenters turned each episode into a headless, over-lit and cheesy office party. In this context, when the Smiths were on the show performing 'This Charming Man' or 'What Difference Does It Make?' they were like gatecrashers from another planet, bringing with them a heavenly dose of reality.

When I interviewed John Taylor of Duran Duran, I told him all this, even though I felt a bit mean doing so. I did know that when he was a teenager in the 1970s, he'd liked a lot of the same music Morrissey and Marr had, including Bowie and Mick Ronson, of course, but that their tastes and their bands had diverged. I told him that every time I got a glimpse of a Duran Duran video, with the band and a load of half-dressed women all aboard a yacht in the Indian Ocean or whatever, in an era of rising youth unemployment and the miners' strike, I just couldn't cope. It was a weird juxtaposition. I told him there's a lot I like about Duran Duran now, but back then we needed the Smiths. John was very understanding and very gentlemanly about it; 'I know, Dave. I appreciate what you're saying.'

On 13 March 1984, the Smiths played the Free Trade Hall in Manchester. My evening started off in a basement bar called

Corbières, as many evenings did (the bar had the best jukebox selection in town). I met Liz Taylor and her friend Kim. Liz had a stack of T-shirts for the merchandise stall, so we went down to the Free Trade Hall early and I tried to sell some copies of my fanzine to the queue. I'd sold a record number of copies of *Debris* (ninety) to people queuing at the Smiths gig in Hanley a fortnight earlier, and this time I got rid of loads again, but with a twist, as my diary records: 'I ended up giving lots away because I liked everyone so much.'

After the gig, I went to the Haçienda, where Sue Ferguson was working that night. Martin Mittler, the bass player for Laugh, was there, and after an hour he persuaded Sue to clock off early and we jumped in his car to go down to the Sandpiper in Wilbraham Road in Fallowfield. The official Smiths after-party was taking place upstairs, which was fitted out like an aircraft, with airline seats and seatbelts. Mike Joyce, the Smiths' drummer, was there, as were Andrew and Tracey from Swing. It was a trendy place to be, but I am not sure I socialised much as my diary records: 'Susan and I sat in a corner and ate loads of sandwiches.'

I made a couple of other visits to the Free Trade Hall over the next few years, including to host a disastrous spoken-word event featuring the American writer Kathy Acker. Only thirty people came, and Kathy was in a bad mood because Graham Massey from 808 State had created a pre-show tape of someone intoning 'Kathy Acker' over and over again and treated it with weird sound effects, so it sounded like 'Kaaaaaaaaaathy Ackeeeeeeurgggggh'. She thought we were taking the piss.

After the Smiths gig there, my next trip to the Free Trade Hall was to see Arthur Scargill deliver a speech to miners and their supporters. I resolved to do more than wear 'Coal Not Dole' stickers and go on marches, so, later in 1984, I organised a couple of benefit concerts to show solidarity and to raise money for the striking miners and their families. I also wanted to push back against the propaganda poured out by the media in order to trash the miners and their cause.

When the government went to war with the miners – the 'enemy within', as Mrs Thatcher called them – there was no post-war plan. Closing mines and the resultant job losses would impact on families but also threaten towns and villages and ancillary industries. All those structures that support a healthy life were under threat; a place of work, local shops, the pub, the community. Citizens were economic units rather than human beings.

Sue Ferguson was dating Jim Khambatta who managed Marc Riley and the Creepers, so I asked them to play and Marc also put a call through to the Three Johns in Leeds who agreed to join them on one of the nights. I'd booked two consecutive Tuesdays in December at Jilly's, a club above Rafters on Oxford Street. The other night featured Pink Industry and Big Flame. These were set to be the first concerts I'd organised since the Marine Girls.

Less than two weeks before the first show, a taxi driver was killed by two striking miners who dropped a brick off a bridge onto his taxi in an attempt to disrupt the transportation of 'scab' labour to mines in Nottinghamshire. The manager of Jilly's phoned me and told me that the strike was now too controversial and cancelled the bookings. I moved the first concert to the Tropicana on Oxford Street, and the second one to the Gallery at the bottom of Peter Street.

I decided the money should go to one particular organisation, Women Against Pit Closures. Just over £400 was raised by the two gigs, but it would have been a little more if I hadn't dipped my hand into the collection bucket at the Gallery and removed some pound notes. I'd invited a dozen miners and their wives from a colliery near Leigh to come and see the gig. I used some of the cash to buy a round of drinks, or maybe it was three rounds. Anyway, it was a great night out.

Through that winter, my reasons for going to the Haçienda multiplied beyond watching gigs and selling fanzines. I began to be asked to DJ before and after bands, not as cover for Andrew, but in my own right.

In January 1985, I was the extra entertainment on a night headlined by Marc Almond. Fifteen minutes or so before Marc was due onstage, there was a knock on the DJ-box door. I opened the top half of it, and there was Morrissey. I ushered him in and told him, yes, for sure you can watch Marc from here, so he took off his coat and stood next to me. We had a great view.

A few moments later, I was peering through the semi-darkness across the club to see if I could see anyone at the side of the stage giving me any indication as to when Marc would be ready to start. I was excited and pulled out my favourite electro track, Man Parrish's 'Hip Hop, Be Bop (Don't Stop)'. As it poured out of the speakers and across the dancefloor, I turned to Morrissey. 'Remember this?' I asked him. Of course he didn't, and he gave me another one of those raised-eyebrow looks. I sometimes speculate what would have happened if that record, that moment, had made a life-changing impression on him. The next day he would have announced to the rest of the band; 'I heard this great record last night, all drum machines, no guitars, no lyrics. Let's sack this rockabilly-tinged balladeering, we're going hip hop.'

Less than three weeks later, I met him again, this time at Rough Trade's London offices on Thursday, 14 February 1985, for a feature in *Melody Maker*. Editor Allan Jones had arranged for Morrissey to be interviewed by six editors of various fanzines (including me, Rob Deacon from *Abstract* and Lesley O'Toole from *Inside Out*).

This is when I quizzed Morrissey about adolescence, and we also talked about Pete Burns; 'I think he's a wonderful person. He's one of the few people I can feel a great affinity with,' said Morrissey.

He also talked about his sympathy for the miners; 'Completely. I mean, just endless sympathy. What can one say? It's more distressing than most people realise, I think. I think it's the end if they go down, the absolute end.'

We also talked about his close relationship to his listeners; 'Everybody needs friends and a lot of people don't have them. And a lot of people who buy records believe that the artists who make the records are their friends. They believe that they know these people, and they believe that they're actually involved in these people's lives and it's a comfort. We shouldn't have a condescending attitude to that.'

I knew that in the past he had relied heavily for lyrics on phrases from Shelagh Delaney, Victoria Wood and others, so I asked him where he had sourced the lyrics for *Meat is Murder*, the new album.

'Well,' he said, and paused, '*Debris* magazine . . .'

On the tape recording you can hear me do a stupid little

half-giggle, even though I knew it wasn't true and Moz was just teasing me.

I have no idea where the follow-up question came from; 'Do you consider yourself to be an ordinary or an extraordinary person?'

No guessing Morrissey's reply: 'I'm probably extraordinary.'

A photographer was on hand taking photographs while we were asking questions and, at the end, attempts were made to get a group photo. The photographer's idea, endorsed by Morrissey, was that he should be sitting on a big chair and that all the fanzine editors should kneel in front of him, with our tape machines pointing in his direction, compliant disciples prostrate at his feet.

I thought this was daft, even demeaning. Someone said, 'Dave, this is your chance to be famous,' but I really didn't care. I reckoned Morrissey of all people would understand that I was allowed to be choosy about how I was represented. Maybe he appreciated the diva-ish nature of my behaviour. He watched as I walked out of the room. I left Rough Trade, went through King's Cross to Euston and got the train home.

It was Valentine's Day 1985 when I walked out on Morrissey, but I guess if you're going to say goodbye to someone – and that someone is the lovelorn Morrissey, the poet laureate of unrequited love – then why not pick Valentine's Day?

7

The Intellectual
Humanist Disco

Apart from twelve weeks on a government work scheme, I didn't have a job. I mean, a proper job, with a boss, holiday pay, any of that. I worked hard on my various projects, though. All day and most of the night, I'd be writing and organising the fanzine, and attending and often getting involved in events at clubs and other venues. Then the next morning I would start again at eight. I really don't know where that drive came from. No one expected or needed me to get up early, except for once a fortnight when I had to sign on.

I had a low-maintenance lifestyle, made more affordable as the DHSS paid housing benefit to cover my basic rent. I wasn't idle and didn't much mind when I was told I needed to get off the dole and go on a government scheme. The Manpower Services Commission (MSC) ran a Community Programme, and if you'd been signing on you were gently encouraged to apply for jobs on it. Salford Education Department advertised a job via the MSC for people to be based at Irwell Valley High School. The idea was to produce brochures and pamphlets and other teaching aids. I was interviewed, and showed some copies of *Debris* as evidence of my initiative. They took me on and, best of all, I sold a copy of issue 4 to each of the people on the interviewing panel.

On day one of the job we had to come up with a project. My idea was given the green light, and I spent twelve weeks researching writers from Salford, which was brilliant. I dug out books and old press cuttings about Walter Greenwood, Ewan MacColl, Shelagh Delaney and others from Peel Park Library, and spent all day every day writing about writers.

I was already a massive fan of Shelagh Delaney. In later years, I've been asked to present talks about Manchester's independent music scene to students or others. One of the usual places to start is by describing the two performances by the Sex Pistols at the Lesser Free Trade Hall in 1976, which energised the generation – Buzzcocks, Joy Division, Richard Boon, Tony Wilson, Morrissey and the rest – that would change Manchester music forever. But sometimes I'll start by discussing a different, earlier cultural intervention, just as inspiring and illustrative of independent, maverick, creative endeavour: the early life of Shelagh Delaney, whose play *A Taste of Honey* was premiered in 1958 when she was nineteen years old.

Living in Salford, a part-time usherette, one-time clerk in a milk depot, with a few notes and a vague idea for a novel, Shelagh Delaney felt her spirit was being held back. 'Tethered' is a word she uses to great effect in a 1960 BBC profile of her by Ken Russell, as she describes the restlessness of the young folk of Salford and particularly her feelings as a young teenager in the mid-1950s; she was 'tethered like a horse' in a circumscribed world frustrating her urge to break free, to find life.

What triggered her decision to turn the novel into a play was a trip to a theatre in Manchester to see a hit Terence Rattigan play called *Variation on a Theme*. Having sat there squirming in her seat, disappointed by its deadly dullness, she returned home. The mainstream was saying nothing to her, so she looked local, setting *A Taste of Honey* in a 'comfortless flat' in Salford and telling the story of a teenage daughter and her mother (who's described as a 'semi-whore'), the daughter's relationship with a homosexual art student and her liaison with a black sailor.

When *A Taste of Honey* was staged by Joan Littlewood's Theatre Workshop in London in May 1958, it hit the theatre world like a jolt. That a young lass born in Salford could produce a piece of theatre so funny, dramatic, current, heartfelt and important knocked British theatre off its axis. In the *Observer*, Ken Tynan was an early enthusiast: 'Miss Delaney brings real people on to her stage, joking and flaring and scuffling and eventually, out of the zest for life she gives them, surviving.'

Artistic activity has no obligation to be comforting. It can be oppositional, challenging, disconcerting. *A Taste of Honey* never went away and, if anything, its influence grew. Tony Warren devised and wrote *Coronation Street* in its wake; set in the same streets and, at its best, glorying in the same colourful cadences of everyday Salford speech.

The days in Peel Park Library were fabulous. Occasionally I'd have a day back at Irwell Valley High School to check in with the managers of the project. That was OK, too. I'd just sit around all morning and then go home and no one ever gave me any hassle seeing as the mission to get me off the unemployment register for three months was being accomplished. The only problem with having to go to the school was that I'd have the kids bothering me. They'd chant 'Skinhead, skinhead' at me and ask where I got my clothes from. 'Oxfam,' I'd say, and they'd piss themselves laughing.

Not having a proper job didn't mean I wasn't working. I was becoming involved in a venture at a club on Whitworth Street, seventy yards down from the Haçienda and opposite the Archway. This club was later called the Venue, but in 1984 it went by the name Cobwebs, although I'd never met anyone who had set foot inside the place. The poster boys told me it was usually empty apart from a few heavy drinkers who would end up fighting well before the end, but occasionally the club would be busy if the owners booked a stripper.

The poster boys were a tight little group of guys who organised and controlled fly-posting around Manchester. Most of the cash came from London-based record companies and live-music promoters who sent them massive posters in batches of a hundred. The poster boys had a few regular sites around Manchester – under flyovers or on the frontages of derelict buildings – where they would paste them. They chased off anyone trying to move in on their trade; even individual gig promoters or innocent students trying to get people to come to see their band could feel their wrath if they pasted up posters on any of their sites or, worse still, on top of any of their posters.

The poster boys decided to take over and run Cobwebs and asked me to DJ. I don't recall how this came about, although they had a base near the Claremont pub in Moss Side, just a street or two from where I lived in Great Western Street, so maybe my proximity had brought me to their attention. One of the friends of the poster boys, Matthew, knew Big Flame so perhaps Dil or Greg from the band had told him that I had started doing a few DJ gigs.

Their list of people to approach would not have been very long. They knew lots of soul and funk and reggae DJs, but they wanted someone who could hit those bases but also attract an alternative crowd, the Iggy Pop and New Order fans. This was 1984, not 1994: not everyone wanted to be a DJ. There were probably more barbers than DJs in Manchester at that time.

The poster boys were a rum bunch but, when I met a couple of them at their place on Claremont Road for a briefing, I soon realised that one of them, Jimmy Carr, was very keen on music and he seemed to be the most enthusiastic about getting me involved. He told me that Cobwebs would be renamed the Wheel in honour of his favourite club, the Twisted Wheel. Jimmy was sweet; we had a great connection.

The other poster boy at the initial meeting was Vini Faal, who was a friend of Rob Gretton's and had been involved in live promotion in the past, including the staging of a Johnny Thunders gig in Chorlton that Morrissey had attended. Soon after the meet-up on Claremont Road, I bumped into Vini out postering with the crew and he introduced me to his brother Mike Faal.

It soon became clear that my involvement in this new venture entailed more than just being hired to arrive at the venue with a whole lot of records in a box, play them and then go home. Two days before the opening night, Jimmy rang on my doorbell. He explained that they needed me to help paint the venue.

The poster boys had been up all night driving their van to lots of building sites, collecting bits of wood. I gave them the benefit of the doubt that they had restricted what they gathered to unwanted two-by-fours, rather than breaking and entering these sites and half-inching the constituent parts of a dancefloor. I'd had a sheltered life and I always try to see the best in people.

We discussed the sound in Cobwebs and realised the best option was to circumvent the tinny little speakers already installed in the club and to hire a sound system from Moss Side instead. Larry Benji was a mate of the poster boys, and he sorted the sound and promised to play some reggae on the opening night. Oh, and then the poster boys told me I was DJing the opening night too. I had little idea what to play, but Jimmy and Larry said I should at least do the first two hours.

The party attracted an incredible mixture of people, a packed crowd. I was twenty-two, probably too young to know what was going on. I still don't know what was going on. Everyone had a great time, but the room had more than its fair share of rogues along with a couple of dozen people I knew from selling *Debris* and being out and about at gigs. I played songs including 'Flesh of My Flesh' by Orange Juice, Lee Dorsey's 'Working in the Coal Mine' and 'Reach For Love' by Marcel King.

Larry took over for a while and I sat down at a table where Susan was entertaining a whole crew of ne'er-do-wells. Half an hour later, it was time for me to play again, but I couldn't stand up. I think it's what's called 'a contact high'. The poster boys seemed extraordinarily happy about everything. Everyone was stoned on everyone else's smoke.

Then Saturday night arrived, and I was there again, ready for anything, but no one attended apart from a few of my friends. Handing out free Red Stripe and encouraging the consumption of marijuana was the perfect way to fill the club on the launch

I'm in the middle; this is probably 1969 or 1970.

Eighteen years old.

Debbie Harry / Blondie at Barbarella's, February 1978.

Lesley Woods of the Au Pairs at Alexandra Palace, 1980: a day of great music.

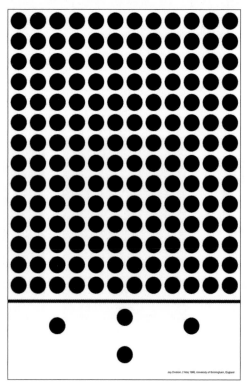

Joy Division at High Hall, Birmingham.

Swing advert printed in *Debris*, 1984.

 MINERS BENEFIT CONCERTS

TUES DEC 11th

PRESENTED BY 'DEBRIS' MAGAZINE

THE THREE JOHNS
MARC RILEY and the Creepers

TUES DEC 18th

PINK INDUSTRY
BIG FLAME ◆ SWIVEL HIPS

JILLY'S (65 OXFORD ST., M'CR)

ADMISSION: £2(£1·50 with UB40). Doors open 8.30 pm.

SOLIDARITY WITH THE N.U.M

VICTORY TO THE STRIKING MINERS

Miners' benefit gigs, 1984.

DEBRIS

PINK INDUSTRY ● MALCOLM X
MARK.E.SMITH ● BIG FLAME ●
TOOLS YOU CAN TRUST **40**p
'WIGAN PIER REVISITED'
CAFE GUIDE TO M'CR ● ISSUE 5

Debris, issue 5.

Carol Morley and Debbie Turner in Tot, 1986.

THE FALL · CHAKK · THE STOOGES · JAMES BROWN ·
INCA BABIES · THE CHIFFONS · ACR · MAGAZINE ·
ORANGE JUICE · T.REX · GANG OF FOUR · ....

ADMISSION £1 (before 11pm)
£1·50 (after 11pm)

ALL DRINKS 70p

EVERY
FRIDAY
at the
VENUE
17 WHITWORTH ST WEST

Flyer for 'The Magic Roundabout' at the Venue.

In the Haçienda DJ box, 'Temperance' 1987.

Kim Gordon (Sonic Youth), at the
New Ardri, Hulme, June 1987.

Thurston Moore (Sonic Youth),
at the New Ardri, Hulme, June 1987.

Amberidge Walk: Sonic Youth slept on the floor
of number 20 in June 1987.

Haçienda, 1990. © Peterjwalsh.com

Laurent Garnier in the Haçienda DJ box. © Peterjwalsh.com

Police raid at the Haçienda, 1990. © Peterjwalsh.com

Poster for the Haçienda DJ tour of America, June / July 1990.

night, but now the realities had hit home. That evening I played Roland Kirk's 'A Sack Full of Soul' and although only eight people danced, that was nearly half the people in the club, so I tried to be positive. There was another reason to be positive about that first Saturday too; the door staff turned away a few regulars who were asking what time the stripper was on, so at least all twenty customers were cool kids. I wasn't going to give up.

The poster boys' interest soon drifted away, though, which turned my first club residency into my most short-lived, but it lasted long enough for me to get gigs at the Wheel for Big Flame and Life (formed by New Order crew member Andy Robinson, they had just released a single on Factory Records). One Saturday, I shared the decks with Hewan Clarke, but the poster boys were nowhere to be seen. The venue closed briefly but the new owner, a Greek man called Andy (full name 'Andy the Greek'), kept in touch.

Jimmy, Vini and Mike went back to fly-posting and their other activities. I still saw them occasionally. One curious event occurred when they took me to an all-day drinking club in Moss Side called the Volta (no relation to the esteemed eatery now located in West Didsbury). They knocked on my door, told me it would be nice to catch up, and they'd buy me a drink. I jumped in the van and we drove round to the Volta. It was about four o'clock on a hot afternoon. There were six of us in total. I have no evidence for this, but I have since wondered if they called for me thinking it would be useful to have an extra body. It may have been a friendly, innocent visit, but there was no warm welcome when we all walked through the doors of the Volta. The room fell silent, one or two people walked out, and we were given free beer. Perhaps someone owed someone some money. Maybe the poster boys genuinely craved my company that afternoon, but I'm not 100 per cent sure.

Issue 5 of *Debris* was nearing completion. For some reason I hit upon the idea of interviewing Mark E. Smith by post. Neil at Swing gave me Mark's address and I wrote to him asking fifteen questions and enclosing a stamped self-addressed envelope so he could write back to me with answers. He did this within a day or two, in his best handwriting.

As well as the interview by post with Mark E. Smith, issue 5 included an interview with Jayne Casey talking about her band Pink Industry. In Liverpool, Jayne introduced me to her partner Kif, and their young son Ra. She told me how her father's violence and cruelty had contributed to her mother's death. 'I saw my mother getting beaten shitless. Images like that stay with you; I could never call them to mind now, but they come out quite often in my music and in my relationships with people.'

In further evidence of my lack of idleness, I was involved in another club, this time with Greg and Dil from Big Flame. They launched a regular Thursday night they dubbed the Wilde Club, hosted at the Man Alive, which was in the basement of Pelican Press on Grosvenor Street. The idea was to provide a stage for interesting bands looking for Manchester shows. A band would perform a thirty-minute set each week and I would play records before and after the live music. The Man Alive held about a hundred people.

Big Flame were a three-piece group named after a revolutionary socialist organisation from the early 1970s, which, in its turn, had taken its name from a 1969 television play, *The Big Flame*, written by Jim Allen and directed by Ken Loach, about a dockers' strike. Big Flame's songs were short, sharp explosions released on their own Laughing Gun label, and then on Ron Johnson Records. John Peel was a big fan; between July 1984 and May 1986 they recorded four sessions for his radio show.

The boys in Big Flame were relentlessly determined to liven things up – not just via the music they made but through lots of extra-curricular activities too: hosting gigs and doing newsletters. Rightly, they believed that it was in everyone's interests to make opportunities for each other.

If you take a snapshot of creative activity in any city in any era, you'll find established major acts taking the headlines and filling the bigger venues, but look harder and you'll also find a mess of struggling musicians, new and emerging bands, young DJs, dreamers, chancers and little scenes at various hard-to-find venues. That's where I like to be, and where I was, very deeply, in the years 1985 to 1987.

Mid-1985, I had my fanzine, a part-time job at Identity in Affleck's Palace and my weekly slot at the Man Alive. My days and nights were filled with fanzines, live music and DJing. I threw myself into activity of all sorts and made, in my own way, a splash or two.

Big Flame created a weekly newsletter to give out at the Wilde Club, which had listings, playlists, slogans, mini-manifestos and, on the front cover, a hand-drawn picture of the Nicaraguan revolutionary leader Augusto César Sandino. We liked new music but we did have old-time heroes including the Pop Group.

I liked that Big Flame were judgemental and rigorous and took things seriously. Goth was a no-no. It was about singles not albums. They'd considered everything – they'd taken a position and were unyielding; haircuts mattered (like me, they kept their hair short). There was an echo of pre-parka, pre-Brighton (and definitely pre-Weller) mod, when the movement and the look were sharp, dynamic, pure. In a manifesto in the first newsletter, Big Flame declared the Wilde Club to be 'evangelist and uncompromising . . . we believe in community, conversation, fanzines, longer weekends, short hair'.

The newsletter plugged upcoming shows – the bands in the first couple of months included the June Brides, Jasmine Minks, Yeah Yeah Noh and Bogshed. The newsletter also included a list of five or so songs that the audience might hear me play: the likes of the Fire Engines 'New Thing in Cartons', Trouble Funk 'Drop the Bomb', 23 Skidoo 'Language' and a song by Singers & Players called 'Bedward the Flying Preacher', which I had heard on Steve Barker's Sunday afternoon show on BBC Radio Lancashire.

There were supposed to be bands on every Thursday, but then Big Flame got news that a band was pulling out and suggested that instead of replacing them, we should dispense with live music that week and just have me playing records. When I picked up the newsletter the next week, they had billed my full debut appearance there on 7 March as 'Intellectual Humanist Disco with DJ Miserable Dave'.

'You have made it sound crap, and no fun,' I said. 'Who's going to come to something called that?'

I disputed with Dil and Greg how miserable I was (they said 'very'). Then we had a short and unhelpful discussion about what an intellectual humanist disco actually was. They told me; 'We don't know. It's the first one ever. You're going to have to define the phrase with whatever you play.'

Forty or fifty people came and I played everything from the playlist along with 'Tell Me That I'm Dreaming' by Was Not Was and stuff by the bands that Big Flame were booking including 'You' by Chakk. The Man Alive served spicy Afro-Caribbean food and had a pool table in one room. The dancefloor was small, but that was OK with me because it made it easier to fill.

A network was developing for the exchange of ideas and for mutual sustenance. Without the benefits of today's digital technology, we relied on letters, telephones and club nights to make connections. One of the people who wrote to Big Flame and got a reply was Richey Edwards, a few months before he joined the Manic Street Preachers. In an interview in 1991 he recalled that, for his circle of friends, the 1980s was 'The biggest non-event ever . . . All we had was Big Flame. Big Flame was the most perfect band. But we couldn't play their records because they were too avant garde.'

In these months at the Wilde Club, I was learning things. I was learning that an undercapitalised crew of people, just a handful, can make something happen. I was learning stuff about DJing; that you have to think about every music choice, to know what each song represents and how it reflects the world. That the music you play has a status, a value, a significance, a specific place in the big scheme of things.

Back then, still and always, a good DJ should have a position, an individual take on what he or she wants to play. From then on, it's about building a bridge to the audience, a kind of negotiation. Total non-compromise is brave but can alienate potential customers; however, ditching your principles and just playing the fifty most popular records in the world ever is far worse. Anyone, or any computer, can do that.

Playing before and after the bands had sharpened my sense of how to make a selection that drew in an audience. The response to what I was doing at the Wilde Club was positive. People danced. If you wanted to hear 23 Skidoo on a Thursday in Manchester in the spring of 1985, there was simply nowhere else to go.

We were marginal in Manchester, but I didn't mind. In some ways, I revelled in it. Things seemed so much more exciting and unpredictable on the margins. So many people whose music and taste inspired me were open-minded, and were drawn to and from the margins rather than the mainstream. And it felt like where I belonged.

Via our primitive network we knew we had allies elsewhere. I was still visiting Wylie and others over in Liverpool. The inspirational people locally were always looking outwards from Manchester and were far from parochial; Factory was still assiduous in building links with New York, with bands like ESG as well as people like Ruth Polsky, Arthur Baker and Mark Kamins.

Big Flame had created an informal alliance between what we were doing and a small bit of the Leeds scene; Age of Chance from that city played a couple of times, and it was at the Wilde Club that I first met James Brown, when he came over from Leeds to sell his fanzine *Attack on Bzag*. Among other positions of authority in publishing, James went on to become editor of *NME*, *Loaded* and *GQ*, and to launch the website Sabotage Times.

I was a big fan of Chakk from Sheffield; they were one of the first groups to play at the Wilde Club and I went over to FON studios to interview them for *Debris*. One of the band, Mark Brydon, later co-founded Moloko with Róisín Murphy.

Eventually, the Wilde Club nights began to be less frequent than weekly, but I'd been given a new opportunity back where I'd done those nights for the poster boys. The owner, Andy the Greek, had kept the dancefloor I'd helped to build but he hadn't kept the name, the Wheel; instead, he'd started calling his place the Venue. Even though my previous experiences there had included playing Roland Kirk to just eight people, he asked me to play every Friday.

I was given full rein over everything that happened on a Friday, aside from running the bar and employing the door staff. I called these Fridays 'The Magic Roundabout' and a number of people who had been at the Man Alive most weeks followed me there, including two young women called Laura and Jackie, John Twang, David Scattergood and Maureen Ward. Within weeks I had new regulars too, including Little Andy.

At the Venue, I didn't have the supervision and mini-manifestos of Big Flame but I stuck to some of the Wilde Club principles, notably to take up a position about what you will and won't champion, and to steer the night with as little compromise as possible. I also realised that a successful regular night needs anthems. By this, I mean that a DJ needs to cultivate certain tracks that people begin to associate with their sets at that particular venue. Even better if those songs are out of the ordinary, and the audience are only ever likely to hear them when they play.

At the Venue, alongside an eclectic mix of the O'Jays and the Clash, there were at least three obscure songs that became big favourites. One was 'Joy's Address' by Float Up CP, who were a spin-off group from Rip Rig + Panic, with members including Bruce Smith and Neneh Cherry. Another was 'I,

Bloodbrother Be' by the Shockheaded Peters, and the third was by the Loft, 'Up the Hill and Down the Slope', a single on Creation Records. Sometimes, DJing, I'd clear the dancefloor but I'd deal with it – I'd find something to rescue the night. I realised that public humiliation was a part of growing up and certainly a part of my DJing apprenticeship; when things go wrong, you become wise.

8

When We Talk About Love

DJing is not about power, it's about sharing. *Debris* was the same: sharing, connecting. You might want to play a record your audience would ordinarily be resistant to, but if you find a context for it, play it at the right time, in among more familiar material, it might work. Similarly, I always hoped *Debris* could introduce people to something new. I was prepared to put myself on the line.

Debris had started getting a little name for itself. Other fanzines would plug the fanzine and I'd mention my favourites like *Hungry Beat. Jamming* called *Debris* 'A brilliant piece of literature from Manchester', and Neil Taylor in the *NME* described it as 'the best fanzine in the world'.

I wanted to be honest, to hoover up ideas and to share passions. Some of the stuff going in *Debris* included reviews of novels, features on Sergei Eisenstein, Shelagh Delaney, Oskar Kokoschka, *Chinatown* and Patty Hearst. I was tempted to devote a whole issue to James Baldwin.

Debris also had detractors. The usual criticism was that it was 'pretentious'. One night on a venue toilet wall someone had scrawled: 'Debris = arty shit'. I developed a thick skin or, at least, tried to; I already knew from DJing that you can't please everybody all of the time and, what's more, you shouldn't even try.

I didn't much mind my work being described as 'arty', a word that's been attached to some of the best things ever, and to the best people. Joy Division referencing Kafka; Devoto and his passion for Dostoyevsky; Linder's collages; John Cale releasing an eight-minute ballad 'Hedda Gabler', loosely based on the Ibsen play.

Artiness is attractive in a person. I like people who challenge greyness and limited expectations, especially when it's a brave thing to do. I'm thinking about Holly Johnson walking down Bold Street in Liverpool in 1975 wearing salmon-pink trousers while brigades of no-nonsense lads threw fruit at him.

I also began including free flexi-discs with the fanzine, featuring barely known bands like Dub Sex, Laugh and King of the Slums. Once, I was at home and live on air John Peel announced he'd just received the new *Debris*, and with a slight scrunch took the latest flexi out of the paper sleeve and played it without listening to it first. It was wonderful to be trusted like that.

I went with my friend Mikey to sample the sound of the machinery at the Manchester Free Press printing the fanzine. The next issue included a track of the sounds we recorded. I was fighting for my right to be arty, but it was too much, maybe. This time even John Peel gave the flexi a miss.

I was a fan of the American short-story writer Raymond Carver, having been introduced to his work through his collection *What We Talk About When We Talk About Love* and the magazine *Granta*. In 1985, Picador, which had just published *The Stories of Raymond Carver*, brought Carver to London to promote the collection and I was desperate to meet him. He was on the cusp of becoming a literary sensation; his reputation grew very quickly over the following year or two, and continued to rise after he died in August 1988.

Carver's schedule in London in spring 1985 wasn't full. There were only four or five UK-based journalists who wanted to talk to him. I was told I could meet Carver at his London hotel, the Sheraton in Belgravia, even though all I had was a little fanzine in Manchester that sold around five hundred copies, mostly to half-drunk people at the Haçienda. I'd never been to a London hotel; I'd never met an American writer.

After the interview was printed in *Debris* this young lad, who I knew was very into his music, came up to me at the Haçienda; he had a bit of a snipe about *Debris* being arty and told me he didn't think people would be interested in the American guy. I said, 'Please read the interview, and if you can, read his stories.'

Two weeks later he was back in the club, and he was gushing. He'd absolutely fallen in love with Raymond Carver. And not only that, he'd made me a T-shirt with one of Carver's front covers on it and presented it to me. I still have the T-shirt. It was such a powerful moment.

I'd thrown myself into the Carver interview, tracking down all the stories I could get my hands on. The encounter went well at the Sheraton. He was well built, with an earnest, doleful manner, like a big bear resigned to being caught by poachers sometime soon, and he welcomed me warmly.

I was wide-eyed meeting him, and out of my comfort zone among the hotel's pastel shades and thick carpets (I was impressed by how the doors closed without making a sound). Having split from his wife, Carver was in London with the poet Tess Gallagher, who offered me tea and biscuits. Not only had I never been inside a London hotel or met an American writer, I'd never been served tea on a tray by a poet.

I was meeting Raymond Carver in the least Carver setting imaginable. He wrote of rundown, smalltown America; all-night cafés, TVs, bankruptcy, dead-end jobs, violence and despair. Many of his characters are insecure, and under pressure from confusing circumstances, the power of the past, their own weaknesses, and seldom do they learn much or find any answers. The stories are told in short, bleak sentences, but they have moments of wry humour, even the story 'Jerry and Molly and Sam' about trying to get rid of the family dog.

Carver married young and had two small children by the age of twenty. Married life was a continual battle to pay the rent and buy clothes for the children. He and his wife could only get a string of short-term, low-paid jobs. When he started to write, there were so many obstacles, including profound alcoholism, the demands of parenthood and financial difficulties. Short stories were all that time and space allowed.

I guess anyone wishing to write, or follow any other creative vocation, could make a list of reasons why they couldn't or shouldn't, but Carver cracked on. I found it instructive, even inspiring, that despite everything he found time to write. 'I just wanted to write more than anything,' he told me. 'The writing was the one thing I was determined to hold on to, it was the one connection that I felt if I could hold on to that, no matter how dim and guttering the candle became, it would give my life some validation. It was that important to me.'

We discussed his inspiration and creative processes and he explained how there's an element of chance in the way a little incident or phrase can spark a story and mystery about what happens next; 'I don't really know where I'm going when I begin to write the story, I don't know the ending. I don't know the middle of the story. It's like groping around in a room in the dark looking for a light.'

I told him that I sensed that many of the characters place some hopeless demands on their love relationships, that people have an intense need for love, but it can be misdirected. He agreed; 'I'm glad you found that there is love in these stories, even though it may be misdirected sometimes. But I think that's true. Many people in these stories do need love.'

There was a second of silence before he summed up; 'Sometimes those who need love the most are the least capable of inspiring it.'

Listening again to the interview thirty years later, and thinking about other interviews and encounters, I realise that, although I have a deep engagement with the work of the interviewee, of course, my line of questioning sometimes springs from my own preoccupations or issues at the time. I think this is OK. It's OK for an interviewer to invest emotion in an interview.

In recent years, I was drawing on my own life when I discussed with Jamie xx the curiousness of being an introvert DJ. And at a time when my inner life was a bit grim, I interviewed John Lydon and I decided to ask him if he had ever had therapy. I thought my question was fair as John had battled through so many incidents and issues in his life – some obvious, some not so obvious – and had written two autobiographies, and he lives in California, the therapy capital of the world. But he seemed perplexed by the question.

When I interviewed Raymond Carver I had a failure of a love life, which I now realise was probably a result of my radar being on the blink. I think there were girls interested in me, but I wasn't good at reading signals. There was a girl called Kris who was taken onto the books of Model Team International. I thought she was way out of my league, and she probably was, except I never found out for sure. She came round once and after *Newsnight* I walked her home; she kept asking me to meet her and she suggested one sunny evening that we should take a walk in the park together, which we did, and then we parted and I never saw her again. I think there were signals – in retrospect, I think they were strong – but I couldn't read them.

Susan and I were housemates, along with Rob Walker, on Great Western Street in Moss Side. One of our closest friends was Paul Morley's younger sister, Carol; she helped sell my fanzine. Carol Morley had numerous sexual partners and plenty of adventures. When taking a break from her chaotic life, she used to sit in the kitchen and eat cashews and talk to me about Samuel Beckett.

At the end of the 1990s, Carol began making a film, called *The Alcohol Years*, a genius piece of work. In the film, she questions me about those years in the mid-1980s and we talk about our relationship. We never had sex; during filming, Carol prompted me to explain why this was so. I realised then that the other factor in my non-love life at the time was that I didn't seem to have much of a libido, which might have been a product of the mild depression I was inflicted with at the time. *The Alcohol Years* includes interviews with a number of men who fucked Carol, including some who paid her for sex. So, a certain cachet ends up being attached to my status as the man who *didn't* sleep with Carol Morley.

The girl who probably got the most messed around by my malfunctioning radar and undemanding libido was Denise Fitzgerald, from Liverpool. We had a lot of mutual friends and she was often in Manchester. If there was a must-see film on at the Aaben, a group of us would go, I'd sit down in the cinema, there would be shuffling around of seats and invariably Denise would end up sitting next to me. When Everything But The Girl played in Liverpool, I arranged for her to get VIP access and she sent a card thanking me.

Denise called me up. It was about ten in the evening and she was on a payphone. 'I'd like to see you, Dave.'

'OK, where are you?'

'I'm in Café Berlin.' That was a wine bar on Bold Street in Liverpool. I'd been there to see a wonderful band called Send No Flowers play.

'Well, I'm here,' I said, meaning I was thirty-five miles away at home on Great Western Street in Moss Side in Manchester (but I guess I didn't have to spell that out as she had called me at home). I was unaware of her ardour and urgency. 'So why don't you call me tomorrow or the next day, and we'll meet?' I suggested.

The payphone was in a noisy venue, conversation was difficult. But we'd already run out of time anyway. It was one of the hazards of payphones; you had to have cash and be ready to feed the meter. Denise, on the phone from Café Berlin, never got the chance to reply to my suggestion of a meet-up in the next few days.

I went off to bed, Susan went out, but Rob was still up, having a cup of tea, which he always made with a pot, which he warmed, and with proper tea leaves (and it took ages). Rob was a filmmaker but, like all of us, he was only in the early stages of his chosen vocation. He spent most days writing to organisations who might lend him £200 so he could make a film called *Land of Cockaigne*, a dark and drug-related adaptation of a medieval myth he was going to set in modern-day Hulme. He was a deep thinker but a man of few words. He'd sigh or shrug his shoulders, run his hand through his hair or raise an eyebrow and you'd have to guess his thoughts. He sighed when I told him Denise had called. I tried to guess the meaning of the sigh; something like 'you have some untangling to do'.

'Night, Robert,' I said to Rob.

Fifty minutes later, I heard a knock on the front door, voices and then Rob shouting 'Dave.' I went downstairs and he nodded in the direction of Denise.

'You've got a taxi from Liverpool?'

She didn't speak. She stared at me.

Brandishing a sleeping bag, I said to Denise, 'I have this for you. Shall we talk in the morning?' She suddenly crumpled drunkenly into a chair. Rob was on another chair; he raised both eyebrows at me. I don't know what the hell he was thinking, but then I have no idea what I was thinking either. Denise got up, pushed past me and ran out of the house.

Rob wasn't giving me any advice, let alone good advice, but I knew I should run after her. It wasn't a great area: a murky park opposite, a couple of all-night shebeens, and prostitutes usually stationed on three of the corners between my house and Princess Road. I was barefoot and wearing just a T-shirt and pyjama trousers, so I started upstairs to get some shoes but then decided I didn't have time to get properly shod, so in bare feet I ran into the street to find her. She had disappeared.

I sat down next to Rob, who offered to make me a cup of tea, but I knew that would entail him warming the pot and the complicated tea-leaves business, so it all seemed too much of a palaver and I went back to bed.

About an hour later, woken by a whimpering sound, I looked out of the window, then ran downstairs and opened the door. Denise was lying on the doorstep crying and half asleep. I let her into the house, and she ran to the sleeping bag and curled up. When I woke up the next morning, she'd gone.

A week later, I got a postcard from her. It just said, 'Sorry.'

I know. What was up with me? I have no idea.

It was over, and it had never really begun.

The next year I got chucked by a girl called Elaine because I was so distant, she said, and impossibly hard to get to. 'You're like a rock in the middle of the ocean' were her exact words.

9

Sonic Youth Slept
On My Floor

Ever since Blondie had awakened my teenage interest in music from New York, I'd had one ear on what was happening in small venues over there, which was one reason why my attention was drawn to Sonic Youth. That and a coincidence; Liz Naylor, who I had met that evening with Morrissey in the pub in Hulme, had moved to London and worked at Paul Smith's label, Blast First, which looked after Sonic Youth in the UK. Thanks to her, I received a pre-release copy of the band's second album, *Bad Moon Rising*.

Sonic Youth were barely known and, in March 1985, yet to play a show in Manchester. I immersed myself in the album and their debut, *Confusion Is Sex*. Iggy and the Stooges were just about the only reference point I had for Sonic Youth's sound, attitude and mindset. A generation earlier, the Stooges had soundtracked 'war across the USA' in '1969', the year the promise of the 1960s crashed and splintered, courtesy of the continuing slaughter in Vietnam, the Stones at Altamont and the Manson family.

Years later, I discovered Sonic Youth's Kim Gordon had grown up in California; the Manson murders were close to home and motivated the song 'Death Valley '69' track on the *Bad Moon Rising* album. Kim's spoken-word style vocals, on 'Ghost Bitch' and 'I Love Her All the Time', seem to find a space in which time stands still.

I would get to see Sonic Youth three or four times between 1985 and 1987. They are undoubtedly the best rock band I've ever seen; the non-standard sound, the discomforting challenge of the lyrics, the way they threw themselves into a performance, Iggy Pop-style. There was also something fascinating about the gender relations in the band, like the Au Pairs, I guess, but on another level of powerfulness.

The first time I saw Sonic Youth was in Leeds on 25 March 1985. The show was so low-key it doesn't even appear in the 'definitive' list of Sonic Youth concerts posted on the band's website. It was in a basement venue, which is now called the Hifi, which in 1985 I think was called the Central. There wasn't even a proper stage – the band were set up on the dancefloor. I sat quietly while Sonic Youth ran through a few songs in the soundcheck before Paul Smith took us all to Pizza Hut. I'd been granted an interview for *Debris*.

Most of what you can hear on the tape of the subsequent conversation is the rattle of cutlery and the Pizza Hut muzak, including the Fun Boy Three song 'The Lunatics Have Taken Over the Asylum'. Bob Bert, the drummer, said nothing at all during the interview; Lee Ranaldo was a little distant; Thurston

Moore was eager, though, and Kim also tried her best to engage with my questions.

Pizza Hut went up a level and provided customers with the Ice Cream Factory – unlimited trips to a large, plastic, ice-cream dispensing contraption – but that wasn't a feature of their establishments in 1985, although the buffet-style salad bar was.

Later Sonic Youth turned out to be a massive influence on Nirvana and were eulogised by David Bowie as 'so important to the Eighties', but my first encounter with the band began a little inauspiciously with us all gathered around the salad bar in Leeds. We each had a bowl and made our selection of bits of lettuce, tomatoes, cucumber slices, coleslaw sludge and unidentified crunchy stuff masquerading as croutons.

Given that they were so unknown, perhaps I should have thought about collecting some general and helpful information about Sonic Youth during the interview. Maybe I should have asked, 'How did you meet?' or 'Tell me about the recording of the album,' but I was crazy for ideas, and earnest, and eager, and after we'd settled down to eat, my opening question to Sonic Youth was this: 'Underneath bland, success-seeking American society, do you think there's an ever-present undercurrent of violence?'

On the tape of the interview you can sense the stunned silence. Lee Ranaldo was eating from his salad bowl and staring at me incredulously.

Thurston, kindly, offered a reply: 'Yes, definitely,' he said.

And Kim helped out; 'Yes, it goes right back. You can see it in early American novels and, later, in movies and comics and things. The whole of our country was born out of violence.'

Lee stopped skewering hard-skinned salad tomatoes with his fork. 'Somehow it's all caught up with the idea of freedom,' he said. 'It's as if freedom and violence are part of the same thing.'

After some talk about how issues from the 1960s 'counter-culture' remained unresolved, and weird guitar tunings, Kim described the sound they aimed for. 'It's a spirit and an attitude. It's always been to do with breaking free, breaking through sexual and emotional repression.'

Sonic Youth were scheduled to play at the Haçienda a few weeks later, supporting Nick Cave and the Bad Seeds, and my plan was to include the interview in the new issue of *Debris*, have it ready for then, and sell shedloads of fanzines at the gig, but I messed up and missed all my deadlines.

Happily, though, my connections with the band stayed strong. A year later, I was offered the chance to stage their first headline show in Manchester, at a club called the Boardwalk. I'd just started running Saturday nights there with a partner, Nathan McGough.

In the mid-1980s, when I was first making and taking opportunities, I had several important allies – Andrew Berry, Big Flame and John Peel. Nathan McGough was a major addition to this list. He was managing the band Kalima and living on Brunswick Road in Withington when I first met him in 1986; he was sharing a house with Suzanne Robinson, who ran the café at the Haçienda, and Franco Brazil, who was an exotic musician genuinely from Brazil. Nathan was in the process of moving on from Kalima in order to spend more time looking after the Bodines, who were signed to Creation Records.

Nathan grew up in Liverpool. His mother, Thelma, worked on Cilla Black's *Blind Date* TV show and, in her youth, had hung out with the Beatles before they were famous. She'd met John Lennon when they were both students at the Liverpool College of Art in 1957 and discovered they had some formative experiences in common, including their fathers walking out on them when they were young children. They dated for a few months, including taking a trip to see Elvis in *Jailhouse Rock*. John was very short-sighted but too vain to take his glasses so, needing a running commentary on the storyline, he kept yanking Thelma's hand saying, 'What's happening now, Thel?'

Their courting petered out just before he took up with Cynthia Powell, but Thelma and John remained friendly until one evening at a school dance in 1959 when they had a minor argument and he hit her. She walked away and they were never close again.

Over the next few years, Thelma briefly dated Paul McCartney, and also had Nathan, but by the middle of the 1960s she was with Roger McGough and running a boutique called Monika. She and Roger later had two boys, Tom and Finn, but were divorced by the end of the 1970s. According to Nathan, his stepfather was the first man in Liverpool to experience LSD, thanks to the American beat poet Allen Ginsberg who visited Liverpool in May 1965 and declared the city to be 'at the present moment, the centre of consciousness of the human universe'. The Liverpool poets – Roger McGough and Brian Patten among them – were Ginsberg's hosts.

Nathan was very likeable and sociable, and, unsurprisingly given his upbringing, interested in art and culture. He had been in the Royal Family and the Poor, and in an early line-up of the Pale Fountains. When he first moved to Manchester, he lived with Tony Wilson's family.

As well as being a musician on the Liverpool scene, Nathan had helped run a few live shows in Liverpool too, including gigs at Plato's Ballroom where I'd once seen Dead or Alive – and also New Order – play. We 100 per cent trusted each other.

Nathan and I began working together, booking bands weekly at the Boardwalk. The Boardwalk was a family business. In 1985, the Sinclairs had bought the building, an old church school dating back to the Victorian era. The last significant activity there before they took over was that one of the floors had housed the Green Room alternative theatre (which later took a site on Whitworth Street). The Boardwalk building included several floors, and you went up the stairs to access the live room, which was the former theatre space. Inside, there was capacity for about 180 people.

In a project headed by Colin Sinclair, the family had turned the basement of the Boardwalk into rehearsal rooms, which hosted bands including A Certain Ratio, Happy Mondays and, a few years later, Oasis. On the top floor, in the early days, there was extra rehearsal space, used by James and the Railway Children. Colin managed the Railway Children.

The Boardwalk opened as a venue on 21 March 1986. A Certain Ratio headlined the first Friday of the first weekend. Nathan and I were booking and promoting Saturdays at the club. We called our enterprise 'The Saturday Club'; the bookings on our opening night were the Pale Fountains supported by the Bodines.

It was a month later that Nathan and I welcomed Sonic Youth to the Boardwalk. All tickets were sold. In fact, the timing was perfect; the band had gained a ton of followers with the heart-kicking brilliance of the newly released album *EVOL*, which remains one of my favourite records of all time.

After the Sonic Youth show at the Boardwalk, Nathan and I and the band decided to go on to the Haçienda. There had been just over two hundred people crammed into the Boardwalk, more than double the size of the crowd in the cavernous Haçienda. I remember the sense of anti-climax, leaving a packed sweat pit that felt like the centre of the music universe and arriving at a big empty warehouse where the DJ was playing 'Ring My Bell'. The Haçienda's resident Saturday night DJ was clearly struggling, pursuing a commercial playlist with no success.

Nathan and I had some kudos in our small worlds; we felt like the new kids in town (to mark the launch of our Saturday shows, the Manchester listings magazine *City Life* commissioned a Kevin Cummins portrait of us both). Nathan loved the ladies and never ducked out of a challenge (he reckoned he could turn a lesbian straight, but I never saw any evidence of this). When we first met, he was just splitting from a steady girlfriend, Eilidh Bradley, who was photographed smoking a cigarette on the front cover of the Bodines single 'Therese'. Nathan already gave off the scent of success, which seemed to feed into his ability to get girls. Although we were comrades in many ways, we were not always on the same wavelength, as any girls we attempted to double date would discover. His target would end up being invited to have sex in the toilets, and her friend would be invited by me to an upcoming art show at the Whitworth Art Gallery.

At our post-gig visit to the empty Haçienda with Sonic Youth, Nathan got it into his head that he would seduce Kim Gordon. It turned into some strange kind of dream. Nathan failed, dramatically, but for about five minutes I stood with Thurston Moore, quietly, uncomfortably, the two of us staring at Nathan trying to do some dirty dancing to 'West End Girls' with Kim Gordon on a virtually empty dancefloor. We didn't speak, Thurston and I – I mean, what could we say? I can't hear 'West End Girls' without recalling that scene. It haunts me.

A year after the Boardwalk show and the 'West End Girls' fiasco, Sonic Youth toured again, with Firehose featuring Mike Watt, formerly of the Minutemen. This time I was co-promoting with Tim Chambers and the gig was at an Irish club, the New Ardri Ballroom in Hulme, a favoured venue for Irish showbands. Sonic Youth were on a guarantee of £600 but there was no extra fee for Firehose.

Tommy, the owner of the Ardri, hired the club to Tim and me for next to nothing. Noel and Liam Gallagher's father, also called Tommy, was one of the resident DJs – some of the staff called him 'the monk' because of his hairstyle. To save everyone money and embarrassment, Tommy Gallagher was told he should have the night off when Sonic Youth came to town as I planned to play hip hop between the bands.

I had moved back to Hulme and it was decided that, to save more costs, Sonic Youth would stay with me on Amberidge Walk, just a hundred yards or so from the venue. I was happy to do my best to look after them; my work diary records that I spent £30 on drinks, which included a crate of Breaker, a crate of Red Stripe, two litres of orange juice and a litre of water.

They were easy, undemanding, guests and had only a few hours sleep, making use of a couple of mattresses and a comfortable chair (Lee took the chair), before setting off in the van to catch a ferry over to Holland for a show the next night. I didn't get to make them breakfast, but I did instant coffee for them, just before they left, still wearing the clothes I'd worn the day before.

The next time I saw Thurston Moore was in March 2014, almost thirty years after we'd first met. It was at Liverpool Sound City, specifically at the conference held there for music industry professionals, bloggers, musicians, students and other interested parties to gather and listen to speakers, panel discussions and onstage interviews. I was interviewing Thurston.

The status of the band was complicated. In October 2011, it was announced that Thurston and Kim were divorcing, following the revelation that Thurston had a girlfriend, art-book editor Eva Prinz. Since then, Thurston and Kim had not spoken about their split at much length but the online chatter was deafening, and the band had stopped writing, recording or touring.

I was excited but also anxious, though, because I needed a strategy. The event was attended by six hundred delegates; I had forty minutes and a long list of subjects I wanted to discuss with Thurston, including his early inspirations, his thoughts on Nirvana and his solo work, but Kim's name would crop up, for sure, and I'd been wondering how to handle his marriage break-up.

I couldn't pretend Kim and Thurston hadn't split – that would have been strange and unnatural – and even if I did decide not to mention this personal issue, then a member of the audience would be likely to ask a marriage break-up question. It was probably my job to frame it sympathetically. Also, of course, it was part of his story – a big part – and part of the story of the band. Delving deep seemed OK, but I didn't want to act like some kind of a gossipy sleazebag.

I met Thurston in a quiet room backstage, where he introduced me to Eva Prinz and we had a drink and chatted to the

Sound City organisers. We had twenty minutes or so before we had to walk down the corridor to the conference room, take to the stage and do the interview. So, while we waited, I reminded Thurston of the handful of times we'd previously met.

These were encounters etched deeply on my memory, and I listed them. 'In 1985 I interviewed you in Leeds, Pizza Hut, for my fanzine.'

'What was it called?'

'The fanzine? *Debris*. And I put on two shows in Manchester, the first at a club called the Boardwalk, the second at an old Irish club, the Ardri. Then you all came and slept in the spare room and on the floor of my flat. It was a bit scuzzy. My apartment. On an estate.'

He looked at me.

'A housing project,' I said.

Thurston, however, had absolutely no recollection of me or any of these clubs, or rooms, or estates, or events, or encounters. He did remember my fanzine, however; 'I remember *Debris*,' he said, looking at me.

'The gigs were good.'

'Right,' he said.

'If they'd been disasters you'd have remembered them.'

'I guess,' he said, and we laughed.

Thurston genuinely wanted to remember our meet-ups. I consoled him. I told him they were fleeting meetings, it was a long time ago and in that era he must have had dealings with a ton of fanzine boys. He furrowed his brow, narrowed his eyes and played with his hair, but still couldn't find me in his memory bank.

Who knows how we influence each other? Or how we evolve

via our meetings, our experiences of other people, their life, or art, or ideas?

I told Thurston the difference between what we recollected of each other tells us a lot about the hero/fan relationship. 'You changed my life, but I didn't change yours. In some ways we're the sum of our encounters, aren't we?' I said. 'And one day I will write a book about all this.'

10

The Mosh Pit In A Gay Bar

In the mid-1980s, we didn't have the means to document what we did in the same way as now – via digital photos and videos – or to maintain connections via email or Facebook. You shared a moment, then it was gone. You met someone, then they disappeared.

Nathan and I invited the Shamen to play at the Boardwalk – before Mr C and the late Will Sinnott had joined them – when they were a psychedelic-type band influenced by groups like the 13th Floor Elevators and Love, and still based in Aberdeen. The agreed fee was £100, lower than Primal Scream but higher than some; we paid the Pastels and BMX Bandits a combined £110, the Beloved got £40 and Pop Will Eat Itself got £50.

These financial arrangements were made after a phone call or two; we had no faxes at our disposal. Occasionally I couldn't find a number so I would write to bands. I wrote to Jason Pierce at his home in Rugby to see if Spacemen 3 would play; they did, on a fabulous double-bill supporting Talulah Gosh, for the princely sum of £50 (Talulah Gosh got £80). Everything was on a shoestring, with bands staying on floors or sofas, with friends or fans.

The night the Shamen played we were in danger of losing as much as £30. They'd come all the way down from Aberdeen and only forty people had turned up. I asked if they'd accept £70 instead of £100 and Colin Angus, the singer, agreed. We were both deeply embarrassed.

I've taken a little less of a DJ fee than expected from a few promoters since then. You can usually tell if a promoter is messing you about. If you believe in something and you put your body and soul into it to deliver a good event and it doesn't quite happen, then it's cool. When you just dick about, look for a short cut, blame someone else, it isn't.

Later in 1986, I worked with another Blast First act from America, Big Black, fronted by Steve Albini. He was later the acclaimed producer of Nirvana's *In Utero* and *Surfer Rosa* by the Pixies (among about a hundred other albums). A band called Head of David supported Big Black in what was probably one of their first gigs; they'd just been signed to Blast First.

In Big Black interviews, Steve Albini came across angry, aggressive, saying things such as, 'I like noise. I wanna feel it whipping through me like a fucking jolt. We're so dilapidated and crushed by our pathetic existence we need noise like a fix.'

The Big Black show took place at a gay club called the Archway, which had opened eighteen months earlier in a railway arch on Whitworth Street West, just down the road from the Haçienda (it was later the site of the Brickhouse). The owners, Harry and Wayne, had established the Archway as probably the most hardcore gay club in the city. They'd given the railway arch a stripped-down interior, which I suppose was a cheap way of converting the space, but also seemed to fit the uncompromising, macho vision they had for the venue. Harry and Wayne both sported handlebar moustaches (in addition, Harry had a favourite cowboy hat). The Archway was supposedly mixed, apart from Tuesdays, which were designated men-only, but I never saw it less than 95 per cent male.

So how did Big Black end up playing there? They were flying over for their first shows in Europe and the itinerary was a little threadbare. Paul Smith called up Tim Chambers and asked him for advice, and he and I took up the challenge of staging a show for Big Black in Manchester on a Monday.

We hired the Archway because it was small and cheap, although they had never had live music at the venue before and we knew we'd have to take in some of the staging. We did the deal; Harry and Wayne seemed to trust us. I gave them just a little background information about the band and told them they were called Big Black; they seemed to like the sound of the name.

As well as venue hire, we paid £100 for the PA (hired from a company called Beast, who also brought the staging), plus a fee for the two bands (£200 in total). The stage went up against the wall facing the entrance. Big Black were a three-piece, so it didn't need to take up the whole dancefloor, although it slightly reduced the capacity, which Harry and Wayne reckoned was 150. We needed 115 people to break even.

John Peel played Big Black and very occasionally plugged live dates, while Steve Barker, who had a Sunday afternoon show on BBC Radio Lancashire, was a Big Black fan. His taste was inspiring; he was responsible for getting me into the On-U

Sound label, among other things. One of Steve's contacts was Alan Woods, who ran a record shop in Wigan, rather prosaically called Alan's, but rather wonderfully stocked. Alan's customers knew their Black Flag from their Big Black; with Alan, Peel and Steve on our side and telling people about the show, we stood a chance of getting close to breaking even.

The toilet stalls in the Archway were extra large, big enough to fit two or three men in them at one time, and around the venue there were posters Blu-tacked to the exposed brick walls advertising forthcoming events and featuring illustrations of bulging crotches, handcuffs and cartoon cowboys with neat moustaches waving engorged police truncheons around.

Albini was an angry young guy with a tough band who said he needed noise like a fix, but I had no idea whether hanging out in a hardcore gay club was a temporary lifestyle choice that would appeal to him. We were probably being over sensitive, but wanting to avoid Albini throwing a wobbler, Tim and I decided to downplay how gay the venue was, so we asked Wayne and Harry if we could remove the posters for the evening.

Albini arrived. He was wiry, a mere slip of a lad physically, and watchful. We discussed the sound and agreed on Big Black's onstage time. He wasn't anything like the fierce fella I was expecting. He was softly spoken, almost academic. He talked in polite, complete, neat sentences.

Soon afterwards, Wayne and Harry turned up, ready to experience the evening's entertainment, just as Big Black were sound checking. Judging from their pained expressions, they were clearly unconvinced anyone in their right minds would pay to experience this noise whipping through them like a fucking jolt. Plus, Mr Albini was neither big nor black.

The audience wasn't enough to fill the venue to capacity but enough for the place to look busy, the locals supplemented by people who'd made a journey to be there from St Helens, Liverpool and, courtesy of Alan Woods, Wigan. The show was a wonderful, visceral noise attack. The guys in the audience in the mosh pit in front of the stage were frenzied, T-shirts off, lost in the cacophony.

Harry and Wayne were standing next to me watching the show. Amazed that people had turned out for the gig, they were now very, very happy. As the gig got even hotter and sweatier, Harry and Wayne seemed mesmerised by the lads in the mosh pit, stripped to the waist, pushing, pulling, clashing into each other, all flailing pleasure and testosterone. After an encore, the lights went up. The youths down the front dragged their T-shirts back over their pale, damp torsos. Harry eventually stopped staring at them, turned to me and said, 'Dave, can we do this every week?'

It turned out that Tim and I were about £10 short of breaking even but the audience had loved the gig, and we congratulated ourselves on avoiding any discussions with Steve Albini about the venue. If he had any inkling of what happened in that space on the other 364 days each year, he kept it to himself. However, when his tour diaries were published, he recalled Big Black's first gig in Europe, in Manchester; it took place, he said, in 'a tiny little homo bar'. I thought he hadn't noticed. But he had. I'm not sure if it was Harry's cowboy hat and handlebar moustache or the size of the toilet stalls that had been the killer clue.

Big Black went on to do their first London show at the Clarendon, and then on to Holland and Germany. The next occasion they came to Manchester, Tim and I promoted the show, this time at the Boardwalk. We filled it beyond the legal capacity and made more on the door than we'd lost doing the Archway. Albini complained about the heat, politely told me I looked 'underfed', got paid and waved goodbye.

Despite Harry and Wayne being so gentlemanly and enthusiastic, I never used their venue for a live performance again. I popped in once or twice for a very late drink after the Haçienda, but the Archway scene didn't last long. Harry and Wayne got ill and died of AIDS-related illnesses. I still think of them as true representatives of innocent, exciting times.

The arrival of the AIDS virus was a feature of the mid-1980s, played out against a backdrop of controversy and homophobia. Less than a month after our Archway show, the then Chief Constable of Greater Manchester Police, James Anderton, remarked that homosexuals, drug addicts and prostitutes who had HIV/AIDS were 'swirling in a human cesspit of their own making'. A year later, Anderton defended his homophobia: 'Sodomy between males is an abhorrent offence, condemned by the word of God, and ought to be against the criminal law.'

Thatcher had declared war on the miners, and recalibrated the economy to the detriment of the north and to the benefit, particularly, of the financial institutions in the City of London. The right had also declared war on the 1960s, a decade in which social attitudes had pushed governments to pass more liberal laws on divorce, abortion and homosexuality. To reactionaries in Thatcher's Britain, including President of the National Viewers and Listeners Association, Mrs Mary Whitehouse, such moves were a cause for regret. The nation's bestselling newspaper, the *Sun*, announced at the time, 'What Britain needs is more men like Anderton – and fewer gay terrorists holding the decent members of society to ransom.'

Even though they were dark days, everyone of a progressive, liberal persuasion could have had at least a moment's glee if we had known what had happened behind the scenes subsequent to Anderton's outbursts: his daughter came out as a lesbian.

It took a while but, eventually, the prevalence of the AIDS virus was seen as a public health matter; in 1987, the government ran a major public information campaign called 'AIDS: Don't Die of Ignorance', which used television adverts and sent an information leaflet to every household. But the demonising of the gay community was still rife.

In *Debris*, I interviewed John Balance of Coil. I went down to his flat in London, he signed all my Coil records, he made me a cup of tea, and we discussed some of the cultural imperatives that lay behind their music, revolution and the leaders of the self-styled moral majority like Mary Whitehouse. 'I'm not saying we can enlighten people,' said John. 'It's just that certain things, we feel, should always be pushed to the surface. People should release and live out anything inside them. And the same goes for society; it should be far more open about everything. It's always the hypocrisies and sexual hypocrisy especially – because it's closest to people – that fuck everybody up.'

Thatcher in Britain and Reagan in America shared so much. Their economic policies coincided, and both were determined to roll back progressive causes. The presence of American military bases in Britain was controversial; both leaders ramped up the Cold War rhetoric. As is often the case with reactionary governments, both also strengthened their power by defining and demonising enemies inside and outside the country: trade unionists, immigrants, homosexuals, foreign governments. Just before his re-election, Reagan jokingly referred to bombing Russia.

In April 1986, following the death of an American serviceman in an attack on a Berlin discotheque, Reagan ordered air raids on Libya. Many of the aircraft that took part were stationed at the RAF bases at Lakenheath and Upper Heyford. A protest march was arranged in Manchester, culminating in a rally on Albert Square where James performed live.

Just after the Libya attack I interviewed Dee Dee Ramone. I asked him for a view on Ronald Reagan; 'I think he's gone a little too far with this Libya stuff and all,' he said. 'That Russian guy, what's his name? Breznikov?'

'Gorbachev?'

'Yeah, Gorbachev; he's a bad guy too.'

He told me that his wife cut his hair ('I used to have a barber but it was starting to cost so much money, like, thirty-five dollars with the tips'), and we discussed new music. He said he'd never heard of Sonic Youth and didn't like hip hop, but his favourite new band was Suicidal Tendencies.

Big Black didn't sleep on my floor, but other bands did. For a while, I lived on Alness Road in Whalley Range. I was living there when Nathan and I staged a concert by the Slovenian band Laibach, their first UK show outside London. Their set at the Boardwalk began with one of them onstage chopping wood with an axe. This lasted several minutes, before the rest of the band began to unleash sonorous, symphonic sounds, like a cross between Krautrock and Holst's *The Planets*. They were serious but with a touch of self-conscious absurdity, and so arty; they were at the heart of the burgeoning – and now much lauded – Neue Slowenische Kunst (New Slovenian Art) collective.

Laibach had come in a van all the way from Ljubljana. The driver was an old guy, very smiley, who fought with the partisans in the Second World War, and, while the band slept on my floor, he slept in the van with all the gear. He was probably the friendliest guy with an axe in a van in Whalley Range that evening.

During my time living in Hulme, it was no problem to me having bands to stay. Hulme flats were squats by this time; there were no tenancy agreements. If you had the key to an available flat, you could move in. I was living rent-free on my own in a three-bedroom flat, albeit grotty and surrounded by boarded-up or burned-out properties. The Pastels once stayed over, along with the Vaselines, who'd come down from Glasgow with them to play the support slot. I also hosted the Butthole Surfers, just.

The Buttholes had a gig at Leeds Polytechnic, with an extra night off before they went down to play in Newport and then on to London. I went to Leeds and then travelled back with them to Manchester, and the lead singer Gibby wrote his review of his own concert sitting next to me in the back of a van on the M62.

Our happy bonding counted for little on arrival at my charmless Hulme flat. We walked in, and Gibby immediately told Paul Smith he wouldn't stay there. 'Look at it,' he said. 'There are no carpets.' He was right; there was heating, hot water and a few mattresses, but no carpets.

Helen Hawkins, an ex-student from Falmouth, lived a few doors down from me. I liked her and put her on guest lists. For some reason, I thought this meant she'd like to be woken up and have me invite the Butthole Surfers to stay with her. She had carpets! My saviour! I called her and reminded her about the guest lists, and the band and I duly trooped around there. There were carpets but no mattresses.

Gibby was still unhappy and decided we should all go back to mine. I had stopped talking to Gibby by this time. Home again, all standing around with beers and no plan C, I addressed Paul Smith: 'Tell Gibby if my place is good enough for Sonic Youth it's good enough for the Butthole fucking Surfers!' It was about three in the morning, we'd all had a long day and some drinks. I couldn't be arsed any more.

The Buttholes stayed two nights. They were scheduled to do an interview while they stayed with me, so the next day some of the band sat in my bedroom with the presenters of the *Meltdown* show on BBC Radio Manchester and journalist Jack Barron from the *NME*. They discussed how they had been accused of setting fire to REM's van but they claimed the van set fire to itself, which seemed unlikely. The rest of the day they had time off and told me they wanted to go take acid somewhere, so I sent them to Lyme Park.

11

Primal Scream,
But No Tambourine

There were a number of changes at the Haçienda at the beginning of 1986 after the appointment of a new manager, Paul Mason. He was poached from Rock City in Nottingham and tasked with trying to turn around the fortunes of the very financially challenged club. Mason was instrumental in deciding to move towards DJ-oriented nights, a move more to do with economics than anything else. The Haçienda was losing money, booking bands was an expensive business, DJs were cheaper (this was 1986, things would change). The weekly Friday 'Nude' night was already showing what could be done. By early 1986, it had a strong identity and a very good following thanks to the DJs, Mike Pickering and 'Little Martin' Prendergast.

Paul Mason was assisted by Paul Cons, who was adept at coming up with ideas, booking some of the entertainment and spreading the word. He had a 'marketing' role but back then we only had a vague idea of the concept and never used the word.

I first saw him when he was a student activist, his red hair resplendent, sitting in a road somewhere on a sitdown demo, and he had started working at the club before Mason arrived.

The two Pauls were aware I had done a few one-offs standing in for Andrew Berry and was making a success of Fridays at the Venue, so they came down to see me play there. The club was busy, but Mason told me he thought the clientele were too 'art school'. Nevertheless, they concluded that the Thursday gig at the Haçienda was mine if I wanted it, £40 a week, starting 1 May 1986.

All sorts of things were coming together for me at this time. Adrian Thrills, one of the *Debris* fans at the *NME*, had asked me if I would write for them. My first request was to interview Happy Mondays, who I had begun to follow and champion. When you were a newcomer at *NME* and living outside of London, they loved it if you wrote about some talent out in the provinces, particularly if you were bigging them up as the hot new thing.

In May 1986, Happy Mondays were being managed by Phil Saxe. He was an ex-DJ – he'd worked at the famous northern soul venue the Twisted Wheel – and in the mid-1980s he sold jeans in the Arndale Market, which is probably where he met the Mondays; they went in there to get jeans. Phil was looking after them, and they'd been signed to Factory Records. The first single hadn't done particularly well and they hadn't got much media coverage.

I journeyed over to a flat on Leicester Avenue, off Cheetham Hill Road, to get some words from the band, but only two of them turned up – two out of six, and they were more interested in smoking dope than talking to me. I asked them who wrote the lyrics. They told me it was Shaun. I asked if they knew where he was. 'Nope.'

I didn't stay long after that, I got the bus back into town and went to track down Mr Saxe in the Arndale Market. He was chattier. He said that Happy Mondays were the new Velvet Underground and he told me some stuff about them, enabling me, eventually, to cobble together a small article from that afternoon in Cheetham Hill.

I didn't rush to do lots of work in *NME* – I preferred writing in *Debris* – but I did chase them for opportunities to write album reviews, which were my favourite commissions. I enjoyed living with the vinyl for a couple of days, constantly turning it over (literally and in my mind), finding ways to describe and evaluate the music, and then seeing my words in print.

An additional positive development was that a double date turned into something promising. Nathan and I took out two girls called Karen and Rachel. Unusually, it wasn't Nathan but me that discovered them or, at least, they discovered me. Rachel had come to the Venue on her first or second week in Manchester, having arrived in the city to start a course at Manchester Poly. With her friend Karen, she began to come to the club every Friday, dance happily, and request records from me. She learned which days I worked at Identity in Affleck's Palace and she'd pop in there to see me and became friends with my co-workers, Tina and Debbie. She dressed like an extra in the film *Desperately Seeking Susan*.

This time, I managed to detect the signals and we started dating. On one of our first nights out, we went to hear DJ Dave Booth at a psychedelic night at the Playpen, a venue on Bootle Street formerly owned by George Best. One of the girls

I knew from the Hulme Crescents whispered in my ear, 'Oh, you're here with your bit of fluff?' Women can be so mean about each other.

After the launch of the Saturday Club at the Boardwalk, Rachel became a regular there too, along with Debbie, Tina, their Identity colleague Lisa and another friend of theirs, Jane. They were all big music fans and a very cool gang.

Despite the lack of cash, the uphill struggles and the carpet controversies, I loved being involved in all this live music, the Man Alive, the early days of the Boardwalk, the Haçienda before it got famous. Nobody cared about what we were doing, but that wasn't an issue. We were indifferent to the big wide world.

The Boardwalk was just around the corner from the Haçienda. When we launched the Saturday Club, the Boardwalk's licence ended at 11 p.m., so we'd usually walk up the road to the Haçienda. The money issues usually worked themselves out. Nathan and I were happy so long as we still had a fiver each for when we went around to the Haçienda after the gig (unbelievably, sometimes the bar staff made us pay for our drinks, so the fiver each was useful).

I have all my old work diaries. Nathan and I paid Colin Sinclair £70 a night to hire the Boardwalk. We paid tiny fees to the bands, but ours was a good gig for them to play and we only charged £1.50 or maybe £2 entrance fee. There was no prospect of making money as the club had such a limited capacity, but we did it because we liked having fun and there were bands we liked who weren't getting gigs anywhere in Manchester, so we thought we should get involved.

In addition to small bits of *NME* work, I'd started doing some freelance writing for *City Life*. I'd end up writing previews for my own Saturday Club events, usually under a pseudonym to camouflage the conflict of interest.

I covered the night Primal Scream played. It was their first show in Manchester, supported by the Weeds. The Weeds were fronted by Andrew Berry, who was now music-making and writing songs. Andrew wanted the chance for his band to play somewhere locally. Nathan, now hanging out with the Creation Records crew, suggested we should find a slot for Primal Scream, who were fronted by Bobby Gillespie and were one of Debbie's obsessions. We put the two together on the bill; the Weeds supporting Primal Scream. The deal with Primal Scream was that we'd pay them £100 rising to £130 if we sold out.

I interviewed Bobby Gillespie. The band had released two singles, neither troubling the top 100. Primal Scream were on the lowest rungs of the ladder to fame and fortune, as I discussed with Bobby. 'We'd love to be huge,' he said, 'like Creedence Clearwater Revival.'

We sold out all the tickets for the Boardwalk gig, all 175 of them, so Bobby would be scooping the jackpot. It looked like Nathan and I had arranged a perfect night. In theory, anyway.

I volunteered to set up the event and attend the soundchecks. Two of the Weeds didn't turn up; apparently they were helping Longsight police station with their inquiries about some drug issue. Meanwhile Tracey Donnelly said she suspected that they had smashed up her car, but with two hours until showtime, I had enough to think about. Next, Primal Scream were on the phone . . .

Primal Scream had been involved in a minor traffic collision on the motorway on the journey down from Glasgow. They were phoning from a hospital in Warrington, their van was wrecked and Bobby had sustained a minor injury to his arm. They said that apart from that, all was OK, but without a van they couldn't make the gig.

'Can Bobby stand up and sing?'

Apparently, yes, but he couldn't play the tambourine.

'Would it still be a Primal Scream gig without the sound of a tambourine?'

Yes, apparently it would.

I rang Angela Matthews who ran the entertainment department at Manchester Polytechnic, which gave her the use of a van. It was driven to Warrington, the gig went ahead without the Weeds, and without Bobby playing the tambourine. He was duly rewarded with £130.

12

Let The Music Play

I was involved with three different venues, hosting 'The Magic Roundabout' at the Venue every Friday, the live shows at the Boardwalk on Saturdays and I'd done the deal to begin DJing every Thursday at the Haçienda. One early midweek afternoon, Andy the Greek phoned me and asked me to go to see him at the Venue. He was a decent club owner and had left me pretty much to my own devices running and DJing Friday nights for him. 'The Magic Roundabout' was going well; it was cool, busy, fun.

'How long have we known each other?' said Andy.

'Two years?'

'Yes, and I pay you thirty pounds every Friday, and we are full every week. We get on well, it's a family here.'

It was a family, he was right; his father had run the club before him, when it was called Cobwebs and fights broke out most weeks and the stripper got paid more than the DJ. And, also, he was right, we did get on. We'd only had one falling out, me and Andy, on a Monday evening in 1985 when he threw a party which included a buffet of cold meats, pork pies and sausages. I was the DJ and when the buffet was served I played 'Meat Is Murder'. Andy walked over to me and gave me a very deep Greek look but he didn't sack me, although my girlfriend Elaine said, 'You are such a dick, Dave.'

'So, you are doing the Haçienda every Thursday?' asked Andy, still in interrogation mode.

'From a week on Thursday, yes.'

'You think it will go well?'

'I guess, yes.'

'So,' he said. 'You have to choose. You stay here or you go the Haçienda.'

'I want to do both, I can do both.'

'I don't want you DJing up the road. I'll give you a pay rise,' said Andy, who seemed to have planned out this conversation and was now about to play his trump card. 'I'm happy to put your wages up to thirty-five pounds a night.'

'Look, I appreciate that, Andy, but it's not about the money. I can't leave the Haçienda, I want to give it a go.'

Andy looked at me. I gave him the name of a few people I thought should take over my Friday-night slot, including Leo Stanley, my boss at Identity. Andy asked me what the Haçienda was like; it had been there for four years, and it was just seventy yards up the road from his club and yet he'd never been in (I guess he thought it was part of a different world). I told him it was arty and cold. He said that's what he'd heard.

The shift to DJ-oriented nights at the Haçienda was slowly being implemented. 'Nude' was already pulling a crowd on Fridays and my Thursdays were about to be launched. Various

DJs had been employed on Saturdays, but that night needed some attention, as I had realised when Sonic Youth, Nathan and I had gone in there after the Boardwalk show.

If I'd looked into things closely, instead of approaching the job with blind passion, I might have hesitated. The Haçienda had already had a number of resident DJs, and with one or two exceptions they hadn't been able to find or connect with an audience. Even a great DJ like Greg Wilson had only lasted as a resident for three months.

I was inexperienced and had given no thought to making a career as a DJ, but creative activity is invariably enhanced by unselfconsciousness; there's too much to express to allow commercial considerations to get in the way, and there's no time or inclination to step back and analyse. I was just enjoying the moment. My instincts prevailed, and that was definitely for the best.

I had something in common with Mike Pickering and Little Martin who were making a success of Fridays. Our apparent amateurism was no disadvantage. 'The local DJs were telling us that you can't do this or you can't do that,' Mike once said. 'It was like there were all these rules. I didn't know what the rules were and I didn't care.'

After the two Pauls had offered me Thursdays, I decided to give myself a pseudonym. I could have used my given name but it was an era when good DJs had interesting names; DJ Cheese, Red Alert and DJ Chuck Chillout, for example. And Mike and Little Martin DJed 'Nude' night as MP2. The one thing I knew was that it wasn't the right moment for the return of the 'Intellectual Humanist Disco with DJ Miserable Dave'.

I chose the name DJ Hedd, a daft almost-steal from Redds

and the Boys; during at least three weeks at the back end of 1985 I considered their 'Movin' And Groovin'' one of the greatest songs ever made. I didn't agonise over the name, as it didn't occur to me that any of this mattered much. In later years, DJing became a career in which a brand identity was important, but in the mid-1980s I had no reason to think anyone cared or had any need to know who the DJ was.

The music policy was being left up to me but we talked about how to spread the word about 'Temperance', as Thursday nights were going to be called. Owing to the location of the club and the music I was playing, we were never going to be a mainstream student choice, but I had faith that an enlightened few would find their way to somewhere arty and cold to hear me playing 'Do the Du'. I also had an extravagant idea that in May 1986 I could somehow channel the spirit of May 1968, and the Paris *événements*. The students in Paris at the time of the insurrection had a slogan: *Cours camarade, le vieux monde est derrière toi* (Run comrade, the old world is behind you).

We gave the idea of a student night a twist by concentrating some of the marketing on students, but not requiring student ID. Beyond the students, I had an affinity with people into new bands – especially Peel-type bands – and I knew I could make the Thursdays attractive to them. I also knew that dole-ites were as likely to go out on a midweek night as a weekend; maybe even more likely, as most people got their dole money paid on a Thursday.

Another demographic I reckoned could be drawn into the club was the city's youth; young men and women, seventeen or eighteen years old (the door staff were never stringent enough to make much of a fuss about the age of the audience); those kids just discovering music beyond the charts, weird stuff, non-mainstream stuff. I wanted the freedom to genre-hop.

The first flyer or two included playlists of records you'd be likely to hear, and included some obscure Venue favourites like 'Stormy Weather' by Fats Comet. I often played 'Hymn From a Village' by James, and 'The Egg' by Happy Mondays ('The Egg' was the nickname the band gave to Paul Ryder's yellow Ford Escort).

On Fridays, with a playlist encompassing electro, soul, funk, reggae, Mike and Little Martin's 'Nude' night had begun pulling in an audience beyond the regulars from the club's early days as a gig venue, including black kids, some of them from jazz-dance troupes like Foot Patrol, and Perry boys. Perry boys was a term used to describe working-class lads who were into what they wore, not always impeccably behaved and, in most instances, pretty clued-up about music; Shaun and Bez from Happy Mondays were two of the era's finest examples.

Many of the people coming to 'Temperance' were also different from the early Haçienda regulars, including lots of local kids too young to have been immersed, or stuck, in the punk era. Noel Gallagher, on the dole in Burnage, became a Thursday regular, and later professed his admiration for bands he would have heard there: the Woodentops, Primal Scream and Public Enemy.

I was hoping to turn people on to the music I liked, getting to grips with audience reaction; every night was like a dialogue with the dancefloor, with me trying out tunes, trying to work out what the audience would go for, or to pick up on their enthusiasms, explore them some more. I soon created a sense of trust with the audience, one of the great things about being a resident DJ.

I've subsequently played in clubs and at events where I've had to deal with a lot of requests, but one of the joys of the Haçienda was that the usual question was 'What was the name of that tune you just played?' and I know this was the same for other DJs such as Mike, Graeme Park and Jon Dasilva. In fact, it had been the same at the Man Alive and the Venue; people would make their way across the club to ask, 'What is this? It's ace.'

The owners, management and I didn't have endless meetings picking over things and we all had other stuff to be getting on with. In the weeks after the launch of 'Temperance', I was busy hosting the Sonic Youth show, among others, and Factory had a big project on: the Festival of the Tenth Summer, marking ten years since punk with a week of gigs and other events, culminating in a show at G-Mex featuring New Order, the Smiths and the Fall.

After a few Thursday nights at the Haçienda, I was asked to DJ on Saturdays as well; they'd decided to replace the 'Ring My Bell' guy. Paul Cons contacted me, asking me to play solo on Saturdays, just as I was on Thursdays. The management came up with a new financial arrangement for me; £120 a week for the two nights. We launched on Saturday 19 July, enabling us to benefit from being the after-show attraction following the big event at G-Mex.

I talked to the Pauls, though, and suggested that on Saturdays I should work with someone else, in the same way Mike and Martin were jointly DJing 'Nude'. Saturdays had to be different to Thursdays, I said, more overtly dancey; and either out of stupidity or good sense I suggested I could buddy up with Dean Johnson.

Dean was one of the club reviewers in the local listings magazine *City Life*, and he had a crew of followers, including zoot-suit jazz types, polo-neck wearers, and Kermit and Anderson from the Ruthless Rap Assassins. He covered jazz, funk and reggae, but mostly played modern soul shufflers, stuff by the likes of Teddy Pendergrass and 'Curious' by Midnight Star. He was the first person I heard play Lisa Lisa and Cult Jam's 'I Wonder If I Take You Home', a truly divine song.

Dean was a connoisseur of black music. The worst adjective he could attach to a record was to describe it as 'white'. He was a white boy from Coventry but, to him, everything and everyone compromised and commercial was best described as 'white'.

In addition, Dean simply believed that anyone who didn't rate his tunes was wrong. I had been to a night he was DJing – he was playing whatever he was playing and no one was dancing, then suddenly he got on the microphone and started shouting at the audience 'You don't deserve this . . .'

You might think that a man like that would not be the ideal DJ to buddy up with, and you might be right, and you might think he sounds a little unqualified for the job of buying into my inclusive vibe and helping to fill a big old warehouse with happy dancing people, but I admired his eccentricity and, especially, his passion for music. He would rarely play anything I would play. We called the night 'Wide', like the music policy.

The Thursday 'Temperance' nights were beginning to build well. I became adept at programming a set over the five hours the club was open (9 p.m. until 2 a.m.). There was continuity week to week, records on the Def Jam label (perhaps 'Sardines' by the Junkyard Band) and Creation Records releases, regular touchstones like 'Sympathy For the Devil', always some A Certain Ratio, plus some less well-known Factory stuff like 'Yashar' by Cabaret Voltaire.

One record I played to the death from day one at the 'Temperance' night in 1986: 'The Official Colourbox World Cup Theme' by Colourbox. Very occasionally I still play it, usually triggering an older customer hastening up to me, to say, 'You know what this record reminds me of?' I know what they're going to say: 'Thursday nights at the Haç.'

I was the only DJ at the Haçienda in the mid- and late 1980s to play New Order records, but I never played 'Blue Monday' because it was too obvious. That was the contrary way you'd think when you worked at the Haçienda; the last thing you'd do is play the biggest hit by the people who owned the club.

Some Thursdays I'd arrive and there would be a record mailer waiting for me in the DJ box, with a copy of a forthcoming Factory release inside, a plain white label without a Peter Saville designed sleeve. I'd only been there for a few months and I had a copy of New Order's 'State of the Nation'. By the end of the year, I'd been given a copy of 'Bizarre Love Triangle'. Bliss.

The challenge of DJing at the Haçienda, and the key to it all, was to play some unexpected choices. That way you made your mark and you fulfilled that Factory philosophy of doing things differently. For example, we hardly ever played reggae, but then occasionally I would.

Morrissey had a thing for making pronouncements about music. He claimed all reggae sounds the same. In response, there was nothing I liked more than following a Smiths song with Shinehead 'Who the Cap Fit' or Wayne Smith 'Under Me Sleng Teng'. These were moments you hoped defined you as a DJ or, at least, made an impact. It worked, I think.

In 1986, Justin Robertson came up to Manchester from his home in the outer London suburbs to study philosophy at university. He became a DJ, later telling an interviewer about his first visit to the Haçienda in 1986: 'I remember walking into this stark, industrial space. Dave Haslam was playing Shinehead 'Who the Cap Fit', which has this electronic backbeat that sounded incredible in there. I fell in love with the place, I started basing my entire life around going there. It was very stark but massively cool.'

Justin, like thousands of others, took a journey through the Haçienda nights and their various musical delights, before settling on Mike's 'Nude' night. Thursdays were often the first taste people got of what was happening at the Haçienda. They'd be drawn in, then become addicted to the club, and move on to other nights. 'Temperance' was a gateway drug for nightlife addicts, opening up the way to harder, purer stuff.

Four years into its life, the club, though, was still losing money; even Tony was now harbouring doubts about the Haçienda. After the Festival of the Tenth Summer – which had been a massive undertaking – he gave himself a break and went on holiday to China. This was August 1986. While he was away, the A-level results were released, on a Thursday. Then, as now, those who'd taken the exams wanted some place to go to celebrate, or commiserate with fellow students. My Haçienda night was packed, the atmosphere was brilliant. The cool sixth-formers we'd hoped would find a home in the club had turned up.

Paul Mason knew that Tony would appreciate some good news, even if it meant interrupting his holiday. Paul went to the trouble of calling him at his hotel and told him the club had been packed, on a Thursday, in the middle of August. Mason was happy his long-term plan to swerve away from live music was paying off. Wilson came back from China with renewed hope in the Haçienda project.

Saturdays were a strain, though. Dean would pick out a record, then, two minutes into it, turn to me with a look of triumph. 'No one else would play this,' he would announce. And secretly I'd think, why would anyone? I'd shut my mouth. I knew he winced every time I played something by New Order. But we bonded over certain records, like '(You Are My) All and All' by Joyce Sims, and somehow those Saturdays at the Haçienda pulled a crowd. Dean and I lasted eighteen months together.

In my time at the club, aside from Paul Cons, my closest allies were people like Suzanne in the kitchen, the hands-on managers like Angela Matthews and Leroy Richardson (Leroy was always super supportive). Paul Mason used to praise me for all manner of strange reasons, including saying, 'I love what you're doing on Saturdays, all the hairdressers are coming in.' I think that was Mr Mason's perfect demographic for Saturdays – hairdressers. It was an old-school way of looking at things, but I understood the logic: girls talk to their hairdressers all the time, so if hairdressers are coming that means they'll tell their customers it's a good night out, which means well-groomed girls will turn up and pay to get in. And if you get well-groomed girls in the club then, sooner or later, you'll get boys as well. And then you make money and then bills get paid and how nice would that be, eh?

I was DJing two nights a week, so I increased my visits to record shops, particularly Eastern Bloc, buying more and more new records, mostly on import, mostly on American labels. Some of them would subsequently appear on UK-released compilation albums, but as a DJ you want to get in early, get the import, even though it was an expensive habit to pursue. An import twelve-inch single could cost anything up to £4.

In 1987, Sleeping Bag, Profile, DJ International and Trax were American labels I always looked out for. I bought the first Skinny Boys album, on the Warlock label, and played a track called 'Rip the Cut'. Listening to 'Rip the Cut' over thirty years later, it's almost unbelievably uncommercial, but I was reckless, passionate, still taking my cue from my instincts, and always inspired by Mike's disdain for 'the rules' and by the desire of the audience for tunes they didn't know. Now, I'm also slightly chastened, realising that I'm probably a lot more conservative in my choices. Perhaps once you have a career – which I have now, but didn't think I had then – there's more to lose.

In recent years, a fair few of my DJ engagements have been private or corporate events. In 2015, I was flown to Lisbon to DJ at an event for Mercedes, as corporate as corporate can be. It was a beautiful venue (a former monastery), very well organised, safe and fully risk-assessed. My choice of tunes, similarly, and a little sadly, was also safe and risk-assessed. It never occurred to me play anything as out there as 'Rip the Cut'.

I don't mind tailoring sets to work for whoever is in front of me wanting to dance, but if I do too many corporate events, I'm soon yearning for a proper night of smoke machines, chaos and surprises.

On one occasion, a girl pushed her way into the DJ box, lay on the floor, took all her clothes off and started pulling at my trousers. Another girl came to the DJ box and asked, 'Do you take requests?'

'Yes, of course,' I lied.

'Will you come back to mine tonight?' she said.

'Sorry?' I thought I might have misheard. She started looking in her handbag for something. I was in the middle of a set, about to flick through my box of tunes and cue up the next record. By the time I'd done this, she'd found a pen in her bag and scrawled me a message. 'Come home with me,' it said. And then in brackets she'd written '(Hyde')' so I knew roughly where I might find myself in the morning. Having struggled for years misreading signals from women, all this was very welcome and made a major improvement to my life.

Away from the club, most of the rest of the week revolved around *Debris*, reading the music papers and taking trips to record shops. It was like searching for some kind of holy grail; the dancefloor filler no one knew but no one could resist.

House music arrived slowly in the record shops, not in a huge wave. Through 1986, the records we'd be playing included two that ended up being commercial hits: Farley 'Jackmaster' Funk 'Love Can't Turn Around' and Steve 'Silk' Hurley 'Jack Your Body'. One record Mike and Martin were playing was Virgo 'Free Yourself' (released by Trax), which made a big impact on me; it was melancholic, wordless and otherworldly.

Dean didn't play house on a Saturday night, but he'd sometimes play something perfect. Nevertheless I learned not to praise anything after the occasion he played 'Let the Music Play' by Shannon, and I'd told him it was my favourite record. He pulled a face and never played it again; I assume the fact of me liking it had somehow turned 'Let the Music Play' white.

Some of the old Haçienda crowd didn't know what to make of the rising number of electronic dance records being played in the club. Particularly to the small residue of punks and goths in the club, disco was the enemy. Even the notion of DJs was hard to handle; older, more conservative regulars were wedded to live acts as the more authentic way to be exposed to music. For some regulars, the best days of the club were over; DJs and ecstasy were a revolution they could do without. A journalist reporting in the *Manchester Evening News* in April 1988 very begrudgingly plugged Mike Pickering's 'Nude' night with these reservations: 'if you can stand the thought of queuing for one hour to get in, for another to get served at the bar and, finally, another hour to escape'.

I had one encounter with an American who had journeyed to Manchester in love with Joy Division and the Smiths, and found what he heard hard to cope with. 'Quit playing to the disco crowd!' he shouted at me. But we were leaving the past behind. *Le vieux monde était derrière nous.*

13

New Order, Untaped

Backstage at the Festival of the Tenth Summer at G-Mex I interviewed Paul Morley for *Debris*. Morley was rising to the top of the game, writing in the culture/lifestyle monthly *Blitz* (he'd just interviewed Norman Tebbit for the magazine), and being a successful part of the team that piloted the record label ZTT and the career of Frankie Goes to Hollywood. His book *Ask: The Chatter of Pop* had just been published.

When I found him, he had just an argument with Liz Naylor that culminated in him throwing sugar over her head (or was it salt?). We discussed all of his various activities, and he was open and talkative. I asked, 'Is the desire for power one of your motivations for writing?' and Morley answered it neatly and memorably; 'No, it's just making the arrangements of the words that I love; arranging the material in a structure. I never think about who might read it or what influence it might have. But it is to do with communication. And it's a kind of reaction; I hate banality, I hate mediocrity and I hate predictability and everything I do is a positive reaction to all that, to fight that.'

I'd admired Morley for so long and was grateful for the conversation. It was exciting for me, meeting characters who had been part of my formative years. One evening I was DJing my little heart out and Mike Pickering banged on the DJ-box door and then walked in with Martin Fry from ABC. I had never met a more pop-starry pop star, even though he wasn't wearing his gold lamé suit. I was trying to act nonchalant so maybe he didn't see my look of love.

My excitement grew in September 1986 when the *NME* invited me to write a double-page feature on New Order to coincide with the release of the *Brotherhood* album. A visit was arranged; I made my way by bus to the New Order studio and rehearsal room in an old Gas Board building in Cheetham Hill, where I had the opportunity to listen to some of the tracks from the album and to have twenty minutes or so with each of the band.

The curious thing is, I'd not had a proper conversation with any of them before. I must have seen New Order play six or seven times by this point, and was currently employed playing every Thursday and Saturday in their club. But the only times I'd come close to them were occasions when Hooky or Bernard had knocked on the DJ-box door and brought in wives, girlfriends or mates to take a look at the view of the club from our vantage point on the balcony above the dancefloor. We'd exchange hiyas.

For seven or eight years, from the first days of hearing Joy Division on John Peel, I was a devotee, bewitched by them and their world, and there I was, an *NME* writer clinging to my old cassette recorder and my pages of questions. All afternoon, I listened intently to their answers, taking everything very seriously. Having waited for years for this to happen, I wasn't going to be offhand or casual, I was going to get this right.

The studio was where Jonathan Demme had filmed the video for 'The Perfect Kiss'. I interviewed them, doing my best, but I wasn't relaxed and they weren't particularly talkative. When my time was up, Hooky said he'd give me a lift back into town. I made crap small talk. I'm not interested in cars, I never have been. But when it's small-talk time, anything goes. I told him, 'This is a lovely car.' I even asked how long he'd had it.

Hooky dropped me off on Newton Street, a few yards or so from one of my regular haunts, a greasy-spoon café called the Alesia (on the ground floor of the building the Roadhouse later occupied). I was so thrilled by the opportunity I'd been given to interview New Order, but also having trouble believing it had all actually happened. I stopped in a doorway, and turned on my cassette recorder to hear the voices of one of my very favourite bands in the world, their words ready for inclusion in my first major *NME* feature. But I couldn't hear anything. I turned up the volume. Nothing. The tape was blank.

Crouched in the doorway, trying to work out if I'd made some mistake in the process of pressing record and play at the same time, or whether I'd been hit by some other disastrous technical malfunction, I knew I couldn't go back and do it again. Instead, I lamented how I'd trashed my reputation with New Order and the Factory crowd, and how brief my career as an *NME* feature-writer was now destined to be. I felt like a small boy who'd slept through Christmas Day.

I took my plastic bag with a notebook, interview notes and my stupid untrustworthy tape machine, and sat in the Alesia, drinking some tea and eating white toast soaked with margarine. After five minutes of leafing through my notes, including the questions I'd prepared and my various scribblings as the tracks from the album were played to me, I grabbed my notebook and decided to start writing anything I could remember any of the band saying. I wrote for half an hour, my list of potential questions triggering more and more memories of what the band had said to me, and my intense concentration during the interview paid dividends.

The New Order interview appeared over two full pages, with photos, and it looked good. Tony Wilson was delighted with all this, and me. He didn't quite get DJing, but he could tell I was doing whatever his DJs were supposed to do; attract a good crowd into his club by playing exceptional off-centre music in a non-showbiz way. But he had more of a handle on the press and knew that having a local writer who could get national coverage for Factory bands was a big asset. I didn't have anything like the space in the *NME* or the influence that Paul Morley once had, but I'd championed James when they were on Factory and I'd also done that brief first Happy Mondays interview in the *NME*.

No one knew how I'd crafted the quotes by New Order. I liked Dave Harper, New Order's press officer; I never told him what had happened, but he seemed pleased with the piece. I was disappointed it wasn't the front-cover feature, but at least I still had my life on track.

14

Bez Against The Nazis

I had known Tim Booth, the singer from James, when we were both students; he studied drama, and we had a number of mutual friends back then (also, he was the first vegan I'd ever met, and the first man I knew who practised yoga). I went to a lot of the band's early gigs, I'd warmed up for them at their performance at DeVilles in Manchester way back in May 1984, I'd interviewed them in *Debris*, and I'd given their album *Stutter* a great review in the *NME*. At the end of 1986, I hosted a *Debris* party featuring James (with Tot supporting) at the Capri Ballroom.

The Capri Ballroom was a first-floor venue on the corner of Platt Lane and Yew Tree Road, owned and managed by one the world's grumpiest men. He really took against us from the moment we started loading in the gear up his ridiculously steep stairs. One of the reasons for his enmity was that I had misled him into thinking it was an office party, invite only, whereas I had been selling tickets for £2 to pay for the PA equipment and the hire of his godforsaken room.

Even when all one hundred and fifty of the crowd arrived to drink his bar dry, he was still pulling a face and cursing under his breath. Then Tony Wilson walked in. The grumpy manager sidled up to me almost immediately, and asked, 'Is that the Granada news guy?' and when I said yes, his whole attitude changed. I don't think he'd ever had a man off the telly in his crappy venue before. This was the first time I properly understood that Tony's profile had won him recognition in the big wide world beyond local bands and indie singles. He'd arrived fashionably late, a man of destiny, standing out, in a big coat.

I didn't tell Tony the truth about the New Order interview even when he thanked me for writing it. We talked mostly about Happy Mondays, who were so low down the Factory pecking order they hadn't been given free tickets for the big Festival of the Tenth Summer gig at G-Mex, which Factory had organised.

You have to remember, the guys in the re-formed Stone Roses and Happy Mondays, now in their fifties, were once young kids giving the Haçienda a bit of a shake-up. Now some of them are grandads, but in 1986 they were the new generation. They were the young ones trying to make their mark.

The audience at the 'Temperance' night in its first year or two included some people who might have identified themselves as part of the so-called C86 scene – fans maybe of the bands that Nathan and I staged at the Boardwalk, including the Pastels, the Vaselines, the Shop Assistants and Talulah Gosh. Although it's an overlooked phase of indie music history, I liked its passionate network of fanzines, flexis, DIY gigs and small labels. I liked also the prevalence of female artists in the C86 bands, and consequent lack of macho bombast.

There was something nouvelle vague-ish about the 'Temperance' girls. The boys sported Smiths-style quiffs or haircuts inspired by the look Bernard Sumner had back then (short, and extra shaved at the sides). But fashions and styles weren't uniform; a reflection of the variety in the music.

The Stone Roses and their friends used to come to the Haçienda in paisley shirts and flares, the Happy Mondays had a Perry-boy look that also incorporated flares. The Liverpool version of Perry boys called themselves 'scallies', but I don't think you'd have found anyone wearing flares on Merseyside even by the end of 1987.

Happy Mondays got themselves a new manager: my comrade Nathan took over from Phil Saxe. In 1986, Nathan and I shared an office on Princess Street, which sounds like a grand way of carrying on, but really it wasn't. I'd been in the building a while, having rented a small room on the second floor, which I used as a *Debris* office, but also it served a useful purpose as I was moving house all the time. I went from Hulme to Moss Side to Rusholme and back to Hulme via a rented room in Whalley Range, so I used the office space to store back copies of the *NME* and a ton of records. I moved onto the first floor, Nathan took the adjoining room, and we shared the phone bill, a fax machine and our thoughts and plans. We established a small record label called Play Hard, and continued staging shows at the Boardwalk on Saturdays and occasional other days.

Early on in Nathan's reign – around October 1986 – the Mondays had a gig in Blackburn at King George's Hall and Nathan asked me to go up there with the band and play a warm-up DJ set. As the name suggests, the venue was old-fashioned, a semi-ornate building. The audience had more than its fair share of football hooligans, a dysfunctional and pretty drunk crowd keen to smash the place up. For them, that was part and parcel of what made for a great night out in Blackburn. Sometimes you can just feel it, can't you? It's going to kick off.

Sadly, a few songs in, the first fight broke out and then some Nazis started *Sieg-Heil*ing at Bez, and the whole room turned into a riot. Bez's dad is a policeman and as a result Bez is very hot on law and order. He grabbed his maracas and waded in.

I know that the best thing that could have happened in terms of me telling this story is if I had taken a couple of hooligans out with a punch to the head and then skimmed a twelve-inch single across the crowded room to knock out a Nazi who was about to attack Bez, but actually what happened when the fight started is that I hid under the DJ decks at the back of the hall. From there, I could hear roaring, shouting and the sound of breaking glass. The only time I looked up, I saw some guy run in from the adjoining room wielding a pool cue. There's a weird unwritten rule of nightclub brawls: there's always someone with a pool cue even if there's no pool table in the building.

Nathan gave me £50 and suggested I could take a taxi home, and I did, promising to reconvene at the office the next morning. It turned out that nobody was injured, everything was good and the band had even been paid.

The Happy Mondays debut album, *Squirrel and G-Man . . .*, was due for release in March 1987 so Nathan was embroiled in various practical day-to-day activities, helping them make sharp exits from potentially incendiary encounters, paying their Boardwalk rehearsal fees and doing his best to get them where they needed to be. His first important challenge was to take things up a level, to build up some momentum.

I said I would get myself in line to review the album for the *NME*, and Nathan and I arranged a live show for the band on the last Saturday of January 1987 at the Boardwalk, inviting Inspiral Carpets to support; Graham Lambert from the Inspirals was a very keen Boardwalk gig-goer. We budgeted £150 to pay the Mondays, and £20 for the Inspiral Carpets. Admission was £2 (£1.50 for students and the unemployed).

Happy Mondays needed to prove they deserved the acclaim being given to them by the likes of Johnny Marr, but their task was hampered by various self-created obstacles. For example, Nathan and I had a problem with the fax machine in the office or, rather, it not being in the office. One morning I discovered we'd been broken into and someone had stolen it. I called Nathan and he said he'd already heard about it from the Mondays, and he'd call a few people to see what could be done.

I then got a call from one of the Mondays telling me the fax machine had been found and one of their mates would bring it in, but he'd need twenty quid for its safe return. Then, on cue, one of their mates turned up, unwrapped the fax machine from a black bin liner, and I gave him twenty quid.

This happened again a few nights later; and once again, the following day, a mate of the Mondays turned up with the stolen fax machine and I gave him twenty quid for it. I told Nathan I couldn't keep doing this, he needed to reimburse me, so Nathan went to the bank and drew £40 out of the Mondays' bank account.

I also said to Nathan that it seemed like an inconvenient way for the Mondays and their mates to access their own cash. He said that it wouldn't happen again, but then it did. One afternoon, two of the Mondays' mates walked in and told me they'd come to steal the fax machine. I tried to explain, 'It's ours, you know, and we need it, we have business to do, this is an office. Mr McGough might want to send a fax to Mr Wilson, you never know.'

'All right, mate. We'll come and get it tonight.'

I said, 'If you do that how much will it cost for me to get it back tomorrow?'

'Twenty quid.' This seemed to be the standard rate, and there didn't seem much room for negotiation.

I told them to come back later while I phoned Nathan, who was at home and still in bed, as it was only two in the afternoon and he was going through a phase of not coming in until four because he said that, with the time difference, that's when the music industry in LA starts work. Most of the calls we got were from the Boardwalk asking when the Mondays' rehearsal-room hire fees would be paid or from venues the Mondays had just played in, like the Citadel in St Helens, wondering where some piece of backstage furniture had gone. Yet the main thing for Nathan was that if a big shot from LA got into work and called him up, he'd be ready to take the call.

I told him we were victims of some insanely stupid protection racket and asked whether this time we could just give the fax thieves twenty quid now directly out of the Happy Mondays' bank account, and tell them to go away and thus avoid the whole charade of a theft tonight, a ransom tomorrow, the subsequent recovery, my loss of cash and, via Nathan, Happy Mondays eventually reimbursing me from their own bank account. He said OK, and came into town and went to the bank. The lads had walked a few times around the block, came back eating a box of chicken from KFC and Nathan gave them the cash.

After they'd gone, I discussed this with Nathan. I suggested he should tell the band that if they ever needed twenty quid for themselves or their mates, we would give them the cash and maybe they could sign for it. I said I assumed most bands could access cash directly from their manager; as usual, this was me being the sensible one. It was therefore agreed that if the Mondays could call up we'd arrange to get their money anytime, during office hours – Los Angeles office hours, of course – and the fax machine could stay with us, permanently. I said I doubted Bono's friends held U2's manager's office equipment to ransom.

There were one or two occasions when I thought maybe the Happy Mondays manager needed a manager, but Nathan was clearly the best man for the job because he could get on their wavelength when required. Of all the possible candidates living or dead, no one could have steered the Happy Mondays ship as adroitly as Nathan did.

The relationship between the Stone Roses and their manager Gareth Evans was less clearly a good marriage. Gareth was based at a club called the International, on Anson Road, out of town on the edge of Longsight, and also sometimes used an old Irish club called the Carousel, which was dubbed International Two. He was a bit of a mystery and I'm not sure he totally knew what he was doing. Tony, Rob Gretton, Nathan and the rest of the Factory family weren't exactly smooth operators, but what they did have was a striking history, much credibility, a ton of good press, and lots of industry connections and allies.

That Gareth didn't really know anyone in the music business sometimes worked in my favour. He was convinced that Nathan and I were big players in the world of pop music, despite the fact that neither of us owned a car or had two brass farthings to rub together and kept having our fax machine nicked. He'd give us free beers at the International. Not just a can each; a crate between us. I went to the International at the end of June 1987 to review the Stone Roses for the *NME*. A couple of years later, the paper was obsessed with them, but at that point I had to fight to persuade them to run even a small live review. Reni 'is the best young drummer in town', I wrote, and Ian Brown is 'a born winner . . . he bobs about the stage like a man on the quayside who knows his ship is coming in'.

The review further boosted my status with Gareth. He'd phone me up and say things like 'Dave, I need to phone the biggest producer in the world right now. Who is it? Where do I find him?' somehow believing I was pulling all the strings in the world of music.

15

Hip Hop, Tarka Dal

I was putting together an issue of *Debris* in the weeks leading up to the general election of June 1987, so I wrote a polemic to mark the occasion, with some focus on the language of the far right, buzz words Thatcher and others had taken to using, including 'freedom' and 'patriotism', and criticising their imagery too; Norman Tebbit had been filmed pasting up a Tory party poster featuring a bulldog, which was one of the Tory attempts to appeal to voters from the far right. It was instructive that the National Front decided not run any candidates in 1987 (they'd had more than fifty in the 1983 general election); they didn't need to.

Maybe some older people look back at their youthful anger and idealism and squirm, but I recently reread the polemic and I loved the young man who'd written it, and I agreed with every word. I like that I quoted the poet Gerard Manley Hopkins, 'Dare-gale skylark scanted in dull cage', a phrase evocatively describing frustration and oppression, the desires of the free-spirited skylark denied. The polemic ended with me writing, 'We need to stab the bulldog and set the skylark free.'

This was the general election campaign in which Labour enlisted various musicians in Red Wedge but, to me, the most urgent and engaged music at the time was the hip hop coming from America. It was a great year for hip-hop albums, not least Public Enemy's *Yo! Bum Rush the Show*. The samples, the rage, the challenge joined the dots between the state of Reagan's America and the civil rights era.

In May 1987, just before the election, I saw the Beastie Boys at the Apollo, supporting Run DMC. Six months later, I went with John Peel to watch Public Enemy at the Apollo. Peel was the DJ who had the biggest influence on me; he loved to share new music with his audience and, as he got older, he never got jaded or nostalgic. He was never much of a fan of the Stone Roses, though; at the same time, he had a few favourite bands he never managed to turn me on to. One example: the Wedding Present. I met singer David Gedge; he was a nice fella, but the band didn't float my boat. Often people would recommend bands to me. In 1989, Peter Hook told me a few times that the House of Love were great, but I couldn't hear it.

Peel was in Manchester because he'd been commissioned to review the show for the *Observer* and he knew I'd been to see the Beastie Boys earlier in the year, so he invited me to be his plus one. I met him in Piccadilly Records, which was then on Piccadilly Gardens. We went for a drink and then we went for a curry in a basement restaurant in Chinatown. John was a vegetarian, but there were plenty of options; he chose tarka dal. I remember him saying, 'Tarka dal is the best way to judge an Indian restaurant.'

We were talking about Mark E. Smith – John was a big fan of the Fall and intrigued by Mark, but I don't think he had even met him. Peel said he didn't much care for hanging out with musicians. There was a shyness about John, but I don't know if that's the whole explanation for this. Perhaps it was also because he found singers and musicians boring or intimidating or he didn't want his illusions shattered – or all of those things – but he recounted at length the story of his relationship with Marc Bolan as some kind of morality tale or warning, perhaps.

Peel had championed Bolan before Tyrannosaurus Rex had even released a record. John said that, at that time, he had become good friends with Bolan, very good friends, and they hung out together. Marc and his wife and John and his wife Sheila spent weekends together, went to hippy festivals, and John pushed gigs Bolan's way, as well as playing the first Tyrannosaurus Rex records on his radio shows.

Bolan split from his bandmate Steve Took, ditched the hippy-type sound of Tyrannosaurus Rex and, as T-Rex, began to have hit records with 'Hot Love' and 'Get It On'. Peel was less interested, less keen, but in any case Bolan suddenly had a ton of other supporters and was surrounded by new fans. Peel said he'd lost contact and friendship at this time. He said he was hoping to get together one weekend with Bolan and so phoned him up. Somebody answered the phone and said Marc would call him back, but he never did. 'And that was that,' said Peel. He looked hurt, still.

Just as we were making plans to leave the restaurant, a mouse ran across the carpet and disappeared under a neighbouring table; only we noticed, and it made us laugh. As we went to find a cab to go to the Apollo, I asked Peel about the tarka dal. 'It was great,' he said.

We took our seats on the balcony at the Public Enemy gig, surrounded by a young audience with lots of energy, all of it positive. When they were asked to put their hands in the air they did (although John didn't). We were chuckling when we came out, amused at how wide of the mark the press reports of hip-hop shows had been. As we left the Apollo, instead of being confronted by riot vans, we saw only a phalanx of parents waiting to give their children a lift home.

Hip-hop records were being played on all the Haçienda nights, and Mantronix performed one of the best live shows the club had ever witnessed. We were clearly in a new era. Mike Pickering and Little Martin's original 'Nude' playlist of electro, soul and funk was being augmented by hip hop and also, increasingly, by early house. Mike was championing the Chicago house sound, not just via the decks but in other ways too. He booked and hosted a midweek special in March 1987 featuring Adonis, Fingers Inc. and Frankie Knuckles. I was a massive fan of the Adonis track 'No Way Back'; when I met him that evening he signed a copy of the record for me.

Mike created T-Coy alongside Simon Topping and keyboard player Richie Close. Test pressings of 'Carino', their first single, were played by all the Haçienda residents. An instrumental, it brought together minimalist drum machines, great keyboard lines and a joyous Latin feel.

Other big British-made records for me at this time included 'That Greedy Beat' by Coldcut, a hip-hop-influenced cut-up of mainly James Brown tunes, but, most of all, 'Pump Up the Volume' by MARRS, a deceptively simple and irresistible mix of house rhythms, and repetitive, sampled mini vocal slogans ripped from records by Public Enemy and the Criminal Element Orchestra, among others.

'Pump Up the Volume' found its way high into the charts. I'd play it every Saturday, much to Dean's disdain. When it went to No. 1 and I still played it, Dean couldn't even look at me. We were still holding it all together but every few weeks Paul Cons would call me, asking me to tell Dean to adjust his music policy, but the alternative route he could have taken was to slam on big tune after big tune, which to me was a far worse crime than occasionally clearing the dancefloor.

Meanwhile, my Thursdays in 1987 were full of young kids, with waves of joy, New Order lyrics and teenage lust pulsing through them, some uncool or drunk enough to end up snogging along the back wall of the balcony when they weren't jumping around on the dancefloor. Peter Saville once told me that Tony Wilson and Rob Gretton always understood the Haçienda was going to be 'a gift to a new generation'. I'm not sure this is exactly what they'd planned in 1982, but that's certainly how it turned out, in a neat display of praxis.

We'd found an audience. In the late autumn of 1987, in the months before ecstasy, the DJ-oriented nights at the Haçienda had taken off. A great space had been created where like-minded strangers met, hung out and danced together, turned on to music they couldn't hear anywhere else. The club was still off the radar and your average person didn't have a clue what was going on. Under the mirrorball hanging precariously from the leaking roof, we had such a lovely collection of music fans, dancers, drinkers, Factory-ites, fashionistas, models, musicians, scallies, students, hairdressers, naked girls and skinny boys.

16

Acid? Acid House?

French DJ and producer Laurent Garnier begins his auto-biography, *Electrochoc*, not when he was a young man growing up in France but on a rainy night in spring 1987: Laurent's first visit to the Haçienda, a Friday. He told me more about this when I interviewed him at Silencio, a small but beautiful private members' club in Paris designed by David Lynch. I explained to the audience that at the time we were getting a thousand people a night but most other people had no idea what was happening at the club or, more generally, in the Manchester music scene. We were on an island, away from anything that was happening anywhere else.

Laurent told how he had attended catering school in France and got a job in the elegant surroundings of the French embassy in London. He was eighteen years old, madly into music and partying, frequenting Camden Palace and clubs like Philip Sallon's Mud Club on Tottenham Court Road. There, he first began to take note of the DJs, their role in making a success of the night. He was especially a fan of Mark Moore. Laurent was impressed by the way he took risks at the Mud Club. According to Laurent, 'You couldn't just play any old music there, it wasn't simply entertainment.'

Laurent left his job at the French embassy and with his girlfriend decided to move up to Manchester where there was a job waiting for him at her sister's restaurant. He'd not done a lot of research for his move to Manchester but he knew that the Factory-owned Haçienda was somewhere he should visit. 'There was nothing special about it from the outside. It was stuck in the middle of nowhere.'

At his first visit to the club, he was enjoying Mike's selections and then heard one particular record, featuring a powerful kick drum, a heavy rhythm and a soaring vocal; Farley 'Jackmaster' Funk's 'Love Can't Turn Around'. Laurent's life turned around. The track sounded great through the Haçienda's sound system. Stripped down and uncomplicated, it cut through the club's poor acoustics in a way that the clattering mess of live rock bands often didn't. 'The Haçienda's sound system pumped out huge bass sounds. I just couldn't believe it.'

The first person Laurent got to know at the Haçienda was Dani Jacobs, one of the lighting engineers (the lighting boys also had a video-making company, Swivel). Laurent gave Dani several mix tapes in the hope that he might pass them on to Paul Cons. Eventually, Paul Cons got in touch and Laurent was installed as a co-resident DJ at 'Zumbar', a new regular Wednesday night aimed at a fashion and music crowd, trendy and dressy, with cabaret performances scheduled every week.

Paul loved booking performers. He used to get bored only having us resident DJs to publicise, and would occasionally surprise me with some extra element he'd decided to throw into the night. Once I turned up to play and Paul told me that he'd flown a female contortionist over from New York. It was a Saturday night. I had to stop the music for ten minutes while she tied herself in knots.

The first 'Zumbar' took place on Wednesday 7 October, 1987, and Laurent made his debut behind the Haçienda decks. He began his career using the pseudonym DJ Pedro. As far as the music was concerned, the DJs still had free rein or, as Laurent might say, 'carte blanche'. Laurent remembers how fraught with nerves he was that first evening, but also the one tune that kickstarted the party: 'Pump Up the Volume'.

By the end of 1987, house music was also evolving beyond the Chicago sound into harder, darker, more instrumental tunes characterised by the use of the sound of the Roland TB-303, an electronic drum machine that produced acid basslines. Virgo, the creator of 'Free Yourself', also had production credits on 'I've Lost Control' by Sleezy D, which featured a fabulously bleepy acid line, intertwined with dramatically pitched-down vocals intoning 'I've lost control'.

Derrick May and Juan Atkins were among the producers behind this darker, bleepy, wooshy minimalism; a sound that would be labelled 'techno'. One of the most gloriously and relentlessly bleepy was the eleven-minute 'Acid Tracks' by the Phuture, which DJ Pierre helped create. It was rave music before anyone really knew what raving was. It was techno before it had become defined. Plus, I hadn't yet heard the phrase 'acid house'.

To my ears, computer-aided dance music was part of a tradition that also included Kraftwerk, Giorgio Moroder, New

Order, some of the things DJs like Hewan Clarke had played (such as 'Don't Make Me Wait' by the Peech Boys) and the record I urged Morrissey to embrace: Man Parrish's 'Hip Hop, Be Bop (Don't Stop)'. I was playing these Detroit and Chicago imports, just a few records at a time and then I'd go back to playing New Order or something else. One of the Reese & Santonio singles, 'Force Field', wasn't a million miles from Section 25's 'Looking From a Hilltop' released by Factory a couple of years earlier. There was no Year Zero. House and techno didn't render the rest of my record collection obsolete.

Thirty years later, the notion of 'Haçienda classics' is a lot narrower than it should be. For example, pioneering DJs in the late 1980s didn't just play house music. At the beginning of 1988, Graeme Park became Mike Pickering's 'Nude' night DJ partner; in the first two summers of acid house, 1988 and 1989, when they were playing bleepy Chicago and Detroit imports, they were also continuing to play hip hop, tracks by the likes of Big Daddy Kane and Eric B & Rakim, and older electro records like Hashim's 'Al-Naafiysh (The Soul)'.

One story of those early days is the visit to Amnesia in Ibiza by Nicky Holloway, Danny Rampling and Paul Oakenfold and others in the summer of 1987. It was the moment they heard DJ Alfredo, and had their first ecstasy experience. I've heard claims that this story of the DJs, and the impact it went on to have, is key to house and rave in Britain, that the whole scene somehow might never have happened if that visit hadn't occurred; all I can say is, it had no impact on me. I'm not saying it didn't happen, and I don't doubt that it changed the music taste of those guys, and their worldview, or that it inspired Paul Oakenfold and the others to push the London scene in a new direction, but it didn't flick the switch that created acid house nationally. At the Haçienda we had our own thing going on. I, for one, was busy in Manchester, always buying records from Eastern Bloc; I barely knew what was going on in front of my eyes, let alone what was happening in London.

I've talked about the development of acid house with Andrew Weatherall, who DJed at Rampling's 'Shoom', Paul Oakenfold's 'Future' nights and Holloway's 'The Trip'. Weatherall and I did an onstage interview at Beacons Festival in 2014. He told me that Manchester caught on to house music before London did. 'Manchester was first,' he said, and I'll take his word for it.

One Saturday in November 1987, I strung together about four or five of these bleepy, wooshy records from Detroit and a young man came up to the DJ box: Jon Dasilva. I knew him because he'd often come and say hello to Dean, and he'd just started DJing at 'Zumbar' with Laurent. 'That acid house was brilliant,' he told me, but I had no idea what he was talking about. He had to explain that the records from Detroit had a name now; 'acid house', that's what people deep into this scene were calling this bleepy, wooshy minimalist stuff.

A month or so later, I was crossing Piccadilly Gardens with a bag of records when I bumped into Tony Wilson. He asked me what I'd been buying. I held up the Eastern Bloc bag. 'Acid house,' I said.

Tony never assumed he knew everything that was going on and had some favoured people he trusted to keep him in the loop. His Haçienda DJs were among this select group. 'Acid? Acid house?' he replied, interested. 'People take acid and listen to this stuff?'

'I don't know,' I said, because I didn't. But I gave him a quick description of the music: Detroit, Chicago, computer-generated, bleepy, wooshy, you know, Pickering plays it.

To be honest, thirty years later, I still don't know the answer. The origins of the phrase are a little mysterious, although DJ Pierre, the man behind 'Acid Trax', later said that at a club he frequented called the Music Box (where Ron Hardy was the DJ and played Pierre's tunes) people did take acid on the dancefloor.

We had no definitions for what we were doing, or stories, theories or timelines; we didn't have any of this. I was in the midst of a mess of excitement, sourcing and sorting tunes, focusing on the next week's nights, intent on making them better than those in the week just gone.

I knew if you didn't want to spend hours trawling the record shops looking for tunes then you'd never make it as a DJ. A DJ also needs some instinctive grasp of musicology, in the sense of knowing the sonics of what works in a song, in a hall, to make people dance. A mix of psychology and anthropology is also important – to read the behaviour and rituals of tribes and crowds, to get some sense of the music taste of the hundreds of strangers in front of you from how they dress or interact with each other, to connect with people, to get on their wavelength, to find a route into their consciousness.

The synergy between the bleepy, wooshy music and the drug ecstasy was becoming clear. If you're attuned to the crowd, you can sense a change in the atmosphere, which, in turn, can be a product of whatever (apart from music) is intoxicating a crowd. It's easy to differentiate between a crowd using beer, or speed, or weed, or cocaine. From early February 1988, ecstasy went from something a small group in the Haçienda were into to being everywhere in the club.

Acid? Acid House?

Four or five months earlier, I'd woken up to a change in the atmosphere around where Happy Mondays and their mates gathered, to my right under the balcony. They were like a club within the club. Unlike the rest of the crowd, they were doing ecstasy, sourced from Amsterdam. Mostly it was pills dubbed California Sunrise, retailing at £20 each. In subsequent eras, dealers may have been offering three pills for a tenner, but these California Sunrise pills were the real deal. Half a pill did the trick.

One of the ace faces in the crew in the unique little corner under the balcony was Eric Barker. By February, Eric had a look; he'd taken to wearing silk pyjamas and a fez. The pyjamas were a practical choice, or so he claimed. Dancing in jeans all night made him sweaty, but silk pyjamas were a lot cooler and better for dancing in. Bez dubbed Eric 'the Wizard of "E"'.

Nights at the Haçienda were unpredictable, and also uncharted; there were no role models, no media coverage, no online videos, and no one had laid down laws about what was cool and what wasn't – it was very liberating. One thing: people didn't know how to dance to this music, until they saw Eric or Bez on a podium and thought 'That'll do.'

The use of ecstasy spread like a wave from the corner under the balcony, across the club. If you'd visited the Haçienda at the end of January 1988 and hadn't returned until the end of March, you simply wouldn't have recognised the place; a revolution had occurred. It was almost two different clubs.

One of the first casualties of the revolution was Dean. He'd been my DJ partner in the DJ box every Saturday for a year and a half. We'd held it together, even though our tastes were divergent and Dean had continued not to compromise, but Paul Cons called me up and said we needed to have a conversation about Dean. He said that Dean wasn't playing enough stuff that people wanted and avoiding house wasn't doing him any favours – there was too much slow soul stuff and no one knew what was going on. There was a need to streamline the music on Saturdays and he wanted me to work with Jon Dasilva.

I told Paul this was fine with me and a good move. Jon was a music aficionado, with a similar history to me; having been into post-punk in his teens, he'd then DJed in Preston at the Twang club (the town's equivalent to the Wilde Club). Plus he knew what acid house was all about – he knew more about it than me – so it made sense. And he'd been DJing with Laurent at Zumbar on Wednesdays.

Ten minutes later, Dean phoned me. He said he expected me to resign in solidarity. I told him the thought hadn't even crossed my mind. 'I have fought your corner, but it's not working out,' I said.

'You call yourself a socialist?' he replied, slamming the phone down.

We kept the name and the idea of 'Wide'; the house we played was in among funk, hip hop and rare groove. I was usually more commercial than Jon, and would occasionally play things that would make Jon wince, but we were a closer fit than I had been with Dean and the tempo, the delirium and the number of new imports being played on Saturdays all increased. To my ears, 'Theme From S-Express' was a Saturday-night tune and my logic back in 1988 was that if that French chef guy everyone keeps talking about can play 'Pump Up the Volume', then I could play 'Theme From S-Express' (or 'Push It').

Digging out records no one else was playing remained important, though. Record shops were key to the music scene in Manchester. I'd been a habitual Piccadilly Records customer, but I'd also go to Spin Inn on Cross Street, especially if I was on the lookout for electro or hip hop. But when the first Chicago and Detroit records started arriving in the city, I did most of my shopping at Eastern Bloc. I use the word 'shopping' but it was more like 'hanging out'. I'd be there two mornings a week, usually a Tuesday and Thursday.

Many of the import releases would arrive in the UK in very small numbers, then the stock would be divided between multiple outlets across the country. Eastern Bloc had good contacts at distributors, so there would be copies of most things available there. I'd want to be one of the few customers who bought the best brand-new release; my copy might be one of only thirty in the whole of the north of England. It was exciting hearing something like 'And the Break Goes On' by the Break Boys and picking up a copy, knowing that it was hot, rare and – to my ears – an immediate floorfiller.

All the Haçienda's resident DJs had audiences that trusted them and had no resistance to unfamiliar tracks or new music of any kind. This is where record shops, and my trips to Eastern Bloc, came in. Martin Price there was helpful in finding me imports, bootlegs or semi-official releases, but he could also be mocking and opinionated. In 1987, he was working with Gerald Simpson and Graham Massey in Hit Squad Manchester, a hip-hop crew, I guess you'd call it. Graham was an established face among Manchester musicians. I first met him when he was in Biting Tongues, who were signed to Factory; I'd often write about them in *Debris*. By the beginning of 1988, the Hit Squad shifted to an acid-house sound and changed their name to 808 State. They recorded an album of

169

material, which was released on Price's label Creed, operating out of Eastern Bloc.

Specialist record shops can be a challenge to visit. Being a DJ who spent money regularly put me near the front in the pecking order of who got best looked after, but, on the downside, I'd have to listen to Martin telling me the Haçienda was a middle-class supermarket and that local guitar bands were jumping on a bandwagon. He also had some unspecified issues with Tony Wilson. But I would always leave Eastern Bloc with a bag of great tunes.

As the summer approached, house and techno were gaining new converts but, although occasionally tunes would break through into the charts, it was always with a considerable time-lag. Some records that were played at the Haçienda didn't enter the top ten until some six months later. We weren't living in an instant world.

Up in the DJ box I was recognising and locking into the change in the atmosphere. I was only a very occasional ecstasy user, partly because I was in clubs working and careful to keep a relatively clear head to make the million right decisions I needed to make. In addition, in August 1988, my son Jack was born. The responsibilities of parenting I couldn't and wouldn't duck, which ruled out saying 'yes' to everything I was offered or feeling the need to be the last person to leave every party.

No one knows how best to run their life; in fact, most people in the summer of 1988 had trouble just knowing what to wear. 'Do we wear shoes or trainers with this music? Do I wear a T-shirt?' On Thursdays, for sure, band T-shirts were a big thing. On Saturdays, the hairdressers and their clients were caught on the cusp of change; in early 1988, there were still people coming to the Haçienda in suits with shoulder pads, then all of a sudden they were in dungarees.

Pyjamas and a fez didn't catch on, but soon the Haçienda audience found a loose-fitting outfit that allowed for extensive dancing: baggy jeans, T-shirts and trainers. It was a look for both boys and girls, which reflected a less predatory atmosphere at the club than at traditional discotheques. There was no sign of girls in a circle dancing around their handbags; people danced together, on the dancefloor, on the stage, under the balcony.

By the end of 1988, there would be dancing in the queue outside too. I was there in the DJ box twice a week every week, feeding the fervour. There's a phrase in the T. S. Eliot poem, 'Burnt Norton': 'the still point of the turning world'. That's sometimes how I felt, stationed behind the decks, sharing the moment but not lost in it, surrounded but separate. Down below: the dancefloor, lit by the relentless flicker of the strobe, a circus of colour and noise, and beautiful half-crazed chaos.

17

The Gig That Changed
Liam's Life

It takes years of hard work to become an overnight success. At the end of 1987 the Stone Roses were barely talked about. They had released 'Sally Cinnamon' on a small label based in Wolverhampton, but were looking to sign to an established indie or a major label. In this task, Gareth, their manager, was working alongside Tony Wilson's first wife Lindsay Reade, but with Gareth's idiosyncratic way of doing things, Lindsay's life wasn't easy.

Inspiral Carpets were very proactive; they never expected anything on a plate, so made things happen for themselves. When their guitarist Graham Lambert gave me a bootleg cassette of the Sonic Youth gig at the New Ardri, he'd surreptitiously put two Inspirals tunes at the end of the recording so I'd have to listen to what they were up to. During 1987, they distributed a proper cassette of their recordings, entitled *Cow*. In November 1987, they supported the Stone Roses at the International.

Nearly twenty-five years later, the Stone Roses sold 225,000 tickets for their reunion shows at Heaton Park, but back in November 1987 demand to see them and the Inspirals was so slack that Gareth gave out hundreds of free tickets to boost the audience at the International. It was a great gig, notable for being the first time Mani performed with the band; he'd recently replaced Pete Garner and brought a more explicit sense of a groove to the music. Thanks mainly to Lindsay Reade, an indie route was open to them; Rough Trade were in pole position to sign them. Gareth, however, had been pursuing his own leads, aiming for a major label deal. In the end, the band were picked up by A&R man Roddy McKenna from Zomba.

Early in 1988, I phoned Gareth as I had a favour to ask the band. Paul Cons and I were involved campaigning against Clause 28 of the Local Government Act 1988, which set limits on the ability of schools to talk openly – let alone positively – about homosexuality, thus, in practical terms, demonising young gay people and sabotaging the ability of schools to give pastoral care and support to their students. Paul and I wanted to raise money for a new group then being set up, the North West Campaign for Lesbian and Gay Equality. I wanted to ask Gareth if we could use the International Two for the anti-Clause 28 concert, and also I was hoping the Stone Roses would join the bill. We set a date in May 1988, and agreed a hire fee of just £50.

I'd already asked James to headline, and they'd accepted. I knew James supported progressive causes; they had performed on Albert Square at the protest against Reagan bombing Libya. The Stone Roses were less of a student-friendly band and with no track record of performing at benefit gigs – but I knew the event would have more impact if I could involve someone unexpected. They accepted without hesitation. On the night, Ian Brown put down a heckler who questioned why they were onstage for a pro-gay cause like that. The band weren't feigning support for the cause either; I later heard that Ian, John and Reni had been among the 25,000 marchers at a huge rally against Clause 28 in Manchester in February.

I promised Gareth the gig with James would be full, so he didn't need to do his usual thing of giving away lots of free tickets – anyway, as I told him, it was inappropriate to give out free tickets for a benefit show. I set an admission price of just £4 in advance and £5 on the door.

I spent far too much time going back and forth between the two dressing rooms. The Roses didn't want to suffer the usual fate of a support band: to play in front of a less-than-full house. They hung on and hung on, Gareth making excuses for why they were running late, doing everything he could to delay their set. Meanwhile, James – Tim in particular – were annoyed and wound up by what they considered to be unprofessional behaviour.

Eventually, the Roses took to the stage, around an hour later than had been agreed. The story of the backstage shenanigans has been exaggerated in the telling, to the extent that there have been claims that the hall was empty when James played as everyone had left to get the last bus, but while it's true that the Stone Roses nearly sabotaged the James performance, the venue stayed busy and the atmosphere electric. James were a big draw in Manchester in 1988, and a great live band.

Later, it transpired that a large proportion of the cash raised was spent on fancying up the office and the operation never properly got off the ground, which was very disappointing, but the Roses performance was a genuine triumph. This was partly down to Mani's influence, but also to their persistence and willingness to evolve; it was as if they had absorbed the euphoric spirit of acid house, then helped to further that spirit. Ian Brown still considers the benefit gig at International Two one of their greatest shows.

Liam and Noel Gallagher both claim that if they hadn't gone to this gig, Oasis would never have happened. The two brothers attended the gig (although, true to form, they went separately). Noel struck up a conversation with Graham Lambert, who was attempting to tape-record the show. It was his first encounter with an Inspiral Carpet; he went on to work for them on the road and at their office on New Mount Street.

For Liam, the intensity, the power and the pleasure of the gig, specifically Ian Brown's onstage swagger, inspired him to get involved in music. He later claimed, 'That was my favourite gig of all time, killed me dead, changed me fuckin' life. If I hadn't gone that night, I'd probably be sitting in some pub in Levenshulme.'

The instigators of the Haçienda, Rob and Tony, and New Order and Mike Pickering were all at least four or five years older than me, which seems a lot when you are in your early twenties. Ian Brown, Shaun or Graeme Park, say, were my generation, a generation that had helped transform the scene, but now you could sense that passion and the urge to participate were also in the hearts of people four or five years younger than us.

The *NME* always needed writers clued-up about what was happening in music cities like Manchester, and in 1988 a real bright spark emerged: Sarah Champion. A lot younger than me, she was an avid *Debris* reader with her own fanzine, *Alarm*, and, later, a fanzine co-produced with Alison Martin called *SCAM*. Sarah's enthusiasm and writing talent were spotted by James Brown at the *NME*.

Sarah threw herself into documenting what was going on in Manchester – the bands, the clubs, the labels. In 2012, she reflected on those years and that anti-Clause 28 gig at the International Two in particular, describing it as the occasion that crystallised the sense of euphoria in the city. 'I think "Madchester" was born that night,' she said.

The word 'Madchester' hadn't yet been coined, but the phenomenon was clear to all, as Sarah Champion describes: 'Excitement in Manchester was building week by week. It's not just myth, somehow the drugs and music were combining and something *big* was happening. We really felt we were the centre of the universe.'

Madchester had one drug but two strands of music. The likes of Martin Price would be scathing about the local bands, and plenty of James fans would have run a mile from hardcore acid-house clubs like the Thunderdome – in the same way many aficionados of Detroit techno never went near a Stone Roses concert – but the clubs and the local bands couldn't be disentangled. They fed into a common energy. In the spirit of the times, many people embraced both. After all, EMI's A&R man Dave Ambrose, who signed Duran Duran, once said, 'Manchester kids have the best record collections.' It's often attributed to Tony Wilson, but he just picked up on and popularised Mr Ambrose's phrase.

Even Noel Gallagher, who has a reputation as a dyed-in-the-wool classic rock fan, when he was in conversation with rock journalist John Doran, touching upon an early Oasis cover of Cartouche's 'Feel the Groove', confessed those years had made an impact: 'When the acid house thing started in '87, it fucking blew my mind and it continues to do so.'

In addition to the anti-Clause 28 show Noel and Liam had attended, May 1988 also witnessed the Haçienda's sixth birthday. I scribbled the set-times down in my diary. I was playing eleven until twelve, preceded by the new kid in town, DJ Pedro, or, in the words in my diary, 'the French guy'. Mike and Graeme took over from midnight onwards. At our talk at Silencio, Laurent also recalled there was a firework display inside the club. Neither of us were exactly sure how that worked, but agreed that somehow, luckily – given the circumstances – no one was injured.

Not long after the Haçienda's birthday event, Laurent got word from France that he had been called up for French National Service starting in August. 'Zumbar' was drawing to a close anyway, as Paul Cons had decided to reinvent Wednesdays at the Haçienda again, with a night called 'Hot'. Laurent left for France at the end of July 1988, taking with him his decks, records and mix tapes, and an 'Acid Trax' T-shirt.

'Hot', launched in July 1988, became the quintessential Summer of Love experience as crowds descended on the club, in dungarees, bandanas and smiley T-shirts. A swimming pool was installed next to the dancefloor, and bleepy Detroit techno, airhorns and whistles filled the air.

In May 1988, both *i-D* and the *Face* had run features on the emerging rave scene nationwide, and as that summer progressed, tabloid newspapers alike picked up on the parties. There have been various studies since revealing how tabloid coverage of acid house changed, from initial enthusiasm (including competitions to win smiley T-shirts) to headlines such as the *Sun*'s 'EVIL OF ECSTASY'. By November 1988, to the authorities, media and general public, acid-house ravers had become a classic case of a 'deviant group'.

The profile of Manchester was still rising and Factory Records decided to change the way they were doing things to reflect the commercial potential of Happy Mondays. The *Bummed* album had been recorded in August 1988. Prior to its release, in November, the band got a new press officer, Jeff Barrett.

The ad hoc and low-key strategies Factory had used for promotion were ditched in favour of a more focused approach for the release of *Bummed*. The Mondays went to London, taking part in a playback event first at Heaven (where the record was played in full to invited media), and then going on to Dingwalls to headline a live show. Nathan later said that the band had made more money selling ecstasy to the journalists at the playback event than they did playing the gig.

The *Bummed* album had been recorded on the cusp of our music culture changing. The rhythm section certainly had a groove but the songs weren't loaded with the revolutionary sonics that marked the new era of house and techno. As our world started shifting, it was reasonable to find a way of giving some of the songs an extra twist or two. Nathan arranged for 'Wrote For Luck' to be remixed twice: firstly there was a Vince Clarke version, then a version by Paul Oakenfold and Steve Osborne.

Philip Shotton and Keith Jobling were two video makers from the north-east who dubbed themselves the Bailey Brothers, with a base in an office building on Sackville Street, just down the corridor from Central Station Design who were responsible for the design of the Mondays record sleeves. Phil thinks of the Bailey Brothers video for the Mondays' 'Wrote For Luck', along with others, like this: 'You could say we were making adverts for the scene.' This makes sense. It was an era before social media and instant global communications; your attention might be drawn to a hot band or a busy venue, but getting a sense of all the elements of a scene – especially the visual, lifestyle element – was a challenge.

The 'Wrote for Luck' video was shot in October 1988 at a club called Legend (later known as 5th Avenue), just around the corner from the Bailey Brothers office and closer than the Haçienda. Eric Barker had begun a regular night there; it was a sign of how alive the scene was that there were a number of key characters, like the Wizard of 'E', had got bored of the Haçienda before the world had even discovered it and gone to other places to establish acid-house enclaves.

The concept for the video required a crowd of ravers; not actors, genuine people on the scene. The band duly arrived. Everything was ready; the crowd had assembled, Dave Rofe was already playing the tunes, everyone was dancing, and there was space for the band to get on the dancefloor, but there was a slight hiatus. Shaun said he wouldn't move until more ecstasy arrived and kicked in. Dave Rofe played on. Then Shaun was ready, the cameras rolled, and it was all done in two takes.

It's an extraordinary three and a half minutes; a trippy, authentic, strobe-fest awash with freaky dancing. After a brief discussion about whether the enthusiastic use of strobe lighting in the video would destroy people's brains or not, *The Chart Show* broadcast the video less than a week after it was made.

The record went only to No. 7 in the indie charts, not troubling the proper top 100.

The scene was still to be discovered. This was true not just of the Mondays and the Roses, but the dance music being played in clubs like the Haçienda too. Some hits broke through belatedly, but DJs were playing music that was barely receiving any radio play (certainly outside specialist shows like Stu Allan's on Piccadilly Radio). MTV weren't champions of dance music; they'd been cajoled and ridiculed into playing hip hop, and house was not yet on their agenda.

This made the Haçienda experience even more exceptional; to hear new house tunes you had to visit a club. You couldn't watch or hear DJ mixes online, you had to leave the house, take heed of rumours or word-of-mouth recommendations. People would travel from all over for their only chance to hear the music and share the atmosphere. A floorfiller couldn't be Shazammed and then downloaded or streamed. It would only exist just for the five or six minutes it boomed through the speakers.

At 2 a.m. no one wanted the night to end, creating a demand for after-hours venues likes the Kitchen in Hulme, or encouraging a quick taxi dash to the Reno in Moss Side. This was in addition to the illegal warehouse parties, where ravers would invade a makeshift space for several hours. Towns like Blackburn and Nelson would become hotspots for warehouse parties, but Manchester's first warehouse party of the acid era took place on 6 October 1988 on Store Street (below Piccadilly Station). Mike Pickering was the DJ, and the organisers were the entrepreneurial ravers Chris and Anthony Donnelly. They were the brothers of Tracey from Swing, and would later to be the founders of the Gio Goi clothing brand.

One person who was now missing out on the action in Manchester was Laurent Garnier. He had left England and the Haçienda, but the Haçienda stayed with him. After his military service, he came back to England to play various venues in the north of England. In France, he helped establish the Rex club in Paris as the spiritual home of the city's techno scene and has since made countless successful records, and created the ground-breaking F Communications label with Eric Morand. In 2017 he was awarded the prestigious Légion d'honneur for his services to music over the last thirty years. After the announcement of this, Laurent said, 'This distinction is not only the consecration of my thirty-year career, but that of a collective history.'

Our individual histories have become part of a collective history, of the clubs, the audiences, the city, and of the people from those years who gravitated towards the Haçienda and then graduated from there, going on to make a mark in music; people like Laurent, Justin Robertson, Sasha, Noel Gallagher, A Guy Called Gerald and the Chemical Brothers. The club also served as a catalyst for Sacha Lord-Marchionne. His first club promotion was at the Haç in July 1994. He is now head honcho at the Warehouse Project, the highest profile twenty-first-century Manchester club.

I love Vincent Gallo, for several reasons, including for his film *Buffalo 66* which I adore, and for the way he jumps untethered from acting to painting to releasing solo recordings. I heard a recording of an interview he gave to film critic Elvis Mitchell in 1998 in which he talks about how artistic activity can be hampered by the available audience. His argument is that if nothing great is happening, you maybe have to blame not the artists, filmmakers, musicians – but the consumers. Gallo talks about clubs like Max's and the Mud Club in New York in the early and mid-1980s, and how the scene worked and played out. He says a band could improve because the audiences were intimately connected to the music, wanting evolution and revolution. The audiences at the Man Alive, the Boardwalk, the Haçienda, however small they sometimes were, had that attitude; connected, adventurous.

Our other link with NYC was that in the 1980s Manchester was going through economic hard times. In the late 1970s New York was said to be financially bankrupt, but to me it seemed like the creative epicentre of the world. You could say we were also confirming the maxim uttered by the Russian film director Andrei Tarkovsky: 'Art is born out of an ill-designed world.'

In addition, the Madchester generation was part of the long tradition of hedonism. Friedrich Engels had stepped over drunken Mancunians lying in the gutter in the early 1840s: 'On Saturday evenings, when the whole working class pours from its own poor quarters into the main thoroughfares, intemperance may be seen in all its brutality.' When Engels was writing, for the urban poor after a week of being ground down by factory bosses, a big night out was as much an exercise in reclaiming life as enjoying it.

The way consuming music gave birth to producing music was also an echo of the way punk triggered an explosion of music-making. Certainly, we benefited from the achievements and infrastructure of the 1970s generation, who, in turn, had plugged into Manchester's history of resourcefulness and the kind of self-organisation that led to the founding of the Trades Union Congress in the city in 1868. We were making our contribution at a time when Mrs Thatcher said there was 'no such thing as society'.

In my polemic in the shadow of the 1987 general election, I'd used words from the Hopkins poem to give a sense of how social and economic policies were caging potential. By late 1988, experiences inside the Haçienda felt like an escape, a glimpse of utopia, a sea of possibilities.

The same month Mike headlined the Gio Goi warehouse party, he piloted the release of a compilation of locally made house music on DeConstruction Records called *North*, which included T-Coy's 'Carino' (eighteen months after it was first white-labelled), as well as 'Voodoo Ray' by A Guy Called Gerald and 'Dream 17' by Annette. Sold in a gatefold sleeve, with artwork by Central Station Design, the album included sleevenotes paying homage to the inspiration of Mike and Graeme's 'Nude' night.

The creativity, the twenty-five thousand people marching against Clause 28, the glory of 'Wrote for Luck', the freedom from the predatory dancefloor, the shared bliss, banging basslines; we'd created a community in an era of 'no such thing as society'. Our joy was resistance, escape and celebration. We'd set the skylark free.

18

Exclusive Interviews, Plastic Giraffes

Jack had arrived at the end of August 1988 and every time I held him in my arms or stared at him I felt a rush of love. Rachel and I were the first of our group of friends to have a child, so it wasn't always easy. When people asked whether fatherhood suited me, I usually said it was the hardest job I'd ever had, which, considering the only things I'd ever done were writing a fanzine and DJing, wasn't really surprising.

The sleevenotes to the *North* compilation explained that by the summer of 1988 Manchester had become 'a jacking zone'. So, Jack was born, fittingly, in the midst of 'a jacking zone', in a Summer of Love, just as a new culture was emerging. He had one thing in common with acid house: he messed with my body clock. Everyone knows that a young baby triggers sleep deprivation, but through the last months of 1988 my body clock was all over the place anyway. Rachel took some time off paid employment, but within a year or two she began working with James, in their merchandising operation – which was huge (they sold thousands of T-shirts) – and, a decade or two later, became Lisa Stansfield's manager.

Early in 1989, I was getting used to being a parent, as much as you ever can. Most days, for a few hours at least, I would go into town to the office at 48 Princess Street that I shared with Nathan. But I was also contactable at home, on the landline (I was still a year or two away from my first mobile phone).

One evening in May 1989, the phone rang at home. Sometimes I'd ignore calls and let them click onto answerphone, especially if Rachel was out and I was playing with baby Jack, and also because I had to wend my way through a mound of toys to answer the phone. Fortunately, that afternoon I picked up; it was Johnny Marr calling. He said that he was now at the point when he was up for talking about the Smiths, the split and his current activities, and he wanted to know if I was interested in an interview.

Johnny Marr left the Smiths in 1987. It was nearly two years later, and he hadn't given anyone an in-depth interview. Now he was offering *Debris* a world exclusive. He said he trusted me and invited me to his house one evening, any evening that suited me. He made it sound like I'd be doing him a massive favour if I interviewed him, while I struggled to avoid collapsing in a heap of excitement on top of a wooden train and a family of plastic giraffes.

I kept myself together, arranged a date and made plans. Johnny had spoken to Todd Graft, a photographer around town, and arranged to meet him after the interview close to where I lived. The photos ended up being taken near St Bernadette's Roman Catholic Church on Princess Road.

I hadn't had a proper conversation with Johnny for several years. I'd seen him many times, though, from afar. And all the times I saw him perform with the Smiths he was always assured, and riveting, although he went through a bit of a Keith Richards thing I couldn't quite get.

The Queen Is Dead, the band's third studio album, was released in June 1986 after being delayed for months by a legal dispute. By this time, Johnny was exhausted by the Smiths' recording and touring schedule, and drinking too much; he said he had been 'extremely ill'.

The North American tour promoting *The Queen Is Dead* was cut short in September 1986. Work on the next album began almost immediately and the recording of *Strangeways, Here We Come* was completed in spring 1987, by which time Johnny had left the band.

I was sitting in his house alone in the living room while he went to get me a drink. At first glance, the shelving all along one wall looked like a wonderful book collection. As you might expect, I went for a root through, but they weren't books, they were VHS videos. He had tons of videotapes; I think he must have had more videos than anyone else in Bowdon back then, including the nearest branch of Blockbuster.

After a brief bit of casual catching-up, we talked about his decision to walk away from the Smiths. I was intrigued by the timing, between the recording and release of *Strangeways*. But, if anything, Johnny seemed to have considered he'd hung on longer than he could have, confessing, 'I was unhappy for at least a year, or even a year and a half, before the split finally came.'

The promotional and touring experience after *The Queen Is Dead* had been problematic, a new album was on the horizon, the circus was about to start again. He couldn't bring himself to sign up to a heavy schedule of gigs to promote the follow-up: 'If we were going to go off and tour and try to promote the record with the bad atmosphere that was around, the situation would have got even more hideous than it was. I thought if we had carried on, then none of us would have been able to take it.'

I asked Johnny if he thought fans would ever stop pinning the blame on him for ending the Smiths. 'People seemed to think that the most important thing in the world was for their favourite group to stay together,' he said. 'They didn't know anything about the way things were. They'd have preferred me to have died, rather than split the group up. That was their sense of what mattered. But that wasn't what mattered to me. They wanted me to die, they wanted to see me die in some rock 'n' roll graveyard.'

The band were more successful than ever, but clearly success was hiding tensions. 'In all honesty, I can't remember a time when there wasn't a problem lurking somewhere,' said Johnny.

After the sacking of Joe Moss, so many and various people had been active managers of the Smiths – there seemed to be a new name every month or so. Meanwhile, most of the burden fell on Johnny to sort out personnel issues, for example. And money. And both him and Morrissey were dealing with stuff that a well-run management team could have sorted.

He'd walked away from the Smiths, but subsequently had never talked about any of this. I had no idea what his answer would be to some basic questions, such as, 'Do you regret the fact that there's no Smiths any more?'

'No, never, not at all,' he said. 'And people around me who care about me feel the same. I can see it in their eyes. I was ill and away from home and I've no idea what would have happened to us musically. It was mad. Also, we were together for four or five years and that's enough for any group.'

The Smiths fanboy in me kept hoping he'd say something positive, and eventually he did. 'Having said all this, I don't think about the Smiths in any other light than wonderful, because it was like some really fantastic adventure that happened to me when I was young.'

He talked enthusiastically about Morrissey's lyrics: 'The lyrics are brilliant. I loved all that stuff, and the ideas.' And he told me *The Queen Is Dead* is his favourite Smiths album.

I'd always enjoyed talking to Johnny about music. In fact, until that evening I don't think we'd talked about anything else. Twenty minutes into the interview, we were reverting to type. He told me he'd been listening to the De La Soul album and to Happy Mondays (the latter, 'the best group on the planet'). He said something I doubt Morrissey would ever say: 'Going to clubs is a good way to hear new records.'

Johnny explained that for the last few years of the Smiths, the music he was being played by friends – like Donald Johnson and Jez Kerr from A Certain Ratio, and Bernard from New Order – was mostly electronic dance. 'Towards the end of the Smiths, I realised that the records I was listening to with my friends were more exciting than the records I was listening to with the group. Things have changed. All those house records from Chicago . . .'

To satisfy his desire to start working with machines, Johnny had teamed up with Bernard, working under the name Electronic. There had been no room in the Smiths for the music he was listening to with his friends; 'One thing about any group who create a certain style and create a certain political aspect to what they do, it gets to be a club, and some things are in and some things are out.'

The Smiths had emerged in a period when synthesisers were all the rage but, perhaps unsurprisingly for two people who first said hello to each other at a Patti Smith concert back in 1978, Morrissey and Marr had given synth pop a wide berth. The Smiths were going against the grain, taking up a contrary stance. In 1983 this was refreshing, as Johnny pointed out: 'At that time there weren't any other guitar groups going on about Leiber and Stoller and the Shangri-Las, and nobody had Brian Jones haircuts.'

Morrissey was dogmatic about many things, in a way which ruled out compromise or evolution. What had started out feeling refreshing – maybe a little revolutionary – turned stale. Johnny put it like this: 'Eventually we'd got ourselves down a musical and political cul-de-sac.'

Synth pop, videos and hip hop were all anathema to Morrissey. He was also especially hostile to the music that was turning Johnny on, telling an interviewer, 'I could never ever begin to explain the utter loathing I feel for dance music. That two people can sit in their bedroom with a little bit of machinery and come out with this huge wall of sound is sterility at its utmost. I want to see real people on stage, playing real instruments.'

I pointed out to Johnny that Morrissey's position was de facto the Smiths' position, and that of the fans too, such was the strong bond between Morrissey and the fans. 'Yes, he led them in his own way. I was fascinated by that, and when I stopped being fascinated I left.'

In the last decades, Morrissey has treated us to his views

on immigration. In 2017, he was on BBC Radio 6 Music claiming that a recent vote for the new leader of UKIP had been rigged against the most anti-Islam candidate Anne Marie Waters (a woman who had gone on record proclaiming 'A lot of people need to be deported. Many mosques need to be closed down.').

By 2017, of course, Morrissey had lived away from England in tax exile for decades, and still preferred to exist in a particular version of a disappeared world; kitchen-sink films, Cilla Black, his adolescence. In 1987, I'd already heard and ignored his declaration that 'all reggae was vile'. I already knew that his music tastes were reactionary, in contrast to the audiences who responded so positively to my DJ playlists. From my first night at the Haçienda, the idea of inclusivity was embedded into the music policy. I aimed at building bridges not walls.

After *Debris* was published, Johnny called me. He said he'd picked up a copy at Piccadilly Records, it was perfect, and he thanked me. You know what? I could hear emotion in his voice, as he thanked me again and called it perfect again.

It was good to get the appreciation, but listening back to the interview now, I regret that I didn't go a little deeper. My strategy had been to be inconspicuous in the interview, neutral, providing a platform for Johnny. But maybe it would have been better for me to have had a bit more edge. Johnny had said what Johnny wanted to say, he'd got stuff off his chest, but I wonder if he would have explained a little bit more why his lifestyle had become so dangerous, the pressures and issues that led to his misuse of alcohol, for example.

The following day, the *NME* called me up wanting to reprint the interview and Todd's photos. I'd barely spoken to them over the previous couple of years, and most of the local coverage was being very ably done by Sarah Champion and Stuart Maconie. I was DJing twice a week at the Haçienda and, in truth, that was a lot more satisfying and fun than hustling for freelance work reviewing bands.

Despite having no regrets spending time on *Debris*, the fanzine didn't last much longer after the Johnny Marr issue. I made some plans for one final one and asked Tony Wilson if I could interview him, and he agreed. I'd been working with him on his television show, *The Other Side of Midnight*; in August 1988, he'd called me his 'critic at large' and sent me and one of his team, Bob Dickinson, to Liverpool to present a tribute to the leftist writer and theorist Raymond Williams.

Williams was a Welshman who spent most of his career at Cambridge, so I have no idea why we did that piece in Liverpool, although I suspect it was something to do with the Granada cameramen. Working a little in TV, I was getting used to the quirks of the industry; schedules would be arranged around the working practices of the cameramen (always men) and (most importantly, it seemed) their breaks. I guess a team were doing some filming in Liverpool and it was cheaper for us to go to them than for them to come to anywhere we deemed appropriate. I also remember not taking the time to work out exactly what I was going to say, sitting in a café looking at a camera and hearing my words coming out, knowing they weren't the right ones. The day after it was broadcast, Mark E. Smith phoned me up with some advice: 'Next time, get a script . . .'

Tony Wilson came to my house for the interview. He wasn't even forty but for some reason I asked him if growing old worried him. 'I don't fear growing old,' he said. 'I realised in

1976 that I was going to remain immature, that I was never going to grow old. I'm a father now, and that is the only true change we ever make in life . . .'

Tony looked around at Jack's washed baby clothes hanging on all the radiators to dry. 'Can I namedrop?' he asked. 'Leonard Cohen said to me, "There's only one important change in a life. When you have a child, you have up until then always been centre-stage in your life, and when you have a child you're no longer centre-stage." And that's the only kind of maturity that will happen to me.'

I wondered if one aspect of that immaturity was faith in youth culture. Tony didn't quite answer the question, but his reply was great: 'I will always retain my love for the avant-garde. And by "avant-garde" I don't mean "experimental", I mean the early art of people who are going to be great artists.'

Doing a fanzine was time-consuming, the Haçienda nights were booming, and I wanted time to look after Jack; as a consequence, the celebratory final issue of *Debris* featuring the Tony Wilson interview never happened. I sat on the Wilson interview for a few weeks, then passed it on to another fanzine, *Recoil*.

I had enjoyed creating *Debris*; not just the creating but the connecting too, the sense of being part of a network. Also, it set me off into the life I wanted; to consume, and to document, but also to intervene in culture.

Apart from personal issues, an underlying reason for the demise of *Debris* was that for most people on the Haçienda dancefloor there now wasn't the same curiosity about who made the records and the background to it all. A Smiths fan might want to know all about the band and Morrissey's favourite books and his opinions about things, but at the club we were playing lots of imports, white-label records, tracks by unknown producers or producers with opaque pseudonyms.

I found this facelessness liberating, this not knowing or caring if I was playing records made by white people or black people or whether they had albums out, let alone whether they were, say, vegetarian. It was pure too, somehow; it wasn't about the sleeve, or the label, or the artist, or the postcode or personality of the artist. Everything was down to the impact of the music in the groove.

19

What The World Is
Waiting For

Gareth Evans asked if I could get the Stone Roses a gig at
the Haçienda. He said I was a Factory person, he didn't
generally mix with Factory people, and didn't know who else to
ask. On my nights off, I was as likely to be at his International
club watching bands as the Haçienda, but for him those venues
were like two separate camps. I told him I'd sort the gig and
also that I reckoned that I could get the band on the BBC2
show *Snub TV*. Gareth was very interested.

Coincidentally, around the time Gareth had asked me about
a Haçienda gig, I had been discussing an idea with Paul Cons of
running a short series on Monday nights, featuring bands with
me DJing. I'd suggested we should call it 'The Monday Club'.
The name was already in use by a bone-headed far-right faction
in the Tory party that was all for the Union, law and order,
Christianity, the whole shebang. I said we could appropriate
the name. Cons knew his politics, he got the reference. So I

called him, told him we had the Stone Roses and we sorted the details at a meeting the next day.

I still have the notes from the meeting; scribblings rather than spreadsheets, of course. We couldn't quite work out a ticket price, before settling on £4 in advance, £4.50 on the door. The Stone Roses were guaranteed £2,000, with an extra £950 if we sold more than a thousand tickets.

King of the Slums were one of the bands Nathan and I released on our Play Hard label, so I gave them the support slot and £150. They were a very original, sarky band who made a lovely noise featuring a very scratchy violin. Nathan used to get wound up because Charley and Sarah from the band insisted on taking their Alsatian dog with them everywhere. They'd be in the office every other day, Charley hassling me for petrol money to get them to a gig at Norwich Waterfront or somewhere, and the Alsatian would be with them. They also took the dog to a *Melody Maker* interview with Simon Reynolds.

The Roses at the Haçienda was a sell-out, and the *Snub TV* footage was brilliant. It was the first of a handful of special Stone Roses shows that marked their rise. In August 1989, their followers took over not just the Empress Ballroom in the Winter Gardens complex in Blackpool, but the town itself, thousands of people descending for a Saturday show on a sunny weekend.

The band didn't want a support act, just DJs. Ian had come to believe that no band was worthy enough to share the stage with the Stone Roses, which was funny, and maybe even true. Their thinking was influenced by those intense experiences every weekend at the Haçienda and elsewhere. The Roses captured the wistfulness of 1960s bands like the Byrds but in their music and at their gigs they also wanted that surging euphoric club buzz.

For Blackpool, they asked me to DJ, and they also recruited Dave Booth from the Playpen. The atmosphere was so close to hysteria by the time I played, it was electric – it was like Manchester had decamped to that ballroom. They'd set up the decks at the back of the stage and, as I was playing, they were loading a few extra things onto the stage. I played 'Sympathy For the Devil' and then the band came on, but when that rumble of 'I Wanna Be Adored' started I realised that my route off the stage had been blocked by the guitar amps and Reni's drumkit. I was stuck at the back of the stage so I watched the whole gig from behind John Squire. I could feel the audience excitement in an almost physical way, like a wave of thunder that could knock me over.

Back at the Haçienda, I'd lost my Saturday residency after more than three years. Paul Mason called me and told me they were relaunching Saturdays. Mr Mason was the man who craved an audience full of hairdressers and their favourite clients so, in an inspired move, he replaced Jon and me with an actual, real-life hairdresser called Nick Arrojo. To be honest, Nick was a very decent DJ and it refreshed things. No bridges were being burned; Jon was DJing every Wednesday at the club and I was doing Thursdays, which were a weekly, and emphatic, demonstration of the mash-up of successful local bands and cutting-edge dance music for which Manchester was becoming renowned.

Having Saturdays free gave me the chance to do gigs outside Manchester, including confirming a booking to warm up again for the Stone Roses, this time at the seven-thousand-capacity Alexandra Palace in London. The evening had a great sense of occasion, but was marred by a terrible sound. As at Blackpool, there was a very sizeable Manchester contingent in the crowd and before the band played there were loud chants of 'Manchester, la-la-la, Manchester, la-la-la'. I loved Ian Brown's famous response, 'It's not where you're from, it's where you're at.' I think onstage at Alexandra Palace was the first time he used the phrase.

In later years, Ian admitted that on the drive home to Manchester, he and John Squire didn't exchange a single word – they were both too disappointed by the gig. I have a vague memory of Gareth's outfit that evening: a Christmas jumper depicting a giant Christmas pudding.

Despite the sound problems and a certain sense of anti-climax, the gig couldn't have been timed better by the Roses; it coincided with the release of their double-A side 'Fool's Gold'/'What the World Is Waiting For'. Sales were enough to secure them a spot on *Top of the Pops* broadcast on Thursday 23 November. Happy Mondays graced the same episode, performing 'Hallelujah' from 'Rave On; the Madchester EP'. The word 'Madchester' was now in common use, and Madchester had taken over the charts.

The Bailey Brothers had a part to play in the invention of the word 'Madchester'. As well as producing videos, they had begun to make progress with a feature film with the working title *The Mad Fuckers*. There was a line in Phil and Keith's script where one of the main characters, a gangster called Charlie, comes back to Manchester on a Learjet and says something along the lines of 'It's good to be back in rainy old Madchester.'

Scrambling around for some development money to help the film happen, Phil and Keith sent a proposal and some of the script to British Screen Finance but got knocked back. The rejection letter was emphatic; they were told it was *exactly* the sort of film British Screen would *never* fund, and *exactly* the sort of film they hoped the British film industry would *never* make.

Tony was always taking an interest in *The Mad Fuckers*. Keith and Phil showed the letter to him, and he described it as 'one of the best rejection letters ever'. He asked them what development money they'd asked British Screen for, and without a pause told them that Factory would find the cash.

The label had no money (and the film was never made). The Haçienda had huge running costs, notably the need to pay for security; Factory had purchased a new HQ on Charles Street, which took nearly a year to refurbish and fit out; and their biggest act, New Order, seemed a little reticent about going back into the studio to follow up *Technique* (the band itself was in suspension, with Bernard working with Johnny in Electronic, Peter Hook leading the band Revenge, and Stephen and Gillian recording as the Other Two).

However, there was a chance to make some money selling T-shirts. James and the Inspiral Carpets were churning out T-shirts by the box-load, and Nathan and I helped establish a T-shirt company to sell Happy Mondays merchandise from our Princess Street office, but Factory had decided to think about the ifs, whens and Saville designs. Factory was like that; some decisions were snap, others took an age.

In the late summer of 1989, Tony was talking to the Bailey Brothers about T-shirt ideas. They told him they had already been considering doing a T-shirt with a photo of Bez off his face on it, with a slogan saying 'Welcome to Madchester'. Tony picked up on the word 'Madchester'. In a flurry of decisions, theories, commands and action, he left the Bailey Brothers, went to find

Central Station Design in their office next door, and asked them to come up with a Madchester logo. Then Tony called Nathan, who called Shaun; the new Happy Mondays record had been given a new name: 'Rave On; the Madchester EP'. The EP was released in November 1989. Still no one had any money.

Veteran journalist Nick Kent was sent to the recording of *Top of the Pops* to write a story on Madchester for the *Face*. Shaun Ryder later recalled, 'That was supposed to be a big deal, Nick Kent coming down, but I couldn't give a fuck.'

During the day, Kent talked to Tony Wilson, who, when the piece was printed, was quoted as saying, 'Ian Curtis dying on me was the greatest thing that happened to my life. Death sells.' Out of context, it sounded cold and calculating. Tony was furious, and denied he'd said it. He called the editor of the *Face*, Sheryl Garratt, and, as he knew I occasionally wrote for the magazine, he called me. He wanted a retraction.

A few weeks before Alexandra Park, Dave Booth approached me and invited me to join him at 'The Hangout', a newly opened club night he was organising in Manchester with Gino Brandolani. It would be weekly, every Saturday, at a club called Isadora's, under the Corn Exchange.

Dave was the DJ in the main room, playing a mix of retro psychedelic stuff and the Stone Roses and Inspiral Carpets. I did a second room for five or six months playing hip hop like 'Talkin' All That Jazz' by Stetsasonic, new beat, electro and Wood Allen 'Airport '89'. There was no light show in the second room, it was all very rudimentary. I had one giant speaker, which blew up every few weeks due to condensation and/or beer in the electrics, and it took at least half an hour to repair. Gino always said he'd get something sorted.

At Isadora's we attracted a more local and even younger crowd than the Haçienda audience. Róisín Murphy became one of the regulars; her family were in Stockport in those years. A young Fall and Sonic Youth fan, she'd just started visiting clubs – including the Reno in Moss Side. From 'The Hangout' she then graduated to the Haçienda. When I interviewed her in 2016, she told me that 'The Hangout' was her first acid-house experience, but she wouldn't tell me if she'd taken ecstasy there.

New Year's Eve at the end of 1989 was my last night at Isadora's. At about fifteen minutes to midnight the speaker blew again. The crowd started booing. Not only had my big build-up been cut short, but instead of chimes and a big tune at midnight there would be silence.

I knew it would probably take until at least quarter past twelve to get the speakers up and running, maybe longer, and I'd soon start getting customers wanting their money back. There was a rear fire exit onto Fennel Street. I grabbed my box of records, took a left out of the DJ box, pushed my way out through the fire exit, hurried on to Corporation Street, jumped into a cab and I was home by midnight. I didn't get paid and I never went back.

My Thursday nights at the Haçienda were still going strong. I may have lost my Saturdays at Isadora's but I had just started my first foreign residency: once a month at a club in Paris called La Locomotive, next door to the Moulin Rouge – and now called La Machine – where a young woman called Hilda programmed the entertainment and the resident DJs included Erik Rug and Bruno Gervais.

Hilda at the Locomotive was one of the first promoters

anywhere to see how Madchester had the potential to make an international impact. Early in 1989, she'd programmed a mini-festival of bands and DJs from the north of England, including a one-off Haçienda night featuring Mike Pickering playing a pure acid-house set, but it went over the heads of the people there so they decided to invite me to DJ at subsequent events. They reckoned a playlist that mixed up acid house with 'Sympathy for the Devil', the Stone Roses, New Order and other stuff would be easier for that particular audience in Paris to digest. Some of the Parisian gay clubs were playing house and also a few crews were organising warehouse parties, but house music hadn't crossed over into the French rock crowd at the Loco.

I went over to the Loco once a month for about a year starting in December 1989. It was the first time the Haçienda had taken a residency in another club, let alone one in a foreign city. It wasn't always easy playing house and techno records to a thousand people who eighteen months before were jumping around to 'You Really Got Me', but things changed, people changed, and the Locomotive nights continued to draw a good crowd of curious party people. We had live bands most months as well; usually bands from Manchester (including James and A Certain Ratio) or associated with Madchester (like the Farm, later in 1990).

Most months the crowd was supplemented by a coach or two of Manchester youth. They set out on the journey to Paris from the Haçienda at 2.30 a.m., after the club's Wednesday night, and usually arrived in Paris some thirteen or fourteen hours later. This gave them some time to drag their flares along the boulevards before the big night out.

Hilda never stopped championing Madchester. She took me to a radio show presented by an old bourgeois intellectual straight out of the 1950s. Hilda translated for me. When I said (and then she said) Manchester was on the cusp of a cultural renaissance, he replied with a sound best rendered as 'Pffffft' and he threw up his hands in disbelief as if someone had just told him Cheddar was tastier than Camembert.

My connections with the Loco and the magazine *Les Inrocks* were getting me some great Paris gigs. In October 1990, I was on the bill at a three-night festival hosted by *Les Inrocks* at La Cigale, alongside James, the Charlatans, Band of Holy Joy, the Monochrome Set and John Cale. One of the nights, we did an afterparty at the Loco, where Tim Burgess from the Charlatans introduced himself and told me how excited the band had been when they had heard I'd been playing their first single at the Haçienda. My first impressions of him were very positive. I'd met friendly musicians before, but he seemed so heart-warmingly genuine. I've hung out with him many times since, and my first impressions were correct.

That year, the other highpoint was warming up for the Stone Roses again, at their 20,000-capacity show at Spike Island. Having confirmed me and Dave Booth again, Gareth had added a few more DJs, including the Jam MCs. In addition, we got Frankie Bones. To this day, I'm convinced the band had asked Gareth to book Frankie Knuckles, but we got Frankie Bones. I can imagine his logic; he's American, he's called Frankie, he's cheaper than the Knuckles fella. Ian gave me a copy of a Bob Marley album and asked me to play 'Redemption Song' at the end.

Gareth Evans booked some bands for the show, including Gary Clail On-U Sound System, with Adrian Sherwood on mixing duties. This had been a suggestion of mine, having been a fan of Adrian for years and with Gary's 'Human Nature' single doing well commercially. I'd also suggested Barrie K. Sharpe, who had just released 'Masterplan', but Barrie, or his people, turned the gig down.

At Spike Island, the DJ set-up was eighty yards from the stage on a rickety tower also home to the mixing desk, the lighting desk and various techy people. From the tower, I could see the queues, acres of baggy jeans and so many T-shirts. Spike Island attracted a young crowd. People travelled from all over, like pilgrims.

Time seemed to slow down that warm May afternoon. There was a long, long wait from the gates opening until the Roses were due onstage, and I panicked a bit as the audience seemed bored early in the afternoon. Slowly, collectively, us DJs began raising the atmosphere, with the Jam MCs working their magic and Alfonso Buller rasping out his war cry 'Manchester Vibes in the Area'. I remember playing 'Cubik' by 808 State; by this time the crowd were kicking up dust, dancing, a sea of Reni hats and floppy-haired happiness.

The sound seemed a bit inadequate, but the excitement built hugely as darkness fell and the Roses appeared, a sparkling, stylish little gang. Reni lost in the rhythms, Mani always moving and winding up the front rows, John channelling Jimmy Page. And Ian: conducting the crowd.

There was excitement but also informality – the band's closeness to the fans, the grafters with their bootleg T-shirts and posters, the good vibes, the absence of bad drugs, and the innocence that comes before experience.

It didn't all go swimmingly after Spike Island – we weren't far off the Haçienda's temporary closure due to gun violence

– and in the months that followed Ian muttered to me about cowboys taking over, but their gig at Glasgow Green two weeks after Spike Island was as powerful a performance as they've ever given.

I was cursed with so much anxiety about how things were going, and worst-case scenarios always preyed on my mind. I am not sure I appreciated how much of a great adventure all this was. But my final memories of Spike Island are listening to 'Redemption Song' and watching the crowd filing homewards, drained and sprinkled with Spike Island dust, and Bob Marley singing about the power of redemption and songs of freedom. Music drifting off into the night.

20

If The Police Don't Close
The Club, The Gangsters Will

In the three years from early 1988 to the decision to temporarily close the Haçienda in early 1991, Madchester went overground. Momentum picked up following that November 1989 episode of *Top of the Pops* and the Stone Roses at Spike Island. The *Mirror* ran a feature eulogising Manchester's role pioneering new sounds and creating tons of new groups plus a language all of its own ('sorted' means 'OK', 'top one' means 'the best', the paper explained).

It was great being appreciated and talked about, but problems and pressures increased rather than disappeared. As a result of ecstasy use, the Haçienda was targeted by gangs looking to control the supply of drugs in the club. You could say that ecstasy had helped create an extra-thrilling epoch in the Haçienda's history, but also sowed the seeds of the club's destruction.

The first time I witnessed a battle on the Haçienda dancefloor was October 1988. That year, from my vantage point in the DJ box overlooking the dancefloor, I'd seen the spread of freaky dancing, the fashions changing – girls ditching shoulder pads for T-shirts – and the sweat rising, the packed, communal bliss.

I always put my record box at the back of the DJ booth, which meant that between songs, I'd have to swivel around and grab the next twelve-inch to play, with my back to the audience, then turn back, put the needle on the record, cue it up. Sometimes I'd know exactly what I was going to play, sometimes I'd take a minute to flick through the box. Sometimes, there would be a knock on the door and I would half open it to see who had come to say hello.

That particular Saturday evening it was all going well. Every time I cued up a record, when I looked across the crowded club, the smoke machine was blasting out, the audience was a haze of joy, whoops and whistles. Then I turned away, started looking through my record box, taking my time, enjoying the moment, relaxed, unaware. When I turned back with the next record in my hand, the audience had retreated to the very edge of the dancefloor, circling a battle between two or three doormen with pool cues and six or seven lads. I turned the music off. Glass was smashing, more doormen arrived, there was a whirl of shouting and scurrying and flailing, and then the battlers made their way through the crowd and disappeared down towards the fire exit near the bar.

Was there some sort of training manual for how DJs should deal with guys hitting each other with pool cues and baseball bats on nightclub dancefloors? I'd never been briefed by management – there was no emergency procedure. I didn't know how to respond to a major fight in a club, but I turned off the music, waited until the fighting had stopped. Took a breath. Listened to a few beats of my heart. And put on the next record. I'd just started carrying around a pre-release copy of 'Good Life' by Inner City; their 'Big Fun' was already a Haçienda favourite. I played 'Good Life', the dancefloor filled again.

There were a couple of trouble spots I couldn't see – notably behind the DJ booth at the back of the balcony – but whatever happened at the moments when it kicked off, I always had the same plan. As soon as things calmed down I'd reach for a big tune and get the night back in full effect. My go-to tunes were 'Big Fun' and 'Good Life', and 'Know How' by Young MC. Within seconds, the dancefloor, the podiums and the stage would fill, and we'd be back doing what we all loved to do; it was that quick, that easy, that wonderful.

I only saw one gun in the club. I was DJing when I heard a heavy knocking on the door. Usually I looked through the security spyhole to see who was on the other side wanting to gain entry, but this time I just swung the top part of the door open. I was confronted with a guy holding a gun at his side pointing at me. He was just three feet from me, young, black. My attention was drawn and fixed to the handgun he was holding close to his chest, the frame half hidden by the coat he was wearing, the barrel aimed directly towards me. My eyes zoomed in so quickly towards the barrel, it seemed to expand, to fill my whole field of vision, like a movie close-up.

'Your records!' he shouted. I slammed the door closed, my heart immediately trying to leap out of my chest. I just stood, back to the door. Just thinking and blinking and wondering and gulping. I had no means of calling security or management. I assumed he moved off as soon as I had clattered the door shut on him, but I had no way of knowing for sure. I never didn't use the spyhole again.

Violent incidents at the Haçienda were unexpected given that, in its earliest years, the Haçienda was a haven from the violence in mainstream lager-driven clubs like Rotters at the top of Oxford Street. The very few occasions there were fights in the Haçienda, it was always small-scale, something domestic, and fuelled by alcohol.

It had been the same for me at the Venue. There, once we got rid of the punters looking for the strippers, the door policy was dictated by the music I was playing. My playlist was so niche, no random troublemaker would go near the place.

From 1988, though, one big thing was making a difference to door security at the Haçienda; the destabilising effect of the club becoming a market for illegal drugs. In the early months, drugs were passed between friends but organised crime soon moved in. For decades, gangs had traditionally stuck to dealing drugs and running protection rackets in the districts they were based in and took their name from; Moss Side, Salford and Cheetham Hill, for example (although oftentimes there were splits into sub-gangs in certain neighbourhoods). Salford were the first and main supplier of ecstasy. But the Cheetham Hill gang were a rising force in the late 1980s, and wanted a majority share in every market.

Moss Side pretty much steered clear, but Salford and Cheetham Hill began to move into town in the late 1980s to sell drugs in clubs like the Haçienda and Konspiracy. Cheetham Hill were carrying guns; this – the use of guns – was the second thing making a difference to door security in Manchester clubs. In June 1989, gunmen attacked the doormen at the Thunderdome, shooting three of them in the legs, while four hundred people partied inside the venue.

In August that year, Claire Leighton died after collapsing at the Haçienda on a Saturday night. Claire had travelled from Cannock with three friends. Aged just sixteen, she'd been to the club once before (on both occasions she used a birth certificate of an older friend). Her friend Tim Charlesworth bought four Es from a dealer in the club and gave two to Claire, who, at home around 5 a.m., collapsed. She died thirty-six hours later.

The Haçienda was so far from the front pages at that time, even the local papers, word of the tragedy barely spread. The inquest in December did get more media coverage, partly because the club's profile was higher by then. Claire's is thought to be the second ecstasy death in Britain, but the first directly linked to a nightclub.

The security issues surrounding gangs and guns increased. From the middle of 1989 for around eighteen months, many people involved in the club scene in the city had a fraught, even frightening time. It's worth noting, though, that the gang violence rarely affected the enthusiasm of customers, and that ecstasy deaths didn't deter people from using E. Clubs like the Thunderdome had a devoted following; DJs 808 State, Steve Williams and Jay Wearden played hard music, the venue had a real edge, but always there was a sense of something happening, a buzz.

Steve Williams was an underground hero. Manchester DJs such as him and Mike Pickering, Jon Dasilva and Laurent Garnier were soon getting gigs out of town too, at places in Blackpool and in Leeds, for example. This was another major change by the end of 1990; that as well as people travelling to clubs to hear the music, DJs began to travel too, and the music and the rave experience began to spread.

I was getting used to being offered gigs away from Manchester by promoters wanting a little bit of the Haçienda, something a little ravetastic and a bit of 'Madchester' at their venue. Sometimes the experience was more, sometimes less, authentic than others. When I played at Oxford Poly, the promoter was very happy about the music, the crowd I attracted, everything. He even seemed secretly thrilled that the event was the first time that a drug dealer had been ejected from his student disco.

Despite the problems, there were some glorious positives too. Madchester and the Haçienda were sending out ripples of influence internationally. Among the French kids who used to come to the Locomotive in that era were some who would in the future make great music of their own, including Philippe Zdar who went on to Motorbass (and then became Cassius). Other Locomotive customers were Marc Teissier du Cros, later of the label Record Makers, and manager of Sébastien Tellier. The Loco had become a favourite space for French fans of acid house and other contemporary alternative music.

It became clear that the team behind the shooting at the Thunderdome were part of the Cheetham Hill gang, and the rumour was that the person who'd instigated the attack was 'White Tony' Johnson, who'd grown up in Fallowfield, south Manchester. With one of his oldest friends, Tony McKie ('Black Tony'), he'd become accepted as a member of the Cheetham Hill gang even though they were from a district five miles away. By end of 1989, 'White Tony' was the acknowledged leader of the Cheetham Hill gang, or the 'Hillbillies' as they were sometimes called. The Haçienda was also in their sights.

I have since met and talked to one of the major players in the supply of drugs in Manchester clubs in that era, a Cheetham Hill general. He carried firearms and a reputation; he'd been arrested and charged twice with murder, but the charges hadn't stuck. He looked after the dealers as they went about the business at Konspiracy or the Haçienda, and they split the profits, very much in his favour. He was making two or three grand a week from the Haçienda.

I didn't know my gangster contact at the time. Some people in the scene, even some people high in the hierarchy in the Haç, seemed to relish the idea of hanging out with gangsters. My thought was that if you let them have a home in your club, it's over. Furthermore, in popular culture, there's a tendency to glamorise gangsters, but I never found them cool. It took them a while to find the Haçienda and it took them no time at all to ruin it.

With guns involved, we were into a new era as gang conflicts developed into full-on confrontations and shootings in the streets. If rivals found themselves in the same venues, the results were incendiary. Twice in the space of six months in 1990, gangs clashed at the International Two during rap concerts, by Ice T and by 2 Live Crew. At the latter, 'White Tony', wearing body armour, led a Cheetham Hill gang into the building and through the crowd, before firing shots at Delroy Brown, one of the Pepperhill generals (Pepperhill was a Moss Side gang). He was hit with a nine-millimetre bullet. Cheetham Hill, having wreaked havoc in the club, then, for good measure, took £1,000 cash from the till on the front door on their way out.

Unsurprisingly, given the death of Claire Leighton, and the presence of drug dealers and known gangsters in the club, the

Haçienda – along with other clubs including Konspiracy and the Thunderdome – was under intense police surveillance. In April 1990, after undercover surveillance and formal warnings, the police told the Haç that they were going to oppose a renewal of the club's licence at a hearing the following month. In response, the management secured the services of George Carman QC, who, the previous year, had successfully defended the comedian Ken Dodd on charges of tax evasion (which, at some points during the trial, looked like mission impossible).

Flyers carrying a statement explaining that Greater Manchester Police were applying to revoke the Haçienda's license at a hearing on 17 May were distributed in the club. This was the wording:

> The police feel we must do even more about removing the use of illegal drugs inside the Haçienda – and this is where you come in – do not, repeat, NOT, buy or take drugs in the club – and do not bring drugs onto the premises. The prime role of your club is a place to dance to the most important music of the day; the only way it can continue in this way is a complete elimination of controlled substances.

This was signed by the directors (the four members of New Order plus Tony, Rob and Alan Erasmus), the management (the two Pauls and Leroy) and the five resident DJs at that time (me, Mike, Graeme, Jon Dasilva and Nick Arrojo).

In truth, no one expected the regulars to desist from drug use but we half hoped customers would realise that buying drugs in the club wasn't the responsible or subtle thing to do. The note we all signed was also designed to be used in future hearings as evidence that the management were taking police concerns seriously.

The summer of 1990 was the most intense period in the Haçienda's history. Elektra Records financed a Haçienda DJ tour of America – the first time DJs from a British nightclub had toured the States. And yet, all the while, hanging over everything was the threat that the club would be closed almost as soon as we returned home.

Elektra Records had signed Happy Mondays and were looking for ways of increasing the band's profile by pushing the scene with which they were associated. One unspoken reason why us DJs were sent was because the various drug-related misdemeanours the Mondays had notched up precluded them from touring over there.

'From Manchester with Love' was a nine-date tour taking in venues in Miami, Los Angeles and New York, divided up between Mike, Graeme, Jon Dasilva, me and Paul Oakenfold. Graeme and I were assigned shows in Boston, Chicago and Detroit.

I'm a different DJ now than I was then. Then I was more reckless, but sometimes all over the place musically and always technically very amateurish. I turned up, played my favourite records loudly and was pretty adept at putting them in the most appropriate order to keep people dancing. In America, I just banged out the likes of Reese & Santonio 'Rock to the Beat' and the Shamen's 'Pro>gen'. Graeme Park was a much smoother operator.

In Boston, we played to a clued-up crowd, all local apart from a girl from Wigan who had previously heard me DJ at Wigan Pier. I encored with St Etienne's version of 'Only Love Can Break Your Heart'. Then there was a power cut at the hotel.

In Chicago, Graeme and I were at Joe Shanahan's Smart Bar; Joe was, and remains, a strong friend of Factory and the Haçienda. Joe reported afterwards how pleased he was with the racial mix in the Smart Bar for the Haçienda night. Isn't that a great thing to report?

In Detroit, Graeme featured in the main room at St Andrew's Hall alongside Kevin Saunderson and Derrick May, while I played in the basement space known as the Shelter. A few years on, and the Shelter was one of the venues key to the career of Eminem; it features in the film *8 Mile*. I expect I played 'Bizarre Love Triangle', but really I have no idea.

21

Tony Wilson In Upper Case

Despite having flown out of the country knowing the Haçienda was under threat of closure, we returned from the DJ tour of America with some optimism, and not just because the gigs had gone well and we'd been paid in lovely dollars, cash. For one thing, it was the summer of 1990, and an entertaining England football team were making progress in the World Cup spurred on by New Order's 'World in Motion' song; the video, incidentally, was another Bailey Brothers production.

In addition, mid-1990 my Thursdays were at their best. The cross-genre mix I'd been pushing for four years was flavour of the month, with lots of new music fitting perfectly into my playlists: 'Groove Me' by Seduction, the Charlatans' 'The Only One I Know' and various releases by 808 State. Andrew Weatherall's remix of Primal Scream's 'Loaded' was filling the dancefloor at the Haçienda and the Locomotive; in July, I got a pre-release of his remix of the band's 'Come Together'. Another gem.

Furthermore, there was good news at the licensing hearing in July when police demands to close the Haçienda were put on hold. Tony had done sterling work explaining the cultural value of what we were doing to Graham Stringer, the Leader of Manchester City Council. The council's view submitted to the magistrates was that, despite the problems, the Haçienda was a focus for a music scene bringing profile and positivity to the city. Manchester City Council taking sides against the wishes of the police was very rare; James Anderton's police force was used to getting its own way. The club was granted six months to bring the availability of drugs on the premises and the associated violence to an end.

Meanwhile, the Boardwalk had been featuring live music without the benefit of a late licence but Colin Sinclair told me he was planning to expand his club to the floor above and open until 2 a.m. He knew there was a demand for DJ-oriented nights and wanted to know my thoughts. I told him it would work for him if he could find the right DJs playing the right music.

His plans prompted me to think about my Haçienda Thursdays. My music policy had been vindicated, and there were never fewer than a thousand people every week. In the summer of 1990, the A-level results Thursday was even more mobbed than in previous years and the *NME* described 'Temperance' as 'the best club night in the world'. I was wondering whether my nights at the Haçienda were as exciting and as big as they were going to get. But then a couple of incidents pushed me into a decision to walk away.

There was still a lot of insecurity around the Haçienda. The magistrates had been lenient and helpful but on a night-by-night, week-by-week level, the club was plagued by gang activity and things hadn't improved. The management was flailing around a little trying to understand the situation and to find ways to deal with it. Tony Wilson told me at the time, 'The people who run the Haçienda hate every fucking minute of the way it is.'

Behind the scenes, management discussed re-establishing a membership scheme – one had been in operation in the club's first years – hoping it would keep out undesirables. They also installed metal detectors at the door, but the doormen had a habit of turning them off when friends or friends of friends turned up. One Thursday at the beginning of September 1990, without warning, they instituted a students-only policy. I had no idea why my night was suddenly student-only. I knew the management had reasons to tighten up the door policy, but Thursday was always the safest night. After I kicked up a fuss, they relaxed the door policy. It had been in operation for just one hour, so no damage was done.

Then the next week I heard that there had been a meeting at which it had been decided to retire Mike Pickering's Friday 'Nude' night and launch a new Friday, with a playlist almost identical to my existing 'Temperance' night. 'Nude' had done so much to give the club its world-class reputation but security problems had begun to affect the numbers attending. The new Friday DJ was Dave Booth, who had stood in for me on a couple of Thursdays and had been playing indie-dance at Isadora's, which remained a success even after I'd left there through the fire exit on New Year's Eve.

The abiding principles of pushing the music forward and doing things differently were being compromised by launching a facsimile of Thursdays on a Friday. This latest decision, presented to me as a fait accompli, I took badly. So, in October 1990 I left the Haçienda just as the Madchester scene appeared to be at its height. I struck off on my own and returned to a refurbished Boardwalk where I had organised so many live shows a few years earlier, but this time started to stage DJ-only nights. When I left, I thought I'd never go back, but over the next six years I would begin another Haçienda residency, then I'd leave again, and then I'd be invited back (which is how I ended up DJing on the last night of the club in June 1997).

I called the office to tell Paul Mason I was leaving, and the same day I wrote to Tony Wilson. It might sound far-fetched, but before texts and emails there was lots of communication by letter. I told him how opposed I was to any dress-code stuff on Thursdays and how exasperated I was that I had been cut out of decision-making, even things that had a direct impact on my work; I pointed out that having a new Friday mimicking my Thursday playlist would have big implications for my night. I threw a few other things into the letter too, including a whinge that there had been a Factory Records party to which I hadn't been invited until the last minute.

In Peter Hook's book, *The Haçienda: How Not to Run a Club*, he says my decision to leave the club and what happened on the last night of 'Temperance' caused a rift between Tony and me that never healed. Unfortunately, I did fall out with Tony, but that was many years later. In October 1990, Tony understood my decision to walk away from the club. In fact, out of all the senior management and owners, he was the only one who found the time to come down to my last 'Temperance' night.

That was Thursday 11 October, seven or eight weeks before I was launching 'Freedom' at the Boardwalk. The management all knew I was leaving, as did most of the staff, and I talked at length to Tim Chambers, who was designated the DJ to take over my Thursdays.

At midnight I made an announcement explaining I was leaving because I had a few unresolved problems with what was happening at the club, explaining I was starting at the Boardwalk on Saturday 1 December, and confessing I was leaving with a heavy heart as I worked with so many great people and loved the regulars. I said something along the lines of 'The club is the people who come, without you there's nothing.' Then I played 'Vanishing Point'. Two days later, eight people turned up outside the Boardwalk expecting me to be there; they'd misheard what I'd said.

Tony arrived about thirty minutes before I was finishing. We didn't have a discussion about the contents of my letter to him; he just stood watching me work and listening to the tunes. He went to get us a drink each. I finished with the song 'Hardcore Uproar'. The next day he wrote to me, a four-page letter, which he typed all in upper case and sent to me on Factory Records paper. It began 'WE ALL MAKE MISTAKES . . .' and went on to apologise for not involving me in the decisions to instigate a new Friday; 'IT WAS LUDICROUS THAT YOU WERE NOT INVITED.'

He revealed that behind the scenes there was some tension between him and Rob Gretton. When discussions started about maybe bringing an end to Mike's Friday night, which had become the most problematic in terms of security, all Tony's anxieties were consumed by the assumption that such a thing would be resisted by Mike Pickering and by Rob. As it turned out, Tony told me that Mike agreed 'WHOLEHEARTEDLY

AND IMMEDIATELY' to the idea of retiring 'Nude'. Such was the relief that a head-to-head was avoided, the changes were pushed through without much thought given to other issues. 'IT WAS PRECISELY EVERYONE'S UNSPOKEN ADMIRATION FOR THE HASLAM THURSDAY THAT LEFT THE NIGHT UNTOUCHED,' he said.

After an apology about the Factory party invite, Tony went on to bring up a couple of issues he had with me, which he wanted to point out. He was in an air-clearing, slightly retaliatory mood. I'd had my say, now he wanted his. One of them was the ill-conceived Nick Kent interview; 'I WAS SHAT ON BY THE FACE MAGAZINE,' he told me. That 'Death sells' quote had really got under his skin . . .

I'd been an occasional contributor to the *Face*, and had tried to talk to Sheryl Garratt about the debatable quote, but all she could find out from Nick Kent was that he had no tape of the conversation. I'm not sure what other representations were made to the magazine – whether Tony, a lawyer, or the Factory press officer Jeff Barrett had been in touch with them – but Tony had wanted me to dig away until I got a retraction from the magazine and I hadn't: 'I WAS SHOCKED THAT YOU NEVER CALLED ME BACK ON THAT ONE, DAVE.'

Another issue he had with me was that, in the wake of finishing *Debris* without printing the planned final issue, I had passed the interview with him on to *Recoil* without telling him and that this occurred several months after the interview itself. He said that when he saw the interview in there, 'THE WHOLE THING APPEARED CHEAP AND DISHONEST.'

By pointing out these slights, he said he was trying to make a point: 'IT'S A WILD WILD WORLD, WE ALL SPEND OUR

TIME IN A STATE OF SPIN; IT'S EXCITING. BUT IT MEANS THAT WE ALL FUCK UP FROM TIME TO TIME.'

I'm a little embarrassed that my conduct hadn't been great, but the letters are an exchange between two passionate people who cared about what they were doing. And it was good he took the time. He ended with a restatement of the vision he had, but the pressure he was under; 'DO YOU NOT THINK THAT WHATEVER IS HAPPENING IS TO PRESERVE THIS VERY SPECIAL PLACE FOR THE PEOPLE OF MANCHESTER? IT'S TOUGH. THINGS HAPPEN. WE HAVE TO GET ON WITH IT.'

After walking away from my Thursdays, I had nearly three months before the launch of my night at the Boardwalk. In the interim, I guest DJed at numerous venues; at a Northampton sixth-form college, the big record of the night was a pre-release copy of '(I Wanna Give You) Devotion' by Nomad. I also began working on the detail of the Boardwalk nights with Colin. I went to the venue to meet him a few times with Eric Barker – I hoped he'd get involved – but Eric decided it was not for him, although he recommended a young lad about town, Marc Hough, as a warm-up DJ. Marc – or Tintin as he was always known – came on board and we shared the DJ duties. The playlist at my new 'Freedom' night was 75 per cent house, with a bit of St Etienne or whatever thrown in.

At the Haçienda, on the surface things seemed good when, at a hearing on 3 January 1991, the magistrates looked back at the preceding six months and declared there had been a 'positive change in direction' and renewed the Haçienda's licence. But behind the scenes, things continued to get tougher, pressure from the gangs was intensifying, with White Tony and the Cheetham Hill crew making concerted efforts to infiltrate the club. Attempting to refuse admission to someone connected with the Hillbillies, members of staff were threatened with a gun, the last of a number of nasty incidents that persuaded Tony Wilson to call a press conference to announce the closure of the Haçienda with immediate effect; 'When we started up the club, we had no idea that these were the sort of people we would have to deal with. It's the best club in the city, that's why they want to terrorise it.'

Four weeks into the voluntary closure, news came that White Tony Johnson had been killed in a gun attack, leading to various discussions at the Haçienda about what the next step should be. The management there had persuaded themselves that the security issues could be sorted out; in fact, associates of the gang the police suspected of being behind the killing took control of the Haçienda door. The second issue was the music policy. It was decided to invite Mike Pickering to do Fridays, Graeme Park to do Saturdays, and ask me back to do Thursdays and launch a new night called 'Beautiful 2000'.

The club reopened at the end of May but, looking back on it, I'm not sure it was wise to go back to the original line-up and maybe it would have been better to have had a complete rethink. Obviously, I was flattered to be asked back even though I'd been critical of the club back in October when I ended the 'Temperance' night, but we never quite recaptured the excitement of two or three years earlier. We were the safe choices.

To some extent, the Haçienda had become a victim of its own success. Other clubs had eroded our uniqueness. By the end of 1991, over in Leeds, Back to Basics had been co-founded by Dave Beer, who'd had his first taste of acid house at the

Haçienda. In 1992 'Cream' in Liverpool was instigated by a crew of people very conscious of how to learn from the Haçienda; our successes and our mistakes. Within a couple of years, what was going on there eclipsed activity at the Haçienda.

'Beautiful 2000' lasted over eighteen months, into the second half of 1992. Unfortunately, around the same time, Rachel and I split up. My work was all about weekends, so Jack stayed with her Fridays and Saturdays. He came back to me on a Sunday. I'm grateful that my friendship with Rachel survived our break-up.

My weekends without Jack were spent at the Boardwalk. I was still doing 'Freedom' but I'd also launched a Friday night there too, which I called 'Yellow'. 'Freedom' was mostly Italo-style piano house, but for 'Yellow' I went for funk, soul, party hip hop. This was against the grain in many ways, as most of the creative DJs around town in mid-1992 were into playing noisy techno stuff. I wanted to push a funkier, softer sound, lots of soul and music of black origin. I invited two younger DJs to join me, and thus the 'Yellow' residents team became a trio: me, Elliot Eastwick and Jason Boardman.

I remember discussing with both the DJ and producer Chad Jackson and Mike Pickering how acid house and the ecstasy boom changed the composition of some dancefloors. It was great to see Mike's Fridays at the Haçienda go berserk, but one of the other noticeable things to me was that the black kids who had been the main dancers lost their space on the dancefloor to the ravers. What had been a Red Stripe and dope crowd had been replaced by a fast-paced, ecstasy-laden one.

At 'Yellow' we played the music that many of us had enjoyed pre-rave – soul, proper disco, classic 1970s funk, stuff by Bobby

Byrd, the O'Jays, Cheryl Lynn, the Salsoul Orchestra – and contemporary releases that fitted: Guru's *Jazzmatazz* albums, the Mo' Wax label, and 'I Should've Known Better' by Mica Paris. Elsewhere in Manchester, DJs like Mark Rae and Andy Madhatter were close to what we were doing but we put a slightly more commercial spin on the music, nurturing a real party crowd. We used to make up names for the genres we featured; promising on flyers that customers would hear 'deep funk, abstract soul and original disco'.

My two Boardwalk nights were thriving but, at the Haçienda, my 'Beautiful 2000' Thursday floundered a little. I just said to Paul Cons, 'This isn't working.' He agreed.

22

Inside Out, Round And Round

There's a line in 'Manchester Meander', a poem by Mike Garry, which goes 'Gorton girls know all the words to songs by Chaka Khan', the truth of which has never been more evident than every week at 'Yellow' at the Boardwalk. And not just Gorton girls, but Chorlton girls too. We also attracted a contingent of Moss Side heads. They were into the music, but had few places around town where they could hear the Fatback Band or Soul II Soul. They weren't into the techno stuff most DJs were playing and, in any case, any venue that attracted much of a black crowd was invariably closed by the police. These Moss Side guys would attend in their big coats, usually with a girl on their arm (often a different one every week). As a consequence, 'Yellow' more or less policed itself. These serious guys weren't like some of the young wannabes causing mayhem; they wouldn't mug a student in the toilets or deal drugs in the club.

Other 'Yellow' regulars included hip-hop producer Johnny

Jay; Rohan Heath and Mark Hadfield of Urban Cookie Collective (nearly twenty years later, Mark co-wrote 'Let Me Love You', a major hit for Ne-Yo); actor Christopher Eccleston; rugby league player Martin Offiah; and my friend Saltz, who had been a dancer in the Jazz Defektors.

Occasionally some of Oasis would join us for the first hour or so; they rehearsed in the basement of the building and were supposed to vacate by 10 p.m. when the club opened, but the cigarette machine was in the club. They'd come feed the cigarette machine, have a drink, then disappear. Occasionally bands who rehearsed there would arrive back from a gig and unload their stuff as we were trying to control the queue. The Boardwalk had become a centre of great activity, bands and DJs, all very local and grassroots.

Saltz was mates with Mick Hucknall, who would sometimes pop in, and he hung out with Ryan Giggs and Paul Ince. A number of other footballers came to 'Yellow'; perhaps most surprisingly of all, Roy Keane. I'm not sure what had led him to come to the club. He never showed a sign of being interested in deep funk, abstract soul or original disco up until then or, indeed, subsequently. My theory is that he had been keeping himself to himself in the dressing room, but overheard Giggs and Ince talking about a Friday night out with Saltz at the Boardwalk, and, undeterred by not having a friend to accompany him, decided to explore the club for himself.

We seldom gave footballers or anyone else VIP treatment, which was part of the charm of the Haçienda and the Boardwalk, and, to be fair, something I always admired about the likes of Giggs and Offiah, and Chris Eccleston; they'd come in not expecting special favours, wanting only to be off-duty and relaxed. They'd get some attention from some of the customers perhaps, but nothing they couldn't handle.

The one time anyone got any VIP treatment was when Ryan Giggs brought Dani Behr, a presenter on the Channel 4 TV show *The Word*. Always well turned-out, Dani was lauded for her beauty and gave off a very posh London vibe. We were a little shocked that Ryan had chosen to take her to a club with no VIP area or champagne, a cloakroom that was full by 10 p.m. and toilets modelled on the ones in Strangeways. The staff rallied around to try to make her feel comfortable and loved. The couple moved on from the club, though, and Dani soon moved on to Les Ferdinand.

It was one of the doormen, Charlie, who alerted me to Roy Keane's presence in the queue. Charlie, a passionate supporter of Manchester City, spent pre-match hours on the door of the Parkside pub close to Maine Road and he didn't think Roy needed inviting to the front of the queue. In fact, let him wait was the general consensus.

Roy Keane got in eventually, after paying the £5 admission. He then queued at the bar behind Chris Eccleston, bought himself a Guinness and took up a spot on the edge of the dancefloor, just watching what was going on, no expression on his face. Every minute or so he took a sip from his pint. When Jason dropped a great remix of the Bomb the Bass tune 'Bug Powder Dust', he didn't respond, but continued to slowly survey the club in full swing in front of him. When he finished his drink, he turned, put the empty pint glass on the side of the bar, walked past the Moss Side guys in their massive coats and the Gorton girls belting out the chorus to 'I'm Every Woman', went down the stairs, exited the club and never came back.

Those seven years of 'Yellow' at the Boardwalk were wonderful, week in and week out, and the sense of achievement was even greater because we'd originated the night from nothing. We were up there with some of the other great nights in the city in the mid- to late 1990s, including 'Electric Chair' and 'Bugged Out'. Unfortunately, the badness kept seeping into our little venture.

The night-time economy came under pressure when violence swamped the city like blood lust through a herd of young tiger sharks. We were in the so-called 'Gunchester' era in the mid-1990s. Gangs fragmented, and scores were settled. In May 1994, someone attempted to murder the poster boy Jimmy Carr, in an incident in which Chris Horrox, a young helper working alongside him, was killed. As he lay bleeding and apparently dying, Jimmy named Marcel Williams as the gunman. Against the odds, Jimmy survived. Marcel duly came to trial at Liverpool Crown Court where his defence team focused on Jimmy's character, and alleged he was engaged in a host of blackmail, gun-running and protection rackets. Marcel was acquitted and Jimmy went into hiding. No one has ever been convicted of Chris Horrox's killing, and I've never seen Jimmy Carr since.

Most of my weekends from about 1994 were stressful. One Friday at the Boardwalk, two guys wearing all black, hoods up, came into my sightline walking across the dancefloor; the first two were followed by two more, and then two more – several in balaclavas, all in jackets buttoned up to the neck. The guys were predominantly black but not exclusively so. They kept coming, at least fourteen, sixteen, a brigade, a troop, a small army. The customers scattered to the edge of the dancefloor, into the corridor behind the stage and out of the back of the building. The small army calmly walked through three hundred people without laying a hand on anyone. I turned the music down but not off as they walked past me in formation, through the door and up to the upstairs bar. A minute later, having walked once around upstairs, they came back down the stairs, and I watched the doormen usher them onwards and out through a fire exit, and I changed the record.

They'd been looking for someone – if they had found them then the visit would not have been so calm and incident-free – and it increased the attention the police were giving us. 'Yellow' was a great night but the police used to get agitated that various criminally minded guys with big coats were regulars. Undercover cops would come in, make a note of what was happening and on Monday morning send a fax message to Colin, who would forward their message complaining about known gangsters in the club to me. Colin would explain the police's logic; it's the music policy, he'd tell me, if you play anything vaguely hip hop the police think you are deliberately attracting the gangsters.

I wasn't going to change the music policy, so I needed a different strategy. This is where 'Upside Down' by Diana Ross became useful. I'd play it if there was undercover police presence in the club. The door team would clock them arriving, word would reach me and on would go 'Upside Down'; not a record you could ever accuse of having a special attraction for known gangsters. I loved the idea that the police in question would return to the station and make their notes on the night. They'd spot some villain from Moss Side and associates of Cheetham Hill, and Roy Keane. They'd make a note of all that. Then, they'd note that the DJ played Diana Ross records. I knew it wouldn't make sense to them, but it made sense to me. 'Yellow' lasted seven years.

That was Fridays at the Boardwalk. Saturdays were more problematic because it was a more housey crowd who liked their class-A drugs more. Among the disruptive elements was a lad called Billy. Billy liked to party and was on the outer edges of a predominantly white gang in Salford, with access to ecstasy at wholesale prices. This led him to begin supplying the drug to some of the regulars at 'Freedom'. It was off the premises and lower than low-key, as these things need to be.

Billy had a younger cousin called Simon, who occasionally he would bring to the club. But one evening Si came alone, with a brief from Billy. He arrived early, positioned himself at the door to my right, leading up to the mezzanine. He approached everyone arriving at the club, going upstairs for a first drink, tugging at their sleeve and showing them the pills he had in the palm of his hand. If Si had put on a massive scrawl of red lipstick, a red nose and come dressed as a clown he couldn't have been more conspicuous.

We were under regular police surveillance; one false move and the place would close, with negative repercussions for Colin, his elderly parents, his team, the DJs, the bar staff, and the doormen and other people employed there. It would also be a blow to the regulars, of course, who would be deprived of their favourite club and the highlight of their week. I didn't think twice about what should happen next. I went to the head doorman and asked him to remove Si from the building. I was looking after my business, and my mates, and I was beyond irritated that he could be so blatant and so daft.

Half an hour later Billy arrived, seething. He stood in front of the DJ box, stared straight at me and ran his index finger across his throat. He pointed at me, and then repeated the throat-slitting gesture.

Ninety-eight per cent of the customers on Saturdays were loyal and loving, but because of the other 2 per cent, it continued to deteriorate. A guy stubbed a cigarette out on my forehead. Another attacked me on the stairs and my two front teeth were knocked out. To defuse the situation, I decided to keep Fridays but end Saturdays. My girlfriend Catherine was pregnant; it was also time to look after people around me a little more. The last night was in May 1996. Robert Owens headlined and it was blissful.

I didn't go looking for Billy, or want to think about him. A couple of mutual friends told me that despite everything he was a good lad. Six or seven years after the end of the Boardwalk, another mutual friend updated me further. He'd ended up owing money to a dealer higher up the chain, a relatively small amount, a couple of hundred pounds. The debt dragged on, until Billy was killed. He was attacked with an axe and decapitated. The body of the guy who had threatened to slit my throat was then put into bin bags and left in his mother's back garden. I don't like bad endings. The moment I heard the story, I felt a punching surge behind my eyes, I shook my head slowly, I was empty.

Some of the Boardwalk nights were so fraught and so exhausting that, after Salmon Cabs had collected me and got me safely home, I'd arrive jittery and anxious, sweaty as well, but, once I'd closed the door, relieved too, so relieved. If I'd been a believer I would have fallen to my knees and thanked the Almighty.

It's worth remembering that customers had no idea of some

of the problems we faced and that most of the trouble was kept out. A few years later I talked to James Barton of 'Cream' about his club's security issues around 1997, suggesting to him that a lot happens when you're running a nightclub that the customers never know about. 'Yeah, so much!' he agreed. 'But we always had a philosophy: whatever happens outside, inside the doors three thousand kids are having the night of their lives.'

I was holding things together, despite the pressure. Jack was with me five nights a week, and in many ways I'd be glad to have his world to escape to; getting up, helping him read numerous books featuring Biff and Chip, taking him out to the Ice Cream Fun Factory at Pizza Hut or to a bar called Cheerleaders around the corner from the Haç, where girls dressed as cheerleaders served nachos. He loved it there. When I took him to see Oasis at G-Mex, where he got a VIP wristband and everything, he lasted just three songs before turning to me to ask if we could go for nachos. We stayed for one more song, 'Supersonic', then went to Cheerleaders.

So why did I put myself through the stress of running those club nights? Why did I persist? I'd built up those Boardwalk nights, it was what I did and what I loved. I was earning from it, as were other people; in fact, more than several livelihoods depended on the project.

I was sifting through old and new releases, presenting them to people, hoping to turn them on. I relished that challenge of being the selector. It's a public service, almost, or a kind of pact; you come to hear me play, my music will follow threads of emotion, you'll know I've never stopped searching for tunes to enrich your weekend, make you dance and enhance your life.

Despite ending Saturdays at the Boardwalk, I was still doing 'Yellow' there on Fridays. Elsewhere, and now, you might get DJs who are better technically than we were at the time, or better toilets, or better security, but we attracted a once-in-a-generation audience; a brilliant mix of black and white, locals and visitors, Prestwich princesses and penniless students, single mothers from Sale and Droylsden, dental nurses and library assistants, lads in bands, Chorlton girls, Moss Side boys.

It was exhausting being in the eye of the storm; there's no bigger buzz than a massive queue outside a club night you're running, but there's also no hiding from the pressure. But what can you do? There was something political and spiritual in the way we were creating communities, sharing music and good times. As for the pressures, you harden yourself, learn lessons, keep your fingers crossed. They were great nights in dangerous times. You can't let the badness win.

This is life; a joy and a test.

So when Paul Cons asked me to go back to the Haç, I said, 'Of course I'll come back.'

23

Take Your Seat And Hold On Tight

The call from Paul Cons asking me if I would return to the Haçienda came just a month after I'd brought my Saturdays at the Boardwalk to an end. Giving up those Saturdays had freed up time to go and DJ outside Manchester. One of the venues I went to twice was Angels in Burnley.

The resident at Angels, Paul Taylor, attracted a very enthusiastic crowd; enthusiastic for both music and ecstasy. His nights were sweaty even in winter, basslines pumping, smoke pouring out of the machine, no one standing around; DJing there you'd throw on something with a big piano breakdown and everyone in the building would flip their minds like they'd been triggered into a rapturous religious experience. Every week, the locals committed themselves to Saturday night fervour. And why not?

Catherine grew up near Burnley, and liked to travel up there with me. She didn't miss any gigs of mine until her partying was very temporarily curtailed by her pregnancy. Raili was born just a few days before my return to the Haçienda. The local paper conflated the news of my Haçienda return and my daughter's arrival in an item pointing out that it was a cue for a double celebration in the Haslam household. It also explained that her name is pronounced 'Riley', which is true. At the Kendal Calling festival fifteen or so years later, I met up with Ian Broudie of the Lightning Seeds and his son Riley – who was addressed in the Lightning Seeds song 'Life of Riley': 'Although this world is a crazy ride / You just take your seat and hold on tight.' Ian and I introduced Riley to Raili that day too.

One of my other gigs away from Manchester was at a night called 'Golden' in Stoke. In the DJ box about one o'clock in the morning, I found myself talking to an actor from the Australian TV series *Neighbours*, Mark Little. It was never explained to me how the actor who had played the character Joe Mangel came to be hanging out in the DJ box at a nightclub on Glass Street in Stoke-on-Trent and asking me to play 'Hideaway' by De'lacy. It was all part of the circus.

Having now just one night at the Boardwalk, I had more time to write, in theory. But *Debris* had long gone and although I had seen and appreciated Oasis in their early days, I wasn't buying into the Britpop mania of the music press in the mid-1990s, so I had few outlets for all the passions and ideas still churning around in my head. And then I was contacted by the *London Review of Books*. Jean McNicol asked me to write a piece about Manchester, describing some of the context to the music scene and covering Oasis and the Haçienda. I submitted eight hundred words, with perhaps more about Friedrich Engels than Jean had expected. I'd researched his time in Manchester in the 1840s and beyond, read his take on the social conditions and the politics of the city in his book *The Condition of the Working Class in England*. I also read background stuff to his life in Manchester. Engels liked a drink, he liked Irish girls. He intrigued me and became part of my *LRB* piece, in which I attempted to draw links between the conflicts around the birth of Manchester as an industrial city and the strength of the city's contemporary popular culture. Between the Chartists and the chart hits.

Encouraged by a few people, I decided I'd make a start on a book, aiming to expand my thoughts from eight hundred words to a hundred thousand. I devoted hundreds of hours to writing *Manchester England: The Story of the Pop Cult City*. They were almost all the hours I had spare when I wasn't DJing – or preparing or recovering from DJing – or hanging out with baby Raili or walking Jack to school or picking him up. Sometimes worlds collided, like the time I'd worked in Dublin, stayed up all night, got the first flight home, sweaty and struggling, and arrived just in time to take Jack to school. Just as we were leaving the house, I confided to him that I was still a bit drunk from the night before. 'Don't tell anyone,' I said. Jack led me down the road, and guided me expertly through the school gates, before announcing in his loudest voice, 'My dad is drunk.' All his eight-year-old mates, and a few of their mums, came to look. I retreated.

I was hanging out with the poet Lemn Sissay. He'd been published by Bloodaxe but had just moved to Canongate. We began to meet up regularly at a café-bar called Fuel, halfway between our houses in south Manchester. We found common ground talking about our performances; his poetry events, my DJ gigs. We made each other laugh, we made each other think, we encouraged each other to write and write.

It was a good time to research a cultural biography of Manchester, especially as the music scene in the city was still fascinating hundreds of thousands of music fans worldwide. Manchester, to them, was, and remains, a city defined by its music.

Manchester had gained a reputation as a place of opportunity, as it had in the early nineteenth century when the population boomed with incomers looking for work in the factories and mills. Now, the energy of the city's music scene brought people to Manchester, creating that combination of energies the local poet Tony Walsh, in his poem 'This Is the Place', describes as people 'born here' and people 'drawn here'.

There was a big jump in applications to study at the local universities, which was attributed to Manchester's history of iconic bands and reputation for great venues and clubs. Changes in the look of the city also accelerated from the early 1990s. Music had helped usher in the city's post-industrial era; buildings that had been derelict had found new life with ad hoc uses in the late 1970s and 1980s. This continued into the 1990s, but with the added involvement of property developers.

The economic state of Manchester in the late 1970s – rising unemployment and broken buildings – didn't hinder a music scene that was creative and bohemian, and perhaps even helped it, certainly in practical terms. Joy Division rehearsed in the remains of an old warehouse on Little Peter Street. Ian Curtis took a job as a sales assistant at Rare Records, a dingy basement store in Manchester city centre.

The Fall and Joy Division, and – a couple of years later – the Smiths, didn't have an identical sound or vision by any means, but the bleakness of the failed landscape around them seemed to be seeping into their music. Jon Savage told *Melody Maker* readers in July 1979, 'Joy Division's themes are a perfect reflection of Manchester's dark places'.

At the end of 1992, Jon Savage was commissioned by Granada to do a short film about the city's music boom. Mr Savage interviewed Boardwalk owner Colin Sinclair, who pinpointed the contrast between the era of Joy Division and the way the contemporary club scene had nurtured a new image of the city: 'What happened originally was that the landscape influenced the bands, and now we're seeing a change where the bands are influencing the landscape.'

The Haçienda's position was on the edge of town, but the club's success stimulated other businesses to open in the vicinity, especially bars and, notably, Atlas. Other areas were transformed by the city's popular culture; the warren of independently owned retail units in Affleck's Palace housed in an empty department store on Oldham Street was key to the development of what became the Northern Quarter. And pioneering night-time venues had kickstarted new eras for other areas, like Manto on Canal Street, Dukes 92 in Castlefield and Sankeys Soap in Ancoats.

Manchester's night-time economy was far busier than ten years earlier, with thousands of people thronging the town every weekend. One result; the city centre seemed a more attractive place to live. Demand for apartments helped fuel new builds and the reuse of old factory and warehouse buildings by property developers like Tom Bloxham. I first knew Tom when he ran a poster shop called Splash in Affleck's.

There had been an obvious demarcation between pubs and clubs before the mid-1990s. Pubs closed at 11 p.m., and if you wanted a drink – and, of course, a dance – you went on to, and paid to enter, a nightclub. Changes in licensing laws blurred the distinctions, leading to multiple free-entry café-bar style establishments catering to early drinkers but staying open and providing DJs until 1 a.m. or later. Applications for licences for new late-night café-bars in Manchester were virtually unopposed.

'Yellow' had seen off competition from other club nights, and we were surviving all the challenges of venues booking big-name DJs and taking out expensive advertisements in *Mixmag*, but we had an almighty wobble when one particular late-night café-bar started up: Prague 5 at the far end of Canal Street. We managed to keep our audience, but this shift in how people consumed music on a night out was a big new obstacle in the way of promoters wanting to host weekly events in nightclubs.

Clearly, though, Manchester City Council and its think tanks had realised how music and the creative industries were proving to be levers for bringing profile, investment and jobs of all kinds to the city (even if they kept calling all that activity 'an engine for regeneration', which I'm not sure is ever top of anyone's list of considerations when they form a band or buy a pair of Technics decks and start DJing).

However, for the council, it must have felt like one step forward two back. In addition to causing havoc in the night-time economy, violent criminals were targeting some of the new high-end shops that had been attracted to the city. In 1997 the Leader of Manchester City Council, Richard Leese, wrote to Chief Constable David Wilmot pointing out that 'rampant lawlessness' was 'seriously undermining investor confidence in the city centre'.

'Yellow' at the Boardwalk was still a struggle behind the scenes, but a joy behind the decks. Despite the gangs and the competition, it was still packed, talked about and the place to be; which is why I was asked back to the Haçienda by Paul Cons, three years after my last residency there. Mike had left Fridays around the same time I'd left 'Beautiful 2000'. Mike told Paul Mason he was sick of the unsafe atmosphere in the club; 'I can't work here when I'm even telling my friends on the guest list not to come.'

There were persistent security problems, but the Haçienda negotiated the mid-1990s with some success, especially around 1993 and 1994 on Saturday nights with Graeme Park and Tom Wainwright installed in the DJ box. Post-Mike, Fridays had struggled to get a regular crowd at the Haçienda, but Paul Cons was running a very successful monthly gay night, 'Flesh', the loudest, proudest gay event Manchester had ever seen. The 'Flesh' publicity that Paul Cons circulated usually carried an hilarious and very effective warning: 'The management reserve the right to refuse entry to known heterosexuals.' It was a great strategy. The glam gay night did what the metal detectors and huge bill for security staff seemed unable to do – it kept the gangsters away.

In 1996, to freshen up Saturdays, Paul was asked to provide the vision and the promotion. He dubbed the night 'Freak' and offered me weekly Saturdays in the basement (the 5th Man, as the space was known), playing alongside Michelle Kelly. I was more than happy to accept; I was addicted to DJing, and despite the club's troubles and the rise of other big-name clubs, it was still a place where everyone wanted to DJ.

In the 5th Man, I built on the 'Yellow' formula of old school 1980s funk and disco, alongside new things like tracks from *Pansoul* (the Motorbass album) and the Kelly G remix of

'Never Gonna Let You Go' by Tina Moore. Being in the second room, a little hidden away, suited me. Through the 1990s, dance music had gone overground, becoming a part of the mainstream, championed by Radio 1 and featuring on million-selling Ministry of Sound compilation CDs.

Dance music going mainstream was something of a mixed blessing. There was a lot less adventure around now that there was money to be made. Audiences were arriving in clubs hoping to hear what Dave Pearce was playing on Radio 1, endless Ibiza anthems, music by DJ Sonique or whoever. Too many DJs played safe.

I didn't have to worry about filling the Haçienda's big room; Paul tried a variety of DJs up there. The 5th Man sessions in the basement were like extra time to me, a return to a club I thought I'd severed connections with. The music worked a treat. In contrast to my experiences a year or two earlier, when 2 a.m. came around I wished I had longer to play, rather than feeling jittery and tortured by ongoing door issues. Once, I was in such a good mood when I got home, I woke up Raili to give her a hug.

Jack was in the house on weekdays – weekends he spent with Rachel, except during school holidays when the schedules became a little more flexible. Both kids grew up with music in the house. Jack, when he was little, had fun hanging out with Martine McDonagh and Tim Booth's son, Ben; they'd jump around to 'Come Home' (Ben knew all the words). Raili, when she was very little, developed a great love for disco music, which is surely a dream come true for any parent.

I played New Year's Eve at both the Boardwalk and the Haçienda, and both were sold out. As 1996 turned into 1997, the Haçienda settled on Elliot Eastwick in the main room and he did a fine job. Despite the rising costs of security and continuing struggles to sustain regular weekly nights apart from 'Freak', there was optimism at the club, and plans were made for a big fifteenth birthday celebration.

In early 1997 we had good reason to think Tony Blair was going to win that year's general election; the polls, at least, suggested so. A fundraiser for the Labour Party was held at a function room at Granada Studios, attended by Blair and John Prescott, who mingled with the attendees, shaking our hands and thanking us for our support. Catherine and I were invited as guests of Tom Bloxham – networker par excellence – who was there with his wife Jo. He'd also invited Peter Dalton from Manto and his business partner Carol Ainscow; they were the co-owners of Paradise Factory, which was housed in the old three-floor building where Factory Records was based at the time it went bankrupt. I believe that among Carol's properties was the massive warehouse complex in Ancoats that was used for the filming of *24 Hour Party People*. The other couple at the table were Tony Wilson and his girlfriend Yvette.

Yvette was a bit of a Tory. She didn't like me, but smiled sweetly enough when the situation called for friendliness. Meanwhile, Tony got stuck into the champagne and told me about his favourite political speech ever: Jesse Jackson's 1988 Democratic National Convention address.

We'd had a Tory government for eighteen years, so we were clamouring for Labour to win the election and take power. We all assumed that a Labour landslide with the Tories in disarray would allow for a radical left-wing agenda. We were wrong, of course, and were doubly disappointed when Gordon Brown deregulated the financial services industry and Blair buddied up with George Bush to take us into war in Iraq. Locally, New Labour and the property development sector didn't get the balance right in the race to regenerate the city centre; a plethora of apartments and student housing brought gentrification at a price – notably the loss of the sort of cheap spaces the emerging creative industries need in order to take root, and no effective increase in affordable housing.

A couple of weeks after the Blair victory, it was the Haçienda's fifteenth birthday, demand for tickets was massive, queues were huge. My only disappointment was that Laurent was assigned the 5th Man and I was given the job of DJing in the VIP room. I did my best in the VIP room, concentrating on quality rather than commercial stuff, or anything vaguely flavour of the month; D-Train's 'You're the One for Me' and 'New Jersey Deep' by the Black Science Orchestra. One of the people who spent some hours in the VIP room enjoying my tunes that evening was Darren Hughes from 'Cream'.

However, any cautious optimism surrounding the Haçienda proved unfounded following what turned out to be the final night of the club, 28 June 1997. I played for four hours downstairs, through until 2 a.m. Elliot, in his room, ended with the Salt City Orchestra remix of 'Post Modern Sleaze' by the Sneaker Pimps. I closed my room five minutes earlier with 'It's Alright, I Feel It'. The club had been packed and everyone filed out of the front door into taxi queues or down Whitworth Street to the car parks opposite the snooker hall, and the regulars were shouting to each other, 'See you next week.' I was happy with how things had gone; it had been another of those nights when, truly, next week couldn't have come soon enough.

Unbeknownst to Elliot or me, just after half-past midnight, a dispute about a small group being turned away by the doormen had escalated, a car mounted the pavement, a mob from Salford and, it was said, St Helens, battled it out, and then someone got banged on the head by a wheel brace and ambulances were called. This trouble erupted in full view of a minibus of councillors and licensing magistrates being given a guided tour of some Manchester nightlife hotspots by local police officers. The following Monday, the licence was revoked with immediate effect.

Behind closed doors, the owners, directors and management considered their options. Internally, there wasn't unanimous support for attempting to resuscitate the club, given the history of security issues and the reality of the money troubles (the club had huge debts to the bank, the Inland Revenue and the brewery, and no viable options to retrieve the situation).

There was talk of a new company being created to take on the running of the club, but the police put a block on that. They weren't fans of the Haçienda, and suspected that whatever new options were being considered or tried, the baleful and criminal influence of various Salford gang bosses would continue.

Messily, the Haçienda had come to an end, but its role in the history of house music, the excitement of the Madchester era and even the rejuvenation of the city was undeniable. Tony emerged from a string of meetings to take his turn on the local news and give the definitive take; he told Gordon Burns on the BBC that he opposed any attempts to keep the Haçienda open or turn it into a museum.

I was still getting my weekly fix of 'Yellow', but eventually I had to walk away from there. In 1999, I'd heard rumours that the Boardwalk might be sold – it was a sign of the changes in the built environment in Manchester city centre over the previous fifteen years that a building that had cost the Sinclairs a figure in the low tens of thousands was being talked about as having a market value of a million pounds. We had one final party, cramming eight hundred people in there.

In the last years of the 1990s, I had numerous Saturdays playing one-off guest gigs, including an appearance on Saturday 30 August, 1997 in Warrington at a club called Casi. After my friend Mike McCormick dropped me home, I made a cup of tea and sat in front of the television for ten minutes, taking a little rest time to clear my head before bed. That's when I saw the news that Princess Diana had been involved in a car crash. I watched on, heard that her boyfriend Dodi had been killed and that she was hospitalised, then went to get some sleep.

I never lie in much, I don't have the gift for it. Sometimes I joke that I'm still catching up on sleep from 1988, and it's true. It was a noisy house in 1997 anyway; Raili was less than a year old and liked a good scream. That weekend Jack was with me rather than his mum. After I woke at ten o'clock, I heard Jack playing in his room, even though I expected him to be watching television. But Diana had died. Jack was very disappointed that the usual cartoons had been pulled from the schedule in favour of rolling news reports. Not even *Saved by the Bell* was on.

So, that was our generation's version of 'Where were you when you heard JFK had been shot?' That was where I was: recovering from a gig in a nightclub in Warrington that later changed its name to Wired, but was soon closed, then became derelict, and was described in the local paper as a 'former night-club and drugs den'. Very 1990s.

Meanwhile, Darren Hughes had been calling me since the Haçienda's birthday with a plan to bring me nearer the 'Cream' team. He gave me a slot in the VIP area of the first Creamfields – held in Winchester – and gave me a monthly residency at their Liverpool club starting in August 1998. Working for Darren also led me to feature a little way down the bill at a few BBC Radio 1 gigs hosted by Pete Tong.

DJs were fulfilling the industry's need for stars. By the end of the 1990s, a lucrative industry had grown around a handful of superclubs and a couple of dozen 'superstar' DJs achieving the kind of commercial success many of them had worked hard for. When I interviewed Paul van Dyk for my book *Adventures on the Wheels of Steel: The Rise of the Superstar DJs*, I certainly encountered a man who had his eyes on the prize. I saw queues of people waiting to hear the big-name DJs, and the stars deserved all the money they were paid. I took great delight, too, in knowing that the punks and goths who'd harangued me for playing to the disco crowd fifteen years earlier would be finding this turn of events hard to handle.

Occasionally my fellow professionals would make me cringe a little. In the magazines covering the dance music scene, you'd sometimes see DJs sharing an all-time top ten, often including soulful, timeless tunes from the 1970s, or clever, irresistible post-disco boogie from the 1980s. Then you'd look at their current top ten, invariably even less radical than Blair's government. I tried to give them the benefit of the doubt, and believe they truly loved the homogeneous, throwaway trance chart stuff they all played every week up and down the country, but I had my doubts.

Most of the more interesting club nights at this time were nothing to do with big-fee DJs, and one-dimensional, hit-chasing

Temperance
Club
Paris

Appearing live

JAMES

Thursday 22nd February

Tickets: £45 (Transport & Admission)
Available from
The Haçienda, Eastern Bloc, Piccadilly Records

Coach leaves Haçienda
Thursday February 22nd at 2.30am
(After club on Wednesday night)
Returns to Manchester after gig
Arrives afternoon February 23rd

For information contact:
Fac 51 The Haçienda
11/13 Whitworth Street West
Manchester
Telephone 061-236 5051

With James at
the Locomotive,
Paris, 1990.

With Paul van Dyk at E-Werk, Berlin, 1993.

Sister Sledge · 'Thinking Of You'
Tom Browne · 'Funkin' For Jamaica'
Sharon Redd · 'Can You Handle It'
Herbie Hancock · 'Rock It'
Sounds Of Blackness · 'Testify'
Steve 'Silk' Hurley · 'Jack Your Body'
Chic · 'Chic Mystique'
Chaka Khan · 'I Feel For You'
Earth, Wind & Fire · 'Let's Groove'
Brand New Heavies · 'Dream Come True'

Yellow
at **THE BOARDWALK**
little peter street manchester
every friday from march 6th
DJ's
DAVE HASLAM, JASON BOARDMAN, ELLIOT EASTWICK
£3 before 11pm / £4 after 11pm
10pm - 2am

(N.U.S £2 before 11pm / £3 after)
march 6th drinks offer; red stripe 90p

First 'Yellow' flyer, the Boardwalk, 1992.

With Tony Wilson in Dublin, 1996.

Flyer for 'Freak' at the Haçienda, 1996.

24 Hour Party People.

Kevin Rowland, onstage interview at the Trades Club, Hebden Bridge.

Jonathan Franzen in Maria Balshaw's office at the Whitworth Art Gallery.

Tracey Thorn, onstage interview at Gorilla, Manchester.
© Elspeth Mary Moore

Neneh Cherry at Manchester International Festival.
© Elspeth Mary Moore

Onstage with John Lydon at Albert Hall, Manchester.

With Tim Burgess onstage at Gorilla.

Memorial to the victims of the Bataclan attack (photograph taken January 2016).

Guido Cesarsky (Acid Arab) and Sophie Morello.

Pins at Espace B, Paris.
© Alain Bibal

Pete Doherty at the Bataclan, Paris, November 2016.

New Order at Granada Studios, Manchester International Festival, 2017.

DJs; I'm thinking of 'Club Suicide' in Manchester, at the John Willie Lees pub above what used to be the Arndale Bus Station. Since the turn of the millennium, I have had almost all my best experiences in relatively small venues: rooms with a capacity of two hundred to four hundred, including Elemental where I worked with Justine Alderman and David Dunne, and the basement of the Rossetti, which was no bigger than the Man Alive, although a good deal more swish.

Some DJs (notably Carl Cox) deservedly remained close to the top of the tree, but for others in that generation, the bubble burst. At Sankeys, things looked a bit ropey. One Saturday at the beginning of the millennium, an expensive DJ Radio 1 Showbiz Big Name was booked in the main room, and I was booked to play in the room upstairs. When I arrived in a taxi, the Sankeys promoter Dave Vincent hurried over – 'Hang on Dave, we're not opening your room,' he told me.

'Why not?'

'The main room isn't very busy, and if we open your room some people will come to hear you and so DJ Radio 1 Showbiz Big Name's room will be even quieter.'

'Great,' I said. 'Me versus DJ Radio 1 Showbiz Big Name soundclash!'

'That isn't how it works. If his room empties he'll never play for us again.'

'Who cares? Trance is over.'

'Oh come on, don't be like that. I'll pay you, Dave.'

So Dave Vincent goes off, comes back with my full fee in cash, gives me my money and I head back towards the taxi.

But then I ask, 'What happens when people come to hear me and I'm not there?'

247

'We'll give them their money back.'
'What if they're on the guest list and haven't paid?'
'We'll give them some money too.'
'You sure?'
'Yes.'
I got in the cab, he waved me goodbye.

24

Ain't Nobody

Catherine and I got married in July 2000. We had Raili, and a house together, and Jack was part of the team too, so everything good had fallen into place, if not in quite the traditional order. On the big day we had a small daytime event for family and a very small number of friends. In the evening we hired the Shed in Fallowfield, a venue on two floors. Two hundred people came, DJs David Dunne and Goff played rave tunes rather than wedding tunes upstairs, with seats and a more chilled-out atmosphere downstairs.

Mark E. Smith stayed mostly downstairs, hanging out with his sister, who he'd brought to the party with him. I stayed mostly upstairs because if I'm somewhere and there's a DJ I tend to gravitate towards them, as if I need to be near some place of safety. Catherine was dancing; her favourite thing in the world is to be on a dancefloor, sweating, lost in music.

Then Mark moved to the bottom of the stairs leading up to the dance room. He was accosting people in a sociable way, but not everyone could cope with his attentions. He spent five minutes accusing a neighbour of being my dad, maybe slightly too vehemently. I knew all this was malice-free, but I could tell some of the guests were finding it hard to handle.

Word reached me: 'You'll have to sort Mark.'

Instead of solving the problem head-on by asking him to stop bothering people as they went up and down the stairs, I decided to do something to distract him, so I asked him to come and dance with me.

'Sure, Dave,' he said.

The two of us walked up the stairs to the rave room, me trying to be as inconspicuous as possible, arriving just as David Dunne played one of my favourite songs, 'Plastic Dreams' by Jaydee, a wonderful techno record. Everyone stared at Mark and me, and then parted, allowing us access to the middle of the dancefloor before resuming their raving. Mark moved decently, swaying from foot to foot and swinging his arms loosely, all the while slightly hunched. Then he started leaning his head further towards me. Was he talking to me?

I didn't particularly want a conversation with Mark, or him to be raising important issues of the day or making some dig about my jacket or shoes or something, I just wanted to block my mind. I looked over to Catherine, who was in her element, sweat patches galore.

As Mark got even closer and closer to my ear, I realised he was rapping in a freestyle manner, but instead of using words, he was rhyming in a jumble of syllables and random sounds, rolling the techno rhythm, barking stuff at me, noises. I was listening to the record, trying to work out if it was the extended version or, if I was lucky, the short version. It was the short one.

But still; one of the longest, most bizarre, four minutes of my life.

Mark stayed on the dancefloor for a while – he had no shortage of men and women happy to be his dance partner. I went to get him a beer and brought it to him just as David dropped 'Ain't Nobody' but Mark had scarpered downstairs.

'Ain't Nobody' is one of the greatest records ever made. Any crowd has to appreciate it, whatever else they're into – indie, techno, disco, jazz-funk, post-punk, whatever. Back a century or two ago, they'd take a canary down a coalmine to see if there were poisonous gases; methane and carbon dioxide were potentially fatal to the miners, of course. A canary was more delicate than a miner and so the gases would kill the canary first, which would alert the miners and give them time to get out. For me, 'Ain't Nobody' is like a canary down the mine; if you play it and the audience don't appreciate it then you can assume it's all going to go wrong, the test has failed, there's poison in the air and you should exit immediately.

I've never gone to DJ anywhere without 'Ain't Nobody'. It's one of those records I need with me, even if I don't plan to play it. Anyway, I never plan much, I have to allow room to react to the crowd or to act on inspiration. I've never prepared a set to the extent of knowing even 50 per cent of what I might play. Sometimes I set off to play a New Year's Eve without even knowing what the big twelve o'clock tune will be.

In my early, vinyl, days, a certain amount of pre-planning was necessary because I'd only take a box of ninety records to a club, or maximum two boxes, which would still mean I'd have fewer than two hundred tunes to choose from. DJs back then were constrained, your set could only draw from what you had in the box; you didn't have a hard drive with you, and thousands of tracks. At home beforehand you'd have to distil your collection down to one or two boxes, imagining and planning what you would need that night. I still don't work off a laptop, but I burn and use CDs. This means I have three or four hundred, but certainly not thousands, of tunes to choose from.

The first priority is to take with you some guaranteed floor-fillers, which mostly change over time and vary depending on the nature of the booking, but there are some perennial favourites; in my case these include 'Ain't Nobody'. I'll also take into account whether my set is a warm-up or peak-time slot.

Also in my selection of what to take to a gig are at least half a dozen tunes that I reckon will be new to the audience, but exactly what they'd love. These might be brand new or just obscure, and certainly the kind of thing a mainstream party DJ wouldn't bother about. The one thing I still know from the days of the Man Alive, the Venue, the Haçienda and the Boardwalk, is that a DJ has to stand for something, something different. There's no point dropping a hugely popular song, like 'Titanium' by David Guetta, if, firstly, you don't like it or, secondly, it doesn't fit with anything else you play or, thirdly, the club or the client could have found a much cheaper DJ to play it. The tunes that no one in the club has heard before are the ones that will help you make your mark. The challenge is to find the right time to play them, to present and programme them in the right way at the right time so that you win the audience over.

Sometimes what you play might not work, but my thing is: until you're ready to look foolish, you'd be best off not being on a stage. Don't dwell on humiliation; learn from it.

There's another reason to prepare your ammunition, but not to over-plan; you never quite know what the audience will be like. Sometimes you mess up by imagining the event is going to be great, building it up in your head and then falling apart when it doesn't live up to your expectation. Sometimes you don't have high hopes, but you're amazed, blown away.

In 2010, I played the B-Side Liquor Lounge in Cleveland, Ohio, having made contact via MySpace with a guy called Brad Petty who booked the bands and DJs there. I was visiting the city to present a talk about Joy Division organised by Terry Schwarz at Cleveland Urban Design Collaborative. I fancied playing a gig while I was in the area. The B-Side Liquor Lounge wasn't on the circuit of top gigs for international DJs but Brad came across well on MySpace, and he had some cash to treat me to bed and breakfast in a nice hotel.

The next evening, Brad's club night far exceeded my expectations. It wasn't particularly full when I started playing, but it was someone's birthday – they had pre-booked twenty friends to come in, people who had no idea who I was or that I was playing, they just needed a night out that evening. They arrived and loved it. Brad loved it. He got on the phone, started haranguing his mates to come, the audience grew, the dance-floor stayed full.

At the end of the night, he gave me the nicest bear hug, leaving a lovely damp imprint of himself on my T-shirt. The next morning the hotel cooked me an atrocious omelette – but there's no way it could take the shine off one of the best gigs of my life. Cleveland had been wonderful. Terry and Brad had done so well. And it's people who make a city, as we know.

Occasionally I get a booking slightly out of my comfort zone: a corporate event or a party. When that happens, I create a Venn diagram in my mind. One circle represents what I play, the other is what I reckon the audience will dance to. At 'Temperance' and 'Yellow' these two circles almost exactly overlapped.

In the mid-1980s customers knew you could only play what was in the boxes of records you'd carried from home to the club; playing off CDs, I'm also limited, but I guess they are not to know this, being used to DJs carrying a hard-drive's worth of music and, in an emergency, a world of online music to access. I hope members of the audience arrive with an open mind rather than with a desire to hear their personal top twenty, but this doesn't always happen. Problematic encounters ensue. Requesters find your refusal to play their choice an affront, a scandal, a personal insult.

Most requests are dead obvious or way out of the ballpark. My estimate; nine out of every ten requests are rubbish. Having said that, this means one in every ten is good and occasionally they're inspiring. I love a switched-on requester and try to play everything they want.

A bad request could include asking for the Foo Fighters in a northern soul club, or an old school R&B record in a minimal techno club, or it could be asking for something too commercial in an underground club, or asking an ex-Haçienda DJ for something too obvious or overplayed, or asking for a pointlessly obscure record.

Moany requests are dispiriting. Fair enough if the club is empty or no one's danced for hours, but you'd be surprised how you can be DJing and the club is rocking, the dancefloor is packed, sweat is dripping off the ceiling and someone will still come up and say, 'Can you play something we can dance to?' Or the variation, 'Can you play something good?' Usually if you ask them to be a bit more specific it'll turn out they haven't a clue: 'You know, something good.'

'Something they play on the radio'; I really hate that request. Being a reasonable bloke, though, I like to engage in debate even with someone hammered at one o'clock in the morning in a dark club, and sometimes go to great lengths to explain that it's boring if I just play stuff you hear on the radio all the time. 'Wouldn't it be more exciting to hear at least some stuff in a club that was different, unique, secret?' I say. 'If you just want to hear stuff they play on the radio, then maybe it would make more sense not to come out, but just stay in and listen to the radio?'

On one occasion at the end of this explanation, a customer said, 'OK, fair enough, mate,' and walked away happy. More often when I rant like that people just look at me like I'm crazy and go off to some other club and never come back.

Perhaps it's mean of me, but this is how much requests can make me cringe; someone once asked me, 'Play something by Stevie Wonder,' when I was actually playing a Stevie Wonder track ('Another Star'). But there's one particular request that drives me mad. 'Have you got any Black Eyed Peas?' They have maybe two or three good songs but one of them isn't 'I Got a Feeling'. That's a horrible song. But when people say, 'Have you got any Black Eyed Peas?' they usually mean 'I Got a Feeling'.

My judgemental side kicks in when I hear the phrase 'Have you got any Black Eyed Peas?' I know I'm going to sound like a music snob, and maybe I am, but anyone who asks for that record doesn't really even like music much, and probably has no taste at all in anything else. Is that fair? I think that's fair! As I lambast people who judge others by their colour, or their sexuality, I had better hold up my hands and admit I am inclined to judge people by their music taste. So shoot me! Or, at least, sack me.

I got a request recently that, for obvious reasons, I never got in the 1980s. A customer followed up the question 'Are you the DJ?' with 'Great, have you got somewhere I can charge my phone?'

Another time I was lost for words was after I had been asked by someone who had a slightly tacky wine bar in Cheshire if I could do a set there on a Saturday. He'd been employing a DJ who had been pandering to a lowest-common-denominator crowd and he'd got rid of him, and the night I was booked was about the third or fourth Saturday with various DJs playing music that was a bit more interesting.

I'd been playing an hour or so, to a mixed response. A few people I'd brought with me were doing their best, but it was three-quarters empty. I don't think the relaunch was going well.

One fella in a suit sidled up to me. 'What's happened?' he said.

'What? Where? How do you mean?'

'Here.'

I tried to help him work it out: 'The music has changed?'

'It's all different,' he told me, then paused, perplexed. 'Last time I was here it was wall-to-wall fanny,' he said.

One of the most memorable encounters I've had while DJing happened at a birthday party. A big-league party planner phoned me up and told me to put a date in my diary, telling me it was someone's birthday party at Old Trafford, the football ground, in one of the suites. She couldn't tell me whose it was, as all the rights had been sold to *Hello* magazine.

I was intrigued, the money was good, so I agreed, but she left me guessing whose birthday party we would be celebrating. I had theories and hopes that maybe it was one of those Manchester United players who'd visited 'Yellow' or Gary Neville, who I knew was a big Stone Roses fan, which would make for a pretty straightforward gig.

A week before the event the party planner called me back to talk about a few things, and I managed to persuade her to tell me who the party was going to be for, so that I could do a little thinking about my set. It was for TV newsreader Eamonn Holmes – it was his fiftieth. Sensing my slight disappointment at this news, she jumped in to tell me that former *Countdown* co-host Carol Vorderman would be there and that stars from *Coronation Street* would be involved in hosting karaoke.

I imagined the Venn diagram. There was very little crossover between what I play and what they might dance to, but I hoped I could scrape together enough music to entertain them. An hour, probably, before I'd have to start thinking the unthinkable: playing music I didn't like.

There's lots of music I don't like. You learn in life that not everyone likes you and that you don't have to like everyone. You can try, of course but, like music, sometimes that's just the way it is.

I went online to see if I could find out anything about Eamonn's music taste. I discovered that his favourite song is the novelty hit 'The Combine Harvester'. It was big for Brendan Grace in Ireland in 1975 and then also a hit for the Wurzels in the UK in 1976. Which version floated Eamonn's boat the most really didn't matter, the whole thing mortified me.

I had been contracted to DJ for an hour, and told that I would bring the event to a close, following the other entertainment which, in addition to the karaoke, was a performance by an Elvis impersonator.

Kym Marsh was there, and Sir Alex Ferguson and James Nathan, a floppy-haired lad who'd won *Masterchef* the previous year. The crooner doing some Elvis was so well received he did two encores, which luckily cut my time down to forty-five minutes. And then I played, on decks that had been set up almost behind the stage, on a nice little structure they'd built for me which was hard to get to from the dancefloor.

Everyone had plenty to drink and they all seemed happy enough dancing to 'I Want Your Love'. Being a bit detached from the dancefloor was good, it meant that no one bothered me, until, after about fifteen minutes I saw someone clambering over the staging to talk to me, but I needed to cue up the next song, and didn't get a proper look at the person until he was standing right next to me, waiting to talk.

'Do you take requests?' he said.

I realised it was Jeremy Kyle talking to me. I really didn't think I could keep it together. I was just looking at him, slightly mesmerised, thinking, you're Jeremy Kyle, and not really believing it.

'Yeah, I take requests,' I said to Jeremy Kyle.

'Oh, OK, mate' he said. 'Could you play some Black Eyed Peas?'

If you'd told me that one day Jeremy Kyle would request a song from me, I think I probably would have guessed he'd have asked, 'Could you play some Black Eyed Peas?'

I took a breath. 'No, sorry.'

Mr Kyle looked crestfallen. He'd climbed all those obstacles and now the DJ had completely and offhandedly dismissed his request.

'It's for my wife.' he said, but I wasn't sure I believed him.

'Sorry,' I said again.

He didn't get angry, he just slowly made his way to the half-empty dancefloor.

My natural inclination used to be to avoid playing weddings, but 'Yellow' girls were now settling down; I started getting breathless emails telling me they're getting married and how they remember those nights dancing to my music and it would be the best thing ever if I would DJ at the biggest day of their life. I might provisionally agree, but also email them a list of cheesy wedding-party songs I don't play. I point out there's no point asking me to play and then giving me the same playlist of songs a DJ ten times cheaper would play.

I didn't want to put myself in a situation when I'd get bothered by a random relative, maybe some Uncle Jimmy tanked up and down from Scotland for the wedding, bugging me for that '500 Miles' song by the Proclaimers, and my refusal leading to incredulity, conflict even. I know how that would end: with him shouting at me 'Call yourself a DJ?'

Usually I get an immediate email response from the bride-to-be telling me she doesn't want the usual wedding fare, she wants to hear what I used to play when her and her mates would come out dancing, so we come to an agreement. And usually we have great fun.

There was one wedding a few years ago at which the bridegroom's father was paying me a lot of money, and he didn't seem impressed when he gave me the cheque. He'd emptied his bank account for me and discovered I don't even talk between the records. I could tell he resented me a little, even though it was the happy couple who had asked me to DJ.

That was a challenge to me. I thought, *I'll win this guy over*, and from the beginning I was fully focused, the music went well. Once he could see his new daughter-in-law and the groom and all their friends were having fun, he relaxed a bit. An hour or so in, on his way past me to the bar, he even gave me a little conspiratorial wink. A few more visits to the bar and I got a thumb's up. Then, the alcohol kicking in, he started dancing, setting all his resentment aside, bustin' some moves on the dancefloor.

When I took the music a bit ravey, he was all caught up in the excitement and carried on dancing. He was a bit sweaty by now, but he was whooping with everyone else. He'd even taken off his jacket. I felt so good.

At the end of the evening, he came up to me, and said, 'That was amazing. The music; it's like it's inside me.'

I looked at him. I wanted to tell him, 'The party went well, the bride, the groom, your family, your friends are happy. And the music is inside you. And for me, this too is a great moment.'

I'd be telling the truth too; it's no exaggeration, you live for moments like that when you're a DJ. It doesn't matter to me if the person on the dancefloor is old, young, an influential promoter from Liverpool, a poet, a music aficionado or the father of the groom. It's addictive, turning people on like that, helping them towards happiness.

25

Denis Law And The Scene On The Screen

'**G**retton is dead,' he shouted. 'You're dealing with me now.'
It was February 2001; *24 Hour Party People* was being filmed in Manchester. Tony Wilson, played by Steve Coogan, is the central character in the film. I was busy preparing for the club scenes, which were three weeks away from being filmed in a re-created Haçienda in an old warehouse in Ancoats.

Tony had phoned me at nine o'clock one morning. I had no reply to the Gretton is dead comment. I hadn't thought of myself as a mate of Tony's co-director at Factory, or even a major ally. Rob seemed like a sweet guy, we got on well, and over the years I'd done two or three long interviews with him, plus Philip Shotton and I went together to his funeral two years earlier. But I'd never discussed anything deep with him – just talked about Factory and music.

I couldn't work out exactly how I was doing Tony's head in. I said to him, 'There's a film being made about you. We're all running around trying to make it the best film ever. I don't understand why you're not sitting in the Midland Hotel in a big chair, soaking up all the adulation.' At the time, we thought the Midland Hotel was the most elegant hotel in Manchester, but I'm not sure that's the case now.

I'd got involved with the filming of *24 Hour Party People* after sitting on a train to London next to two young guys reading a film script. I was being nosey, trying to catch a glimpse of it. When I saw *24 Hour Party People* emblazoned on the cover, I introduced myself and interrogated them a little on director Michael Winterbottom's project to document Factory and the Haçienda on the big screen. We talked, they scribbled my email address down, gave me a copy of the script to read, and a few weeks later I was invited to meet with Michael and the film's producer, Andrew Eaton.

The film feeds off and into all the mythologies. Tony comes out of it well in some ways, but not in others. But it's not a documentary, is it? It captures the spirit of the times, rather than the facts. It's a comedy; that's how the distributors sold it on some of the official posters.

During the making of the film, Michael and Andrew offered me a small fee in exchange for some input into choosing music for the film; Martin Moscrop from A Certain Ratio was another of their music advisers. Only a few months earlier, the site of the Haçienda had been sold to property developers and the building had been demolished, but the filmmakers had met with Ben Kelly and were going to recreate the club based on Ben's original designs. Building the film set in the Ancoats warehouse was the easy bit, but then it would get complicated; after all, there is one definitive version of the building, but so many differing versions of the history of what went on there.

As well as discussing the logistics of filming the Haçienda scenes, they quizzed me about some of my hands-on experiences at the club and at the Boardwalk, which intrigued them. I hadn't meant it as some sales pitch, but the next day they called and upped my money and asked me to sort the DJs and the music, but also tasked me with sorting the bar and bar staff, the security and, in addition, with finding seven hundred extras to feature in the Haçienda scenes.

One issue I confronted was the age of the extras. It was 2001 and I needed clubbers around the average age of the people who would have been on a Haçienda dancefloor, rather than filling the scenes with people in their forties who'd been there, done that, got older. I tracked down the extras by arranging for application forms to be handed out by flyer-distribution company Exposure in the street outside clubs in town. Those people wanting to be involved were invited to fill in an application card and send it to a PO box in Fallowfield.

A week or two in to the project, while I was discussing my progress with Andrew Eaton, he admitted that Tony had recommended that the guys who ran Paper Recordings should be involved in the staging of the club scenes on the film set. I had no idea there had been some wrangling. I said I'd talk to Tony but they suggested that I didn't, explaining that he was annoyed they'd asked me. They'd had some differences of opinion with him, too; Tony thought the recreation should reflect some of the violence that dogged the club in the 1990s. He expected to see trouble on the door and drug dealers on the set. According to Andrew, Tony had been telling people,

'There'll be riots outside, and fighting, and we'll film that as well.' Andrew confirmed that he'd prefer there not to be riots.

I received hundreds of applications from potential extras. I asked Mike to DJ and he agreed, as did Graeme and Jon. There was talk of some of the original lighting being used. I was bringing together bar staff, with the help of Athena from the Boardwalk, and a door team, again using Boardwalk contacts. The security, as far as I was concerned, needed to be as low-key as possible.

Things were going well until that call from Tony shouting at me. He was in a rage, telling me I had muscled in on the Haçienda recreation. He told me it was nothing to do with me. 'Michael and Andrew are making the film,' I countered. 'And they're building the set, doing it all and need someone to do this job and they asked me. It's mostly organisation, I know how to do this.'

I was genuinely taken aback by his extreme reaction. Maybe, for all his apparent enjoyment of the limelight, he was feeling a little exposed, as anyone would if they had no control over a script about their life. When a big thing is bothering you, sometimes you fixate on some small thing. Perhaps, having no control over his portrayal in the film, he was focusing in on control over the list of extras in one of the scenes. There was no chance to discuss it further, Tony had gone, the phone line was dead.

Later that morning, I spoke to Andrew, telling him I hadn't signed up to be getting all this grief. Tony and I had worked together, on and off, in various ways, for fifteen years, and obviously I wanted this to continue, I didn't want our relationship to sour beyond repair. He replied that they wanted me to continue in the role they'd given me and promised they'd find a way of placating Tony.

I asked for more money, which is something I almost never do; I very rarely decline or accept a job based solely on what I'll earn from it, but I really needed to find good reasons to keep me involved with the project, as I'd rather have an easy life than a headache. They paid up. I think I earned more money in the two months of being involved in the film about the Haçienda than the first two years I was DJing there.

The filmmakers did a great job building a set that looked like the interior of the Haçienda. The layout was spot on, as was the décor. Mike was visibly moved when he walked in. It felt just like the club; history, ghosts, regrets, memories and all.

The compromise reached with Tony was to make a hundred guest tickets available to him, which he passed on to old faces and other people he felt should be there, but he'd left the set before filming began, like a parent leaving the kids alone in a house to party. Instead, we had Steve Coogan – playing Tony Wilson in the film – striding through the club and occasionally getting on the dancefloor. That was one of the things that made the evening so surreal: a mix of real people and their acting equivalents scattered around the club. Bernard Sumner was there as well as the actor playing him (John Simm), and Peter Hook and the fake Peter Hook (Ralf Little), the fake Shaun Ryder, the fake Bez, the real Bez.

The premiere in London was also a mixture of the actors and the people they played (the guest list also included Tracey Emin, Johnny Vegas, the Pet Shop Boys and Moby). The Manchester premiere was followed by an invitation-only party on the top floor of Paradise Factory. Again, a weird commingling of fiction and reality; it was the very room that had been the Factory boardroom until the label went bust. The dancefloor was where the company's expensive executive table had been (Tony was so proud of the table it was given a Factory catalogue number, FAC 331). The table fell apart when several Happy Mondays sat on it.

A few months after the Manchester premiere, I was in Reykjavik to help promote the film in Iceland, where the local distributors thought they might have a hit on their hands. I had two gigs to do and some magazine, radio and TV interviews. One of the radio presenters was particularly knowledgeable and enthusiastic. We played some songs from the soundtrack and I dutifully read out my crib sheet with the details of where the film was showing in Reykjavik over the following week. Just before the end of the interview, the presenter said, 'Dave, can I play you part of a recording of an interview I did with Tony Wilson?'

'Yes, for sure.'

He pressed play and Tony was talking, he was talking about me. 'I'm going to have Dave Haslam shot, I'd like to shoot him.'

There wasn't any context. That was the extract.

The presenter sat back in his chair and waited for my reaction. I didn't have a clue what to say. I was amazed by what Tony had said, but unsure whether the listeners to the station would be interested in this squabble, whatever it was about.

'I love Tony. I don't really know what this is about. I owe him a lot, we all do. He knows I will always be a fan, it's a shame he doesn't still see me as an ally. He needs allies. We all do.'

Tony's words haunted me, but I stayed positive, doing my best to help *24 Hour Party People* become a hit in Iceland. In the end, though, I don't think it was, but it was not for want of effort on anyone's part. The film distributors threw a little party where some girls asked me if I wanted them to show me their tits.

In Iceland, they have their own version of MTV, where the marketing gurus took me to be interviewed. I was sitting in a backstage room at a TV studio, watching the show on a monitor in there, and it was just like MTV, except in Icelandic.

The interview with me was going out live and was being conducted by a young presenter lad with an over-gelled sticky-up hairdo who bounced around very excitedly. On the monitor the lad was shouting excitedly in Icelandic but I could follow the gist of what was being said, thanks to occasional phrases like 'techno dance party', 'Next up, Puff Daddy', and 'wicked vibe'.

During an ad break I got taken on to the set and sat down on the sofa. The presenter lad looked at me and I looked at him. Then we were on, live. He greeted me, in English. At least we were speaking English. 'Welcome Dave Haslam, superstar DJ from Manchester' and we shook hands. Then he looked down at whatever notes he'd been given on his clipboard and I could see him scanning them wildly, the words in his notes meaning nothing to him; the Haçienda, Manchester, Steve Coogan. It was all stuff that this young guy wouldn't have a clue about, and why should he?

He just looked at me again: 'Dave Haslam, superstar DJ from Manchester, Dave, Dave Haslam.' The silence stretched into a few seconds, then five, then six; six seconds is a huge chasm of emptiness on live TV.

Finally, a question from the lad popped out: 'Dave, who's the most famous person you've ever met?' That was his first question, his first desperate question. My mind just went blank, I was flicking through my memory bank. For some reason, the first person who popped into my head was Denis Law. But I thought that if I think a bit harder I can probably think of someone more famous and also it's no use me saying 'Denis Law' as he wouldn't know who Denis Law is.

My brain whirred. Martin Fry, Tracey Emin, Tony Blair; should I say 'Tony Blair' when all I did was shake hands with him that night at Granada with Tony Wilson and Tom Bloxham? Maybe I should have said Bono because Bono is probably the most famous person I've ever met and had a conversation with, but I said 'Moby.'

'Ah, Moby, yes,' he said. 'Could you tell us about Moby?' I didn't know how long I had or what kind of insight or information he required, so this second question was even harder than his first.

'He's small.'

'Small?'

'Yeah, he's like this,' I said, casually holding my right hand out, palm face down. Bearing in mind, I was sitting on a sofa I was literally suggesting Moby was about three feet six inches tall.

The lad took me literally. 'That small?' he said, incredulously.

'No, not that small, but just not tall, small, maybe like this . . .' I moved my hand up a foot or so, which was still a major underestimate.

'Oh, OK,' he said, 'Thank you Dave Haslam superstar DJ.' We shook hands. He looked at the camera, and delivered his next link: 'Next up, a wicked video, "Oops! . . . I Did It Again".'

That was it. That was the whole thing, that was my star turn on Icelandic MTV done.

The next morning, up early in downtown Reykjavik, I walked into a coffee shop that was almost empty. There was one shaggy-haired guy in the opposite corner who looked like he'd been up all night. After a few moments he came walking across the room towards me. 'You the English DJ?'

'Um, yeah.'

'I saw you on TV on the evening yesterday. Excellent interview.'

We became friends, he took me to an art show and a bar and I met some of his friends. I stayed up all night after DJing, and took a flight back to Manchester via Heathrow.

Soon after I got home from Reykjavik, I called Tony on the phone and left him a voicemail message explaining I'd heard a tape of his remarks, and reminding him he knew where I lived. 'Come find me, shoot me. You know where I live,' I said, and rang off.

Tony had a lot of fallings-out – a major one with Martin Hannett, for several years he didn't talk to Peter Saville, and his relationship with Rob Gretton was often strained. I knew about all these, and I knew he'd also had his battles with Paul Morley, but knowing that I wasn't the only person with whom he'd locked horns was no consolation. Our next encounter was a year or so later, on a side road off King Street. I turned a corner and there he was coming the other way. 'Hiya,' we both said, before our eyes widened, and we realised what had happened; we'd said hello, even though we were supposed to be antagonists. Tony didn't speak to me again.

My Moby nightmare notwithstanding, I began to get more work talking on TV and radio. Researchers at radio stations and TV production companies have lists of experts with a history of talking to broadcasters. The same people tend to appear on TV because the lists are small. Judging by the calls, I appear to be on lists of experts on the following subjects: the Haçienda, Madchester, the 1970s and the role of music in urban regeneration. I also appear to be close to the top of the list of experts on club drugs; this once gave me the chance to delicately describe the appeal of ecstasy on *Woman's Hour*. Afterwards, presenter Jenni Murray said her son wanted to be a DJ, and we swapped email addresses.

I soon found there are few opportunities to nuance a message if you're employed as a talking head on TV. Producers want a fifteen-second soundbite. I'd be less than halfway through a sophisticated analysis of the subject up for discussion when I could see the unease in their eyes as the chances of a fifteen-second soundbite ebbed away. Four months and three chasing emails later, I'd get a cheque for £50.

I also get asked by students to grant them interviews for their university essays. It seems you can study anything from urban planning and geography to music and event management, and still have a good excuse to write a dissertation on the Haçienda. They've usually seen *24 Hour Party People* but I recommend they also watch Carol Morley's *The Alcohol Years*, which was released soon after Michael Winterbottom's film, and is an interesting watch and a great companion piece.

Carol's attempt to piece together her adventurous, troubled, grim, but in other ways glorious teenage years in *The Alcohol Years* is brave and successful, with wide relevance and great resonance. As her brother Paul says in his book about Bowie, 'A story about a person living in a city inevitably becomes a story about the city itself.'

A few years later, *Control*, Anton Corbijn's film about Ian Curtis and Joy Division, was released. I was asked to DJ at the party following the Manchester premiere, which was at the Cornerhouse cinema. I was also invited to Paris to talk at a showing of the film at the Elysées Biarritz and to DJ afterwards.

They employed a warm-up DJ who played all the big Joy Division songs before I went on; she also threw in two or three big Cure records and 'Blue Monday' as well. The audience were very happy with this, but it left me without any obvious floorfillers to play. I'd arrived with a pretty good box of vinyl, though, so I took a chance to play stuff that wasn't obvious, but was definitely relevant. Things didn't go well; 'Dream Baby Dream' by Suicide left only six or seven people on the dancefloor, but the *coup de grâce* was 'Nag Nag Nag' by Cabaret Voltaire. The last person leaving the dancefloor actually had her hands over her ears.

26

The Ruins Of Time

A few years after *24 Hour Party People*, I was working at XFM Manchester, presenting a three-hour show every Friday evening. It was a friendly team there, and I was grateful for the opportunity, but I was a little uncomfortable in this job. It was as if, this time, I'd put myself in the wrong place, walked through the wrong door. Firstly, it took me a while to hit my stride doing all the links and knowing which buttons to press. But, secondly, and more importantly, I was always uncomfortable with the music policy, which was so conservative.

It was my own fault; I stupidly agreed to do a show that was playlisted for me, although I had some leeway to take a few songs out and to argue for a few songs of my own choice. I am not sure why I allowed myself to become a slave to the playlisters when the likes of Tony Wilson and Mike Pickering had trusted me with my music choices at the Haç.

I squirmed a little at the nostalgia that permeated the playlist; an over-reliance on a limited number of Madchester and Britpop tunes. The playlisters and the advertisers had in their sights a demographic that mostly liked straight-down-the-line male-fronted indie bands, and were worried listeners might switch to another station if the music strayed from the unfamiliar. While I was there, I sneaked in plays for Le Tigre, Lonelady and 'Radio Ladio' by Metronomy; the smallest of small victories. Other presenters, including Clint Boon and Gareth Brooks, love their music as much as me, were more professional than me, and relaxed about the constraints of being on a commercial radio station. Meanwhile, I realised if I was less uptight and more carefree I would be enjoying life so much more.

I didn't have control over most of the music on the show but I could pursue my own passions when it came to plugging club and live music on air. Having a show on XFM pushed me to go out more. Not to blag guest lists for big gigs, but instead to go adventuring in Manchester's grassroots, enjoying the sort of places where I felt at home twenty-five years earlier. I didn't want to be banging on about the old days like those forty-somethings in the late 1970s who had filled my ears with tales of the Beatles and Woodstock.

I found and enjoyed Everything Everything, catching them first at the Roadhouse in June 2008, as a result of the bass player Jeremy inviting me to the gig when I turned up at the café-bar he was working in. I travelled to see his band play gigs at the Barfly in Cardiff and the Flapper in Birmingham, fanboying relentlessly. There is no greater pleasure than watching a hungry, not quite fully formed band evolving, working hard, turning people on, gathering an audience and then making it. Fabulous.

One club night I kept mentioning on the radio was called 'Invest in Property'. I really loved the guys involved, Ric Davies and Benjamin 'Human Man' Perry. Another club night, 'Keys, Money, Lipstick', took place in venues including the Star & Garter. The flyer included the message 'no nostalgia, no throwbacks' to put distance between its playlist and the dozens of Madchester-themed indie nights elsewhere in the city. 'Homo Electric' carried the strapline 'Burn the Past' on one of their flyers.

The biggest revelation to me was a night called 'Tramp', at the Bierkeller every Wednesday (it later moved to North). Over the years they featured guest DJs including the Juan MacLean, Justice and MSTRKRFT. One of the club's co-creators said that they would play music featuring guitars but it wasn't an 'indie' club, and they'd play narcotic, repetitive beats, but it wasn't a techno club. When I first walked into the basement, Will Tramp was DJing, playing lots of music I didn't know. It was a great scene, I felt that immediately; the look of the people, the hair, the clothes, it had the feel of something happening, something new.

I had one really lovely project during my time at XFM: I was tasked with researching and presenting a Joy Division documentary for broadcast around the time of the release of *Control*. Producer Kate Cocker accessed some words from Tony Wilson in the XFM archive, and secured short audio clips from Moby and the filmmakers. I scripted and presented the documentary and interviewed Martin Moscrop, screenwriter Matt Greenhalgh and all three surviving members of Joy Division.

In the hour we had, I managed to cover so much ground but, of course, I was aware we were missing one important presence: 'the missing boy' as Vini Reilly called Ian Curtis in the Durutti Column song of that name. So, after the documentary was broadcast, I went for the day to Macclesfield, where Ian Curtis lived and died, I guess as a kind of pilgrimage.

His last home, 77 Barton Street, is in one of the hillier parts of Macclesfield, built in 1850 on a slight slope, with two steps up from the pavement to the front door. There's no showy gentrification; it's on a well-kept street of neat houses, some with plastic flowers in the windows and ceramic house-number plaques on the front doors. Opposite the Curtis house a horse chestnut tree has grown big enough to block out some of the light to the front bedrooms, and surrounding it there's a hotchpotch of lock-up garages and cramped back yards. The nearest shop is a pharmacy.

Near the end of his life, estranged from Debbie, with so much pain inside him and so many heart-breaking decisions to be made, Ian Curtis went to stay with Bernard for a couple of weeks. Ian was numb, and disturbed and frightened by his epilepsy. In the XFM documentary, Bernard Sumner said that Ian Curtis described it to him like this: 'I feel like there's a big whirlpool and I'm being sucked down into it and there's nothing I can do.'

Ian Curtis was cremated in Macclesfield and at the town's cemetery there's a memorial to him; it's one of thousands of kerbstones bordering the lanes and pathways that criss-cross the cemetery. His impact was significant, but the memorial stone is unassuming, almost hidden. In the twenty minutes it took to find the stone, the sun came out and then disappeared behind the clouds again.

There's no birth date on the stone, although the date of his death is recorded, along with the words 'Love Will Tear Us Apart', and a few flowers, sprigs of this and that and a couple of badges rest on it. When I visited, as well as the badges, there was a shoebox-size, watertight, Tupperware box containing thirty or forty cards, notes, photos and letters. Tentatively, I read through several of them; some of the cards dated back to July (his birthday). Sarah from Manchester had written some words of William Blake's on a card ('the Ruins of Time build Mansions in Eternity'); many of the notes thanked Ian Curtis for his inspiration, and some were from people who admitted they were too young to have seen Joy Division play; some promised he'd never be forgotten; others poured out their hearts to him.

There was so much silence, and the autumn morning light changed again as the clouds shifted and cast shadows, and a soft wind blew fallen leaves across the stones and pathways. There's no tourist trail in Macclesfield; nevertheless, visitors from around the world – Italy, Toronto, Greece, the United States and Belgium – have made for this particular patch of ground.

Tony Wilson died on 10 August 2008, just a couple of months before *Control* was released. He'd been ill for a while, with cancer. A week or so earlier, I'd met one of Tony's close friends, Ian Starr, who bought Tony's house after Tony split from his second wife, Hilary, the mother of his children. Ian urged me to go and see Tony in hospital, but I explained we weren't in a friendly phase and it would distress us all if he found my visit unwelcome. I also missed the funeral, even though Nathan was keen for us to go together.

On 10 August, my Friday evening show on XFM Manchester started at seven o'clock. An hour before then, I was in the XFM office preparing when Tony's lawyer friend Stephen Lea called me; despite the awkwardness of the situation, I was still part of the Factory family. He told me that Tony had received the last rites. I told one of my colleagues and she asked what that meant. 'It means he's going to die, this evening, probably soon.' It was decided that if the worst happened, and I got confirmation of Tony's passing from the lawyer, then I would abandon the playlist and play more suitable, Factory and Tony-related music.

Ten minutes after seven o'clock Stephen Lea called me back, and I ripped up the schedules. Even after his life had ended, Tony had achieved something I never managed: to have the Pigeon Detectives thrown off the XFM playlist.

27

Creating, Taking And Giving Opportunities

Tony died aged fifty-seven. I've never seen his long-term girlfriend Yvette since, but I see his two children occasionally. I sorted Iz with some tickets to see the Stone Roses at the Etihad and I went to one of her recent birthday parties with Nathan, her godfather. Oliver parties with my son Jack. Oli calls me up, we go for coffee and a catch-up.

Creating and taking opportunities was the key to getting through my working life. But one of the many things that struck me about Tony was that he also saw the value in *giving* opportunities. He was always encouraging the next generation. Some people aren't like that; they're forever pushing down on the people trying to make progress behind them.

I value people who enable others to participate in culture, and found an ally at the Whitworth Art Gallery: Maria Balshaw, the gallery's director from 2006 to 2017. From 2011, she was simultaneously the big cheese at Manchester Art Gallery in town, and she's now the first female director of the Tate. Apart from one or two events and occasional collaborations, I'd spent a quarter of a century working outside the city's cultural institutions. I'd got a sense that their instincts were to do what they do, and keep the drawbridge up to deter disruption or challenge.

In 2012, however, Maria asked me and curator Kate Jesson to bring together an exhibition at Manchester Art Gallery by Kelley Walker and Cyprien Gaillard, two contemporary artists whose work reflected, among other things, an interest in music in Manchester. Walker is clearly a fan of Warhol, but also of Peter Saville. Gaillard had created a wonderfully evocative short film soundtracked by 'Asleep' by the Smiths. I dubbed the exhibition *Dreams Without Frontiers*.

I suggested that instead of a traditional exhibition catalogue, we should produce a good-looking Dada-inspired fanzine-style A5 booklet. To open up an opportunity for younger creatives, I also suggested collaborating with young designers at Textbook, and commissioned writers including Greg Thorpe, Hayley Flynn and Damon Fairclough to contribute short pieces on various themes relating to urban landscape and artistic expression. I wrote about Linder Sterling. I then pushed for a spin-off event at the gallery, a 'zine fair.

I'd noticed that over the previous four or five years there had been a resurgence in 'zines, homemade and bespoke booklets, and limited edition prints. Music didn't feature so much but there were dozens of 'zines made by illustrators, feminists, poets and cartoonists. Of course, I related what I was seeing to what had gone in the 1980s, but not nostalgically; instead, in the sense that it was gratifying to see restless and resourceful young people using cheap means of artistic expression.

The new 'zines were part of a lo-fi revolution, alongside such things as seven-inch vinyl singles, screenprints and vintage clothes. At the event, all such things were on sale throughout the gallery's ground floor, as well as letterpress demonstrations and stalls featuring small publishers like Corridor8 and Café Royal Books.

During the Kelley Walker and Cyprien Gaillard exhibition, Maria and her team gave me so much support and some amazing feedback. A few years later, Maria told me how delighted the gallery were when so many people turned up for the 'zine fair. I'd brought a different audience to the gallery, she told me.

In 2009, another dynamic and successful woman, Christine Cort, trusted me enough to give me some opportunities to work with another cultural institution, the Manchester International Festival (MIF). When she gave me a budget to spend on some events, I curated a couple of nights of music featuring bands who I believed deserved some acknowledgement and greater exposure; including Everything Everything, Delphic and Lonelady. And I gave Bicep their first proper DJ gig.

Another door opened when Tim Burgess and his comrade Nick Fraser invited me to contribute to events for their Tim Peaks project, which they take from festival to festival and elsewhere, hosting live music, new bands, one-offs, DJs and in-conversations. The Tim Peaks events at Kendal Calling are always one of the highlights of my year.

Manchester International Festival also helped push me to deliver one of my own pet projects, one that had languished at the back of my mind for too long. In 1999, I'd had a few discussions with the writer Michael Bracewell about staging onstage interviews. It was a simple and not original format – two people sitting on a stage talking – but we started making lists of important things, great guests and good venues, determined that we'd make an event of it. We were going to start each evening with a game of bingo; in fact, we were going to call the night 'Bingo'. Nothing had come of this because we were both busy, drowning in writing deadlines.

I suggested a series of onstage interviews to Christine, taking place at MIF. No bingo; just talk. The events would be called 'Close Up'. MIF would be able to provide a venue including great production and they'd give marketing support. It was all soon agreed. The first interviews featured Guy Garvey, Jackie Kay and Lemn Sissay.

In the mid-1980s I was staging live music shows. By the mid-1990s I was immersed in hosting club nights and DJing. From 2011, 2012, most of my events have been live onstage interviews, 'Close Up' events, many of which I've originated; seeking out the guest, booking an appropriate room (art gallery spaces, theatres, even – for Jarvis Cocker – Manchester Town Hall), and I sort the ticketing and all the mundane stuff too.

I like organising them myself, bringing some of my experience of hosting gigs and clubs to the organisation and marketing. Sometimes I work with cultural institutions, when my commercial experience can be useful. It sharpens your thoughts to an amazing degree when there's no sniff of an Arts Council grant or any other kind of subsidy; no safety net of any kind. You have to take up the challenge of finding an audience for your event.

Anyone involved in making or staging any kind of creative activity should heed this great quote from the American novelist Saul Bellow: 'It may well be that your true readers are not here

as yet and that your books will cause them to materialize.'
It became my mantra for everything I did or planned to do. Be
brave, have the imagination, collaborate with good people and
put in the work; then whatever the nature of the activity, one
day it will attract an audience.

The first time people who none of us knew came to the
Man Alive, we were astonished and excited to see strangers
paying their entrance money. They weren't friends or friends of
friends, they were people we'd drawn in through our efforts.
An audience had materialised.

The 'Close Up' interviews work because there's a hunger for
live events. When the entertainment potential of the internet
became clear, it was tempting to think folk would stay in
more, watch the screen, play online games, download videos,
get drawn through some digital portal into some irresistible
parallel world. When social media took off, it was easy to
assume that for our links, connections, love matches, hanging
out and networking we'd never need to leave the house.

In recent years, as well as a lo-fi revolution, there's been
a boom in festivals, live music, acoustic nights, DJ gigs, and
social and cultural events of all kinds. It's a reaction against
the notion that what you see on your computer screen is
somehow the pinnacle of human experience, and a reassertion
of the value of the primary experience of living in the physical
world. The physical world where people make things, where
they meet. Being in a room with like-minded folk, sharing the
experience of watching something unique unfold in real time,
is a wonderful thing. In addition, social networks have helped
artists, promoters and event organisers of all kinds to find and
nurture an audience.

28

Interview Revelations

When I had the chance to interview David Byrne, there were some complications about the format and the event was something of a disappointment. Mr Byrne was in Britain briefly to mark the publication of his book *How Music Works*. Word reached me that I wouldn't be able to do the event without following his 'guidelines'. I acquiesced, knowing that if I didn't I would miss my chance to meet one of my heroes.

I was told the conversation would have to be limited to issues raised in one chapter of his book; specifically, discussion should focus on the effects of digital music services like Spotify on musicians and the music industry. Mr Byrne also wished to invite media and technology expert Mark Mulligan, who was tasked with explaining to the audience graphs showing that it takes around three hundred Spotify plays of a song to generate the same cash as one iTunes download. And other stuff like that.

On the day in question, David Byrne arrived an hour or so earlier than planned, which was OK; it gave him time to sign the books (another guideline was that he wouldn't do a personal signing afterwards, but signed copies of the book would be made available). I showed him around the venue, the Royal Northern College of Music, and we did a soundcheck.

My event assistant Andrea and I had set up a backstage area, with some food and snacks to pick at, including cheese, fruit, chocolate biscuits and various drinks. We sat there and chatted. He was so polite and charming while we talked about a few things in the book, about the time Talking Heads first came to England supporting the Ramones, and about New York today, and about cycling (I expressed great admiration for his book *Bicycle Diaries*).

Our onstage discussion about the effects of Spotify on the present and future of the music industry was interesting, but not exciting. If you had one hour with David Byrne, is that what you would have chosen to talk about? I could sense some disappointment among the six hundred people in the audience. They weren't to know my casual chat backstage was more interesting than the event they'd paid to see.

I managed to sneak in some questions about his work with St Vincent and the making of 'Psycho Killer', a relatively jaunty song about a dark subject. He said that taking a cue from the words, the first versions of the song were slower, more menacing. But he reckoned that seemed too obvious. Then he said, smiling at me, 'When you say something once why say it again?'

After the event, David Byrne sent me an upbeat email expressing his gratitude and happiness about the event together, but it remained a niggle in my mind that conditions on our conversation had been applied. The chocolate biscuits had never even been opened, so I took them home, called them 'David Byrne's biscuits'. For days afterwards, one of my family would ask if we still had any of David Byrne's biscuits and we'd dig in the box. They went down a storm.

I always have a list in my head of potential guests for onstage interviews. The only criterion is that I am genuinely interested in them, and their life and career. I don't think I could fake interest. My obsession is to get a chance to interview Martin Scorsese at length onstage. Maybe if I write it down, the chances of it happening increase. My fingers are crossed.

Some of the first few I organised were at the Green Room; interviewees included Kevin Rowland, Mark E. Smith and Terry Hall. Afterwards, a number of people and websites asked for footage, but I'd decided not to film the sessions. There were a few reasons, including a practical one of not wanting to be disturbed by cameras and particular lighting requirements, but mostly because I valued the sanctity of the live event. There would be no inferior experience available at a later date on a mobile phone screen. You had to be there.

Often the content is unforgettable. It's a powerful thing, someone being honest and opening up their life and heart to an audience, and it can be emotional for the interviewee too; there have been five or six times when tears have been shed.

John Lydon was on the list and when a chance to talk to him came, I took it. I booked Manchester's Albert Hall, one of the most brilliant venues in the city. We agreed on a seated capacity of seven hundred. For the event poster, I commissioned artwork that paid homage to the cover of the PIL album *First Issue*. All tickets were sold, I read his new book and then I reread his first book. It was great to get a chance to listen again to early PIL; *Metal Box* is phenomenal.

We went through a difficult hour or two before the event when Hannah, from his publishing company, told me that John was having second thoughts about the event, or at least his manager/minder/mate Rambo was. There was a suggestion that John just might talk to the audience direct, or maybe just take questions from the audience. Also, Rambo was adamant he had to be sitting next to John onstage but he wouldn't say anything. I was hoping I could quieten their anxieties about the interview with a quick word with John, but the nearest I could get to a compromise about exactly where Rambo was to be positioned was for him to be stood at the side of the stage, unlit.

I had no idea why Rambo was so paranoid about John's safety. I was wondering why he thought anyone would pay £12.50 for a ticket to a book launch event just in order to cause trouble. His paranoia was justified some eighteen months later at a Public Image Limited performance in Santiago, Chile, when John was hit by a glass thrown from the crowd, leaving a bloody gash.

Lydon gave a lot of thought to the interview, and at least the interview happened, but he very much chose how candid to be and sometimes shut down. I'd got him in a good frame of mind, though, with just a two-minute conversation backstage. Or, rather, a monologue: mine. I told him that my generation had heard the oldsters talking about the Beatles and the 1960s and Carnaby Street like those were the final words in music and culture; we needed signals, a vision of some sort maybe. And then came the Sex Pistols and punk, which gifted us inspiration and a sea of possibilities. I used similar words when I went onstage and introduced him to the crowd. He seemed moved by the reception that he got, and again almost shed a tear when talking about Sid Vicious. 'I miss him,' he said. 'But we will meet again in punk heaven.'

However, he had a tendency to fall into a cartoonish version of Johnny Rotten; swivel to address the audience, with a burp, a shout or a dismissive joke. It was like a defence mechanism; if we were veering away from where he wanted the conversation to be, he'd explode. I concluded there was a struggle there; a hard, no-nonsense punk who's very emotional (you could hear it in his voice onstage, and, of course, you can hear it in songs like 'Death Disco').

It was after a discussion about his childhood, his relationships with his parents, with Malcolm McLaren and with Sid, that I asked him if he'd had therapy. Some of the audience giggled, nervously maybe; as if it was unseemly for two middle-aged men to be talking deeply. He said he hadn't had therapy and was contemptuous of the idea, almost to the point of suggesting people should just get on with it, pull themselves together. But I wasn't convinced. I think rubbishing the idea of therapy was what felt right for his, er, public image.

The interview was intense and interesting, though. He thanked me for all my hard work putting the show together, and during the signing he gave everyone who queued so much time that it took over five hours for him to sign all the books. It was the first night of his book tour. He had peaked early; we'd had such a huge night in Manchester, he cancelled the event in Liverpool the next day.

I had encountered the last-minute threat that an agreed format would be dumped before, at one of my first 'Close Up' events, when I interviewed the American novelist Jonathan Franzen to mark the publication of his novel *Freedom*. As with Lydon, I had waited years for a chance to interview one of my heroes; in Franzen's case, since I read his novel *The Corrections*. I'd hired a great space, the wonderful South Gallery at the Whitworth, one of my favourite rooms in the city. It was the first place I saw a Warhol in real life; you don't forget something like that.

I'd agreed with Michelle from his publishers, Fourth Estate, that it would be a standard book event – reading, in-conversation, questions from the audience, signing. We'd also agreed the in-conversation would probably last thirty-five or forty minutes.

After I'd booked Franzen, several months earlier, it transpired that it would coincide with a cultural festival in Manchester. The organisers agreed to put my event in their programme but questioned me about who the guy was. As we got nearer to the date, they were messaging me excitedly almost daily; they were thrilled how his profile was building and building. My timing was spot on. Three weeks before the event he was the first author to be on the front cover of *Time* magazine since Norman Mailer; his picture was captioned 'Great American Novelist'. It would only be a slight exaggeration to say that his arrival at Heathrow for his *Freedom* events was the literary equivalent of the Beatles arriving at JFK in February 1964.

One of the first things on the agenda for Franzen's invasion of Britain was a pre-recorded interview for BBC2's *Newsnight*. He read some of the book on camera, hesitated, read on, and then, with horror on his face, told interviewer Kirsty Wark that the printed copy had the wrong – and not final – draft of the book. The interview was still run on the show later that evening – complete with footage of the moment of realisation and an uncharacteristic 'fuck' from the author – but a decision had been taken that all twenty thousand copies of the books already sent out to bookshops had to be recalled, and an emergency print run of the correct version was ordered. His publishers were beyond mortified. Some of the staff spent the following morning sobbing.

Michelle was escorting him on the trip, which also included onstage events in London and then Dublin, but it had not gone well. Owing to the recalling of all copies, no books were for sale and Franzen was a little disappointed with the quality of the interviews. While they were at Dublin airport early on the Sunday morning awaiting the flight over to Manchester and my event at the Whitworth, Michelle called me, reported that Jonathan was dispirited, he wanted the Manchester event to be restricted to a reading and a short Q&A with the audience, but no formal interview with me.

'But it's billed as an in-conversation and I have waited for years for this . . .'

'I know you have,' she replied.

'I've even made a pre-show CD of songs mentioned in his novels. I've even got a Bob Seger track, because you know, Caroline and Gary met at a Bob Seger concert, in *The Corrections*, remember?'

'What?'

'So what can we do, Michelle?'

'He's not happy, I understand where he's coming from.'

I suggested I'd meet them when they checked in at the hotel I'd booked for them a mile or so from my house. I knew that Franzen had an interest in post-punk music. He's around the same age as me, likes Talking Heads, his music tastes formed by college radio, so I gifted him a pack of postcards of Kevin Cummins photographs taken during the punk and post-punk eras. He took the box and began to look through, holding the postcards close to his eyes; I hadn't realised how poor his sight was.

Michelle and I left him to take a rest in the hotel and walked down the road in search of a coffee, although things weren't improved when a passing car went through a puddle and splashed rainwater on her jeans; another demoralising moment in her woeful few days.

Because I cared so much about this event, I had already thrown a lot at it, including asking Michelle what Franzen's favourite whisky was and buying a bottle; making the special pre-show CD; then buying those emergency Kevin Cummins postcards. In addition, I'd commissioned Paul Lambert to design a poster for the event, which was screenprinted in a limited edition of twenty on beautiful cotton paper by Mark Jermyn at his studio in Islington Mill. The design featured the motif of birds on a wire, which reflected both the front cover of *Freedom* and Mr Franzen's love of ornithology. This was how in thrall to Franzen and how excited about the event I was. I wanted him to know I cared.

When I left Michelle and went to the Whitworth to help set up the room, there was some good news; Waterstones Deansgate, which was organising the bookstall, had obtained a couple of hundred copies from the emergency print run, even though the correct version wasn't officially being published until the following day.

Thirty minutes before the event, Franzen and Michelle arrived and we settled in the makeshift backstage area, which was, in reality, Maria Balshaw's office, complete with gorgeous wallpaper.

I showed him the posters, he took one, studied it, loved it. 'Maybe you would sign them?' I asked.

'Sure.'

Andrea was making sure the audience's chairs had been laid out and the pop-up bar was ready, and then set the pre-show tape running. All the while I was sitting in Maria's office with Mr Franzen. I couldn't walk away from him until I knew there was at least some chance of reinstating the interview part of the event. I wanted him to trust me. I explained the tape to him, telling him I'd even included 'Turn the Page' by Bob Seger, which was way beyond the call of duty. He seemed amused by this quirky addition to creating a sense of event. Andrea knocked on the door and I had to follow her to discuss some problem with the ticketing.

Michelle came to find me out in the hall. 'He'll do it the way you'd like to do it. He's happy,' she whispered.

He was thoughtful, with the driest humour, keen to respond accurately to every question, and happy to discuss all aspects of not just the book *Freedom* but the abstract idea too. He talked of the value of accepting who we are, rather than being distracted by what anyone is telling us who we could be; 'I will say this about the abstract concept of "freedom"; it's possible you are freer if you accept what you are and just get on with being the person you are.'

As we were in Manchester, and having begun our encounter bonding over Kevin Cummins photos, we finished the interview discussing the appeal of English punk and post-punk music. He admitted he was generalising broadly and there were some notable exceptions, but, he said, 'I feel like English musicians have a pretty good sense of humour, so the kind of sense of fatalism and tragic/comic sensibility that I look for in literature seems to be in a lot of the music that comes out of some of these English cities.'

A day later, Franzen was at a party in London and someone stole his spectacles and threw them in a lake. His hours in Manchester were his favourite hours of his trip to Europe. Franzen sent me a lovely email and we had a polite exchange of messages. I told him I'd gone to see Warpaint at the Deaf Institute. Five years later, he came to Manchester again with Michelle, and we went for a whisky in a curry house behind the Novotel.

I'm always grateful when interviewees are prepared to open up just a little; these things don't work if the audience only learn what they could have read in that person's Wikipedia entry. Not all of them give much away, but that's OK; I'm the last person to demand fake bonhomie from my interviewees. The point of the onstage interview is that the guest reveals something of themselves, which can be that they are guarded, or garrulous, or funny, or shy, or even a bit boring.

One or two guests who have spent a lifetime throwing themselves into live performances have turned out to be very uneasy in the onstage interview, including Kim Gordon of Sonic Youth. Perhaps the music is so much the medium for their thoughts and ideas, conversation isn't so easy. I've met many songwriters and poets who have said more in their work than they would express in real life to those around them; such as Jayne Casey, talking about the treatment of her mother by her father. If the guest is uncomfortable with my line of questioning, I would never persist.

In addition to the Franzen and Lydon episodes, I've had

other last-minute calls requesting a change in the format, and cancelling the part of the proceedings that involves me asking questions. I'm disappointed, not because I want to share the spotlight but because the subject will be someone I admire and the research I'll have done will have consumed me for days. These events aren't well paid; the reward is meeting people, the interview, learning things, sharing good times.

I got a phone call on a train to Preston to interview Jeanette Winterson telling me that the plan might have to change. That after a short introduction from me, Jeanette was going to go it alone. But this turned out not to be the case. She consented to having her photo taken with a fruit bowl, in homage to her novel *Oranges Are Not the Only Fruit*, and spoke passionately to me and the Preston audience in a very direct, honest way.

Some interviews are a breeze, such as the occasion one year at the Liverpool Sound City conference when I interviewed Wayne Coyne of the Flaming Lips, who was chatty and happy to have some fun, although, admittedly, this was after a glass or two of red wine. He treated the audience to a Bruce Springsteen impersonation and showed me his tattoo of Miley Cyrus's dead dog Floyd.

I also interviewed Viv Albertine of the Slits at Liverpool Sound City. Way back in time, at the Fighting Cocks, I remember the DJ playing 'Typical Girls' by the Slits. Musically it stood out, a sparkling, intelligent song you could dance to. Our conversation started with a discussion about masturbation. She has never masturbated, never wanted to, although tried to once half-heartedly when she was nagged so to do by a friend. I'd launched into talking about the subject because she brings it up at the beginning of her memoir, *Clothes, Clothes, Clothes. Music, Music,*

Music. Boys, Boys, Boys. throwing us into the deep end, setting us up for one of the most honest autobiographies I have read.

Later in the interview, she told me the circumstances around the writing of 'Typical Girls' when she was living in a council flat in Highgate with her mum, in a tiny bedroom surrounded by her posters, records and books. She was curious about life and ideas, she'd done sociology GCSE, she'd been to art school; as she says, 'I wasn't naive, I was aware.'

She might not have been naive, but she was bored: 'There was no TV, no telephones, no long conversations, nothing. I was just stuck in my room. I remember going through some sociology textbooks I had, and one of them I think was actually called *Typical Girls*. I thought it was a great title. I was bored, so I thought I'll just write a song. That's why we all did what we did; not to be in magazines, not to be famous, but because there was nothing else to do. The song came out quite easily, this list of what a typical girl was supposed to be.'

She made a riff to go with it, and with singer Ari turned it into a song. Viv's boyfriend, Mick Jones of the Clash, gave them some advice: 'Mick wanted us to put it in 4/4 time because he said we'd have a hit with if it if we put it in 4/4 time. We didn't even know what time it was in; some looping, God-knows-what-time.'

'You kept it how it was?'

'Yes, we refused as we always did! We refused any advice from anyone who made suggestions that they said would make the music a bit more commercial. We'd refuse but then we kept saying, "Why aren't we famous?"'

I reminded her that the song starts with Ari saying 'Don't create . . . don't rebel', and asked whether that was random or whether those two things come at the start because they are key to the song.

'It's those things that make a girl "ugly",' said Viv. 'To be too creative is threatening and to be rebellious is unfeminine and ugly. I am still those things.'

I waited for her to say more. And she did: 'I still find it hard to get boyfriends. As I did then, I get guys attracted to me physically; not many of them want to go much further than that, because I am too creative and too rebellious. It's why my marriage broke up, because of those two things. Nothing's changed. I remember when my marriage was breaking up feeling this massive déjà vu, you know, the kinds of things A&R men would say to us back then, trying to knock me down. I was thinking, the only thing I've got to hold on to this second time around is that I've heard all this before.'

I feel blessed when an interviewee is genuinely open. Some 'Close Up' sessions have been honest to the point of shocking the audience; Terry Hall at the Green Room, for example. We began by talking about Terry growing up in Coventry, when at one point a career as a footballer was possible. 'Very early on, like eleven, twelve, but I didn't pursue it,' he said. 'It was a weird period because I went through a lot of weird stuff when I was twelve, so I just fell off it and I just started drinking cider and smoking.'

The issues that seemed at the heart of what the Specials songs were about – opposing racism, for example – felt very real (after all, Lynval Golding from the group was stabbed in the neck in 1982, almost dying in the attack). I said that I knew it was a hard thing to measure, but I asked if he felt that the Specials managed to change anything via these songs. 'Yes, but not massively,' he replied. 'There's only certain things you can change being in a pop group. You try to make people aware of things, and in the last thirty years people have come up to me and told me stories about how that album and that band altered the way they felt and that's a good thing.'

We went off on various tangents. I knew that Terry had a bad memory and had heard talk that he'd had his telephone number tattooed on his leg, but that turned out not to be true.

A little later, I went back to what Terry said about being twelve years old, and asked him if we could talk about a song called 'Well Fancy That' that he recorded with the Fun Boy Three. When he told the story of the song, his words were met with complete silence by the audience. He said that when he was twelve he was in France in the company of a teacher from school: 'I was sexually abused for three days and three nights, and belted about. I often think now, because it was so under the carpet and behind the curtains then, I think now terrible things might have happened; he could have flipped out.'

He told me that things were brushed aside on his return, but he was given Valium. He became addicted to it. He ended up being addicted to it for years. He wrote the song to share it with people, but also, he said, 'just to get it out of my head'.

The song also triggered a response from listeners: 'I got some amazing letters from all over, some from people who'd been abused by their families and stuff. For me it's always been about communication; that's the reason I do what I do, and whether I talk to one person or a million, it doesn't matter. I'd rather one person really gets what I say; I think that's important.'

Terry said he'd suffered depression badly for decades, but it was only properly diagnosed when he was nearly forty. 'You know something's wrong but you self-medicate with drinks, that's what I was doing,' he said. 'I knew I had a big problem, but I didn't know how to deal with it and it was only when it reached a certain point when I couldn't physically do anything that I had to have help.'

'Was that medication or was it therapy?'

'A bit of therapy, mostly medication. It took two or three years to get the right cocktail really, and it's been a hard thing to do, but now it works. My life depends on these drugs every day, which felt like a horrible thing at first but now I just equate it with vitamins or brushing your teeth or something, it's what you have to do; it's part of your daily routine.'

After such an emotional few moments hearing Terry talk about this, I had no idea how to take the conversation further; there was nowhere deeper to go. I called an interval, announced we'd reconvene in twenty minutes. After the interval, I asked him an important question I hadn't asked in the first part: how does someone who grew up in Coventry end up supporting Manchester United? To a mixture of cheers and boos from the audience, he told us: 'You just do. Nobody I knew supported Coventry when I was ten or eleven; we all had different teams, and Coventry wasn't there amongst them.'

29

Talk About The Now

Some of the musicians, artists and writers I've encountered are funny, some are wary. Some become icons by appearing to be all-conquering heroes, but Lemn Sissay made a big impression on me when he told me that, as an artist, there is no more valuable way to connect with people than to allow yourself to be vulnerable.

There have been interviews that have come close to chaos. Like the time, ten years after our wedding dance, I was interviewing Mark E. Smith at the Green Room. During the interview, I told him I heard that when he was younger he earned some extra cash tarot reading. He confirmed he had psychic abilities, but they weren't useful, explaining, 'What point is there knowing what's going to happen in a year's time? It's not much use. If it was the horses or something or the lottery, but it's not is it?'

Mark's malevolence often targeted interviewers, but as long as he didn't take a bite out of my ear, I resolved to consider the encounter a success. At the Green Room, he gave me a very hard time, telling me DJs had ruined music, and chided me for living in south Manchester. As well as talking about Mandrax, we discussed Methodism, and we had a conversation about why he doesn't like touring in hot countries. 'I tend to get a lot of compression in my head . . .'

The audience were laughing. He turned and addressed them. 'This is serious; if it doesn't rain for a week or two, my head starts to hurt.'

The sense of chaos wasn't improved during the interview when his wife Elena started heckling me from the audience. 'Talk about the now,' she shouted. 'Talk about the now!'

I had planned to talk about Mark's current line-up and activities, but his history fascinated me; also, let's be honest, without the past there would be no 'now'. He had a great past, so much of the early Fall material sounds amazing still, the tales of disorder, hallucinations and caustic dissections.

When I talked to Mark about the now, he told me, 'Every day is great for me. I dislike rose-coloured glasses.'

Twenty minutes into the second half of the evening one of the audience asked a question: 'Is it true you once had telephone sex with Morrissey?' In the ensuing uproar, the question never got answered, and I decided to draw proceedings to a close. Back in the dressing room, I was exhausted and full of red wine, and Mark lit a cigarette.

'You are hard work, you know that, don't you?' I said to him, and began counting out his cash on the shelf in front of the dressing-room mirror. Three hundred pounds, which I handed over.

He took a twenty and pushed it along the shelf back towards me.

'What's this?'

'For you,' said Mark. 'It was good.'

I looked at it; he'd given me a tip or a gift of some sort. This gesture of Mark's reminded me of my childhood, when my grandfather or another elderly relative might pass me a pound note at the end of a visit, with a little smile or wink. Throughout the interview, Mark had stuck rigidly to his default position – giving me a hard time – but this was a genuine moment, and such an unnecessary, endearing thing to do.

'Mark, thank you, thanks,' I said and I meant it.

There was a knock on the door of the dressing room and Elena and Mark's mother arrived, and then Catherine and Raili. One of the first times I saw the Fall play, Mark jumped off the stage to punch someone who had thrown a pint glass at the band. At that time, I could never have envisaged that one day he would introduce his mother to my daughter.

Raili, Catherine and Mrs Smith talked, and I spoke to Elena. 'It's hard to balance it, isn't it?' I said to her. 'It's good to acknowledge the past. Appreciate it. Not live in the past; that's crap, but that's different. Appreciating it, understanding it, that's the thing.'

'It would be better to talk about the now,' she replied.

'I guess,' I said.

All the heckling was fair enough, and in many ways I understood it. I was working through a similar issue in my DJing; trying to have a healthy and honest relationship to my past. Seeing the Madchester classics lined up in my playlist at XFM contradicted what I wanted my DJing to be. Of course, it was a past I had participated in and I was happy people were fascinated by it but, at the same time, as I had said to Elena, I didn't want to live in the past.

The Haçienda had been an important part of my life – the scene, I suppose, of my glory days – but the club had been demolished, and Rob and Tony were no longer with us. I was being asked to feature at various nights playing Haçienda classics. The aim of such events is to give the audience what they want and expect. It's a reasonable approach and I knew from experience that it could be fun playing revival and reunion nights, but at the same time I regretted that a club like the Haçienda, with a reputation for being adventurous, was now being represented in very predictable ways.

I'm not even sure I've worked this out yet. When I play now, I mix it up, music from all eras. It's too dull playing the same records in the same order as I may have done five years ago, let alone thirty years ago. According to the late great Muhammad Ali, 'A man who views the world the same at fifty as he did at twenty has wasted thirty years of his life.' I change; the world changes; my playlist changes. That's how it should be, right?

I still had a curious and voracious mind, bored of predictability. In addition, Tony Wilson's fascination with 'the early art of people who are going to be great artists' chimed with how I'd always felt. In 1996, I'd provided this comment for the sleevenotes of a Haçienda compilation: 'Nostalgia is a device created by old people to deny young people their dreams.'

As you get older, it's always worth hesitating before proclaiming that nothing good is happening in the now. That's why I wrote this at the end of *Manchester England*, 'The end of the story is yet to be lived, let alone told.' That's why I wandered across Piccadilly Gardens to the Bierkeller to visit 'Tramp'. It was exhilarating to walk into a basement in 2006, see a full dancefloor and not recognise the tunes; but, even more than that, wanting and wishing to know the tunes.

It was liberating to be able to enjoy and champion new things. In 2007 I saw Friendly Fires in a tiny venue on Sackville Street and started picking up every flyer I could for shows produced by Now Wave, amazing young promoters who were sniffing out ace music early. I was asked to DJ at Florence and the Machine's first show in Manchester; a showcase in a clothes shop. I was so keen to be involved I agreed to do the event in exchange for a pair of Diesel jeans.

I wasn't satisfied just being part of the 'collective history' (in Laurent's phrase), but, in addition, wanted to more proactively configure the future. I know Laurent feels the same; he curates an annual festival in the south of France featuring bands and acts of all sorts. So, when I organised the *Dreams Without Frontiers* fanzine I offered work to young designers and writers. Then at the Manchester International Festival, I found a way to showcase twenty-first-century bands. By the time you're fifty you should be a giver of opportunities, and aspire, at least, to stay hungry for the now and never rest.

In July 2013, Neneh Cherry talked to me about how to acknowledge a past, but not live in it; to value it without milking it. I'd interviewed her in the 1980s, around the time of 'Buffalo Stance'. But now we were talking at the Manchester International Festival, twenty-seven years after 'Buffalo Stance' had been released.

I asked her if, when she saw footage of herself from that era, she felt a close connection with her younger self or, because of the changes we go through as we get older, the young performer seems like a stranger to her. She gave a lovely answer: 'She's not a stranger to me. When I see "Buffalo Stance", I feel very much like I'm holding hands. It's me, it's somebody else. But you have to allow yourself to move on. I can look at those videos and I think, "My God, you were such a baby" – or when I hear my voice on those recordings, but it's all a part of where I am now. It's why I am where I am now.'

She told me she loved her hits but that there was a time and place for playing them. She appreciated that audiences might want or expect to hear familiar and favourite material, but at the Manchester International Festival she had decided to take the opportunity to choose to do some shows with Rocket Number 9 and a setlist of all new songs. She'd taken the decision it was uncreative to retread past glories.

This goes beyond music and every other artistic activity; whoever you are, in whatever circumstances, it can't be good for the soul to find yourself prizing your past over your present and future. Furthermore, on a civic rather than individual level, swallowing myths about things being better back in the old days is cultural conservatism. I'm not a fan of nostalgia, but I'm fascinated by history, where we've come from, learning from others, researching the roots of ideas, tracing the way the patterns of our past are replicating themselves in the present. All that is good, and valuable; that's not nostalgia.

I've been lucky enough to meet people throughout the world genuinely interested, even obsessed, by Factory, by the Haçienda; the how, the why, the effects, the legacy. One Saturday, I was in Philadelphia with a day off from a short DJ tour, so I decided to go to see a Jeremy Deller exhibition at the Institute of Contemporary Art; Deller, of course, is gloriously adept at animating the history of ideas.

303

Sonic Youth Slept On My Floor

The guy working on reception at the ICA in Philly requested my name and zip code so the institution could track visitors in order to collate information useful for funders. I wrote my name but told him I live in Manchester so I only have a postcode, not a zip code, and he asked me if I knew there was a Happy Mondays event in the gallery that afternoon. Apparently, as part of the programme running alongside the Deller show, two guys, Anthony and Dan, had put together a Happy Mondays presentation/talk for the afternoon. Not only that, but one of the rooms in the gallery had been set up as a mini-Haçienda for the afternoon with video projections of footage from the club and a soundtrack of appropriate music.

A few hours later, I found myself in the Haçienda room where a grand total of eight people stood around in the dark. Then one of Dan's friends came in, wearing a frock coat, like something Engels might have worn. Coat guy had a friend with him and he introduced him to me but it was loud so I didn't catch his name. We attempted a shouty conversation; coat guy's friend seemed to be British. He said he had a band but when I asked him what was his band were called I couldn't hear. I asked him again and he said the Ordinary Boys. I realised it was the band's frontman, Preston. Somehow Preston and I had ended up in a fake Haçienda in an art gallery in Philadelphia.

Preston explained he was songwriting in New York. I told him I liked his friend's coat. A girl called Katelynn invited me to a rave in a yoga studio and I told Preston it would be great if he came too, but he said he was going to a different part of town to see a gig by Dean Wareham, ex-Galaxie 500.

The yoga studio was on the top floor of a retail building closed at weekends, so some unlocking of doors and detours through fire exits were required to gain entry. From the top floor and the music, a ladder reached up onto the roof. Katelynn showed me the view over the city, and we listened to the shouts from the street and the noise of nightlife. It got late, the music played on. Soon the sun would be rising.

It's useful to plot or dream about our future, or to appreciate the way the past intrudes on the present, and to try to understand history, but during moments like my late night in Philly – losing all track of time, up on the roof, the kick drum banging like a heartbeat below – it feels just so good sometimes to be so absolutely, wonderfully in the now.

Work was going well. I didn't think I had cause to be despondent in Manchester. It was fun to be in email correspondence with the likes of Jonathan Franzen and David Byrne, great to be scheduling interviews with the likes of Kate Tempest, and a thrill to be in demand as a DJ, travelling to play in places like New York, Berlin, Florence, Lisbon and Ibiza. But that doesn't stop stuff gnawing away . . .

The Philly yoga rave was one of those nights you never want to end, joy intensified by the excitement of travel and being surrounded by like minds. I was a little restless. I gave thought to the idea of staying in Philly. I could be in Anthony's art gang, sign up to do yoga with Katelynn, start a new life.

30

You Sold Your
Record Collection?

I occasionally struggle with hangovers. I'm not much of a drinker, so I don't mean following alcohol binges; I mean, falling into hollow hours following the intense highs of great DJ gigs and other big events. I know it's something bands, actors, performers of all kinds can feel too. The build-up to big events, the all-consuming moments during them, followed by a draining comedown, the need to adjust from the adrenaline boost onstage to your offstage world. And during a DJ gig, you feel so loved by a room full of people; it's something of an illusion, of course, but it's hard to tell your psyche that. You wake up, it's over, the rush has gone. You're not that person any more.

In the summer of 2015 a number of work projects came to fruition, including the publication of *Life After Dark: A History of British Nightclubs and Music Venues*. As always, I'd made a big emotional investment in a book; the weeks after were, again, a little hard to adjust to. Once the book was published, all the thinking space it had taken up was emptied. When it was filled again, it was with doubts and angst.

My habit of questioning everything turned inwards. Some of the questions I'd asked my interviewees I was now asking myself. I'd discussed with Raymond Carver how intense the need for love could be, and sometimes how misdirected. I'd asked Kevin Rowland, 'Should you have worked out a way of enjoying what you do and not taken it so seriously?', and I'd asked Tony Wilson if growing old worried him. I'd discussed with Neneh Cherry whether we stay the same person as we get older or become, in some way, a stranger.

This anxiety was turning into a proper midlife wobble. In addition, maybe there were reasons to be despondent after all, as Catherine told me that she wasn't feeling good about our marriage. We'd been struggling for a while but things were beginning to deteriorate. Now Raili was old enough to go to university, some of the ties binding us had disappeared.

Despite a ruinous family background, Catherine walks on the sunny side of the street. I wanted to be there alongside her, but people change, domestic shit gets in the way. The person who turned your head dancing on a podium in a catsuit ends up being the person who asks you if you have seen the Visa bill and you know we have no bread don't you? Her work hours were excessive and sometimes dragged her down, my work took me out and away; we'd been OK leading independent lives, but our independent lives had become parallel lives.

One factor in our struggle was that unfortunately I was often unable to sparkle. I'd arrived somewhere feeling isolated. Things happened to me I'd never experienced before, including physical symptoms like panic attacks and insomnia. I had a loving family, friends, a house full of things and was leading the kind of life I always wanted. A life that should make me happy. Emotions defy logic, though.

I looked for a way to mend myself, which I thought would help me mend the marriage. I didn't expect or need non-stop blissful happiness, but if I could move a couple of rungs up the ladder of happiness, it would be something. It might not require me to change my life, it might be a case of finding another way of seeing it, a different perspective.

I talked to my doctor, said I wasn't functioning well, and explained the ladder thing, that ten is permanently and blissfully happy and zero is the opposite. I told her I wasn't daft enough to expect to be a ten. But why not a seven? Instead of what I currently was: a five. She thought it was a reasonable goal and we discussed a ton of issues. Talking to her, I was able to rationalise how I felt, but that wasn't the same as changing how I felt. She offered me medication or a chance to join a three-month waiting list for counselling. I knew I needed a jolt. I asked her to put me on the list. I also decided to take some action of my own.

Even writing this down makes me shake my head in wonderment: among the things I decided to do was to sell all my vinyl. The records represented all the music I have fallen in love with since I was old enough to buy albums and since the dawn of twelve-inch singles, but also represented my working life, and tracked the eras I've lived through and the clubs I've worked at. I posted a picture of some of my collection on Facebook, and awaited responses.

I hadn't played the vinyl for years after a couple of incidents.

One was a journey all the way to Peru to play a show with a load of DJs including Derrick May. I packed a big box of tunes, worried about them all the way from Manchester to Lima via Amsterdam Schiphol, but one of the other DJs arrived with a memory stick in each pocket. At least the box had arrived; I'd waited at so many carousels in fear of losing the tools of my trade, including once in Berlin when my box of vinyl was mislaid by British Airways and I couldn't even do the gig.

I wasn't going to go down the memory-stick route, but it was soon after then that I took to burning and playing CDs. I wanted to play things that were not available on vinyl, and many of the best tunes I was listening to weren't. I didn't want not to be able to share them because of some mundane format issue.

I knew I didn't need the records, but the idea of selling them all was sudden and instinctive, and what slightly surprised me was how it appeared that I had lost any emotional connection to them. The only thing that made me half hesitate was my kids. Jack especially had hoped the vinyl was part of his inheritance. I have a wonderful collection of interesting books, but Jack had always had his eye on the vinyl.

All the music I've loved would live on, and my access to it, via the internet, was undiminished. In fact, online I was hearing tunes I wished I had heard at the time of release. One example springs to mind: Mito 'Droid'. If I'd heard that thirty-five years ago, I'd have spent all the intervening time playing it to death.

When I posted news of the sale and a photo of the collection on Facebook, first there were howls of protest from friends and strangers on the internet, but then it also went viral, and the news travelled to the furthest reaches of the globe online via the likes of *Mixmag* posting about it. My inbox went bonkers, including people asking for a specific record. But I'd decided not to cherry pick the best. The offer was to take them all.

A few record dealers came to my house to give me feedback and a price. One dealer was keen on the tunes but couldn't believe how battered the condition of some of the records was.

'It's a working collection,' I said.

'Sleeves falling apart, Dave. And you can see the dust on some of the vinyl.'

'Not just any dust, that's Haçienda dust.'

He laughed. 'True, and that's the value. The collection's connections. Your story, the Haçienda story . . .'

I got two serious offers, both people happy to pay the asking price; one from an art collector in Italy wishing to display them in a converted church in Italy, and the other from Seth Troxler whose delightful first email to me began, 'Hello Dave, my name is Seth Troxler. I'm currently one of the biggest DJs in the world . . .'

I went to Bologna and met the Italian bidder, Mauro, who had a genuine interest and some intriguing ideas about exhibiting the collection and placing it at the centre of an event programme. I also went to Amsterdam, where my friend DJ Esqueezy and I went to watch Seth DJ at a basement party. One thing that Seth did made me smile; within a few moments of me being in the room he played 'Love Tempo' by Quando Quango. It was like Seth telling me he was plugged into my world already.

I let Mauro down and went with Seth. Seth said he'd play them to new generations of listeners. It felt like passing on the baton, a way to leave a legacy; like hosting a contemporary 'zine fair at Manchester Art Gallery, it demonstrated that the past can be inspiration and ammunition for the future.

I put the records into thirty-five boxes. All of them. Mo' Wax, Creation, Sleeping Bag and DeConstruction releases; a ten-inch Big Flame album; music by the Au Pairs, the Marine Girls and the Fall; twenty of the first twenty-five Warp releases (on white label); rare Coil records; Andrew Weatherall's Primal Scream and James remixes; the 'Madchester Rave On' EP; the Skinny Boys debut album; James Brown compilations; early 1990s Italo house; hip hop, hip house and the signed Adonis 'No Way Back'; *EVOL* and other Sonic Youth albums; New Order white labels; and 'It's Alright, I Feel It', the last record I played on the last night of the Haçienda.

Miranda Sawyer called me; she was researching a book about midlife crises. I said I couldn't imagine getting a Harley-Davidson, that actually what I'd done was the opposite in some ways: to resist the tyranny of stuff. The records, somehow, had come to represent the baggage of my past and I needed to lighten the load. 'I'm midlife,' I told Miranda, 'I'm dragging all this past behind me like baggage, it weighs heavy on me; not all of it is bad – a lot of it is fantastic – but it genuinely weighs heavy. I'm past the age that my mother was when she died – she was fifty-two – so I'm aware of my mortality.'

I remembered Neneh's words: the past represents a big part of who I am and where I am now, but you have to allow yourself to move on. I told Miranda that I've always looked for doors opening, and made opportunities. 'What happens next?' I said. 'I'm into the endgame. I'm running out of time.'

31

The Lesbians Who Saved
My Life

I had some cash, an unexpected mini-windfall enough for me to subsidise a self-help plan. The idea of being in Paris for a while had always appealed to me, and I realised now was the time to make a temporary move. The city had always interested and inspired me, and I also knew I had some job opportunities; I've DJed there more times than any other city apart from Manchester.

This wasn't going to be just some expensive holiday. Silencio offered me some DJ gigs. I also hoped to do some writing while I was in Paris, too. To test the water, I offered to interview Jamie xx for the French magazine *Les Inrocks*. Jamie and I talked on the phone about the melancholic, powerful sound of the xx; and the broken-up, fractured version in his solo work, notably in his album *In Colour*. He's not the most effusive interviewee, which may not come as a surprise to his listeners. Even songs of his you could describe as 'anthems' have an introverted, elegiac element to them.

While talking to him, some of my own situation was seeping into our conversation. I was talking about what DJing still brings to my life – social occasions, a chance to make and share connections – and, that whatever else is going on in my life, however tired or dispirited I might feel, I feel happy and at home behind the decks. It's relentless putting myself on the line, but I know I can do it.

Jamie xx seemed distracted by people around him. There seemed to be a party going on in his Japanese hotel room. I'm not sure he was listening to me, but sometimes you have to say things anyway.

I'd promised myself a stay in Montmartre, and was about to pay a deposit on a lovely apartment when the terrorist attack at the Bataclan occurred. I was home in Manchester that November evening, appalled by the reports of mayhem and deaths at the venue and bars in the tenth arrondissement and elsewhere. A club promoter I'd met in 2013 lost seven friends at one of the bars. A journalist working for *Les Inrocks* was murdered in the Bataclan.

I'd seen Trentemøller perform at the Bataclan in 2010, and I'd subsequently visited several bars and restaurants in the tenth arrondissement. I could picture the layout of the venue and the layout of the streets, but at home that evening of 13 November 2015 I couldn't imagine the carnage. How could anyone?

Although I was a little worried, I knew the French would return to the café terraces and the attractions of the city to me were undimmed. I paid the deposit on the apartment, and packed a huge case of clothes and books. I'd have anonymity, a sense of novelty and adventure, and the inspiration of the people, the history, the streets and the mythologies of Paris.

313

Actress Audrey Hepburn starred in four or five films that were at least partly shot in Paris, including *Sabrina*, in which she plays the title character in a story about unrequited love and second chances. 'Paris isn't for changing planes,' Sabrina says. 'It's for changing your outlook.'

The plan was to be in Paris for three months, but it turned out to be five months. The apartment in Montmartre, on rue Lepic, was a few doors up from where van Gogh had lived for a time in the late 1880s. There are other, cheaper parts of Paris – some of which I came to love, including Belleville – so it was a bit of an extravagant thing to do, but I had Seth's cash in the bank and no desire to invest it in stocks and shares.

In the first couple of weeks of living in rue Lepic, finding my feet, I gravitated towards Le Pain Quotidien, even though it's a chain and its roots aren't even French. But it was very close by, the wifi was good, and on previous visits to Paris with my daughter a trip to Le Pain Quotidien had been one of her favourite things to do, so I already had some sentimental attachment to it. Often the first customer of the day, I'd take a seat by the window and watch Paris wake up.

On my birthday, the first Sunday I was in Paris, I went to the Gaîté Lyrique to see the film *Scorpio Rising* with Nadège, an award-winning sound designer, one of several good friends I already had in Paris. Another was Fanny who works on arts and culture websites (I met her at Laurent Garnier's Festival Yeah!). But one of my hopes was to pick up some friendships that began much further back. With Erik Rug, for example, who I had DJed alongside at the La Locomotive and seen a number of times since, including when he recorded for the Manchester-based label Paper Recordings.

Erik had just started featuring occasionally at vinyl-only sessions at Hotel Pigalle alongside some other veterans of the Paris scene, including Loik Dury and Betino, a Paris legend who owns a record shop on rue Saint-Sébastien. Their events – just down the hill from where I was staying – gave me a great reason to leave the apartment once a week.

I had tried to come up with a few informal rules for myself, including to walk a lot; just to leave the house and walk. I was also determined not to sleep in the afternoon – this was something I had recently been doing in Manchester, a little signal that things were not well, a way of tuning out of the nonsense in my head.

I was aware that in Paris, Montmartre, especially the southside, is considered a tourist area. But once you walk a few hundred metres you hit very different versions of Paris, including mini camps of homeless immigrants under railway arches near Métro stations. In Lauren Elkin's book *Flâneuse* she tells of a rumour of a ward at a local hospital where Japanese tourists can seek counselling if they are traumatised by their disappointment in finding that actual Paris is dirty, chaotic and rude, and not the Paris they were expecting – Amélie serving them crème brûlée and streets smelling of Chanel No. 5.

During those first months, I got to know which day my boulangerie shut (Wednesday), which Métro stations were a pain in the ass to change at (e.g. Châtelet), the ritual of raclette, and the little quirks of the city; on the first Wednesday of the month Paris tests its air-raid sirens.

It was an interesting, maybe even difficult time to be in Paris. The city, understandably, was jittery, one year after the attack on the offices of Charlie Hebdo and just a matter of weeks after the Bataclan killings. Walking to the *Les Inrocks* office, I paused to look at the flowers and other tributes laid out on the pavement opposite the Bataclan and I shed a tear. I took it personally. It was an attack on my tribe; hundreds of music fans, and all the party people on the pavement terraces outside the city's bars.

ISIS literature talks about a 'grey zone'. Originally the phrase was used with reference to Muslims who live happily alongside neighbours of all faiths and types (ISIS have a special hatred for their co-religionists who refuse to be jihadist). Now, it can be more generally applied to the space (social/cultural) where views find common ground, where there is a blurring of identity, maybe, and ambiguity.

Furthermore, ISIS have major hang-ups about sex. They had issued a press statement claiming Paris was targeted as it was 'the capital of prostitution and vice'. The Eagles of Death Metal show at the Bataclan theatre was melodramatically and inaccurately described as a 'profligate prostitution party'.

Most of what the murderers seemed to hate about Paris is most of what I love about the city. Of course, there are as many different versions of Paris as there are inhabitants and tourists, but I'm attracted to its avant-garde cultural history, all that mad art, and cross-dressing cabaret, and be-bop jazz. The Paris both James Joyce and James Baldwin felt at home in. And the city that coined the word 'discothéque'.

There were thorough bag searches at the big stores such as FNAC, and at museums and galleries. A couple of months after the Bataclan attack, out to see Foals in concert at Olympia, it was clear that French music lovers were more than just resilient. After going through two lines of security to get into the venue, I found myself in the midst of the most exuberant crowd I'd ever seen in Paris.

I carried Olivia Laing's *Lonely City* everywhere. I was happy in my own company most of the time, but being alone wasn't so appealing in those hours when I felt like I had no escape route from solitude. But Fanny was usually happy to jump on her scooter after work and meet me at Le Cépage for a drink. One weekend, my son came to stay and, on another, my daughter, both grown-up and wise. It was a joy to see them.

On my fourth week, I was walking down rue des Martyrs and came across a small cabaret club called Madame Arthur. Searching Facebook for clues about what went on at Madame Arthur, I discovered a new weekly party was about to be launched there. The event page was in French and so filled with slang I couldn't really work out what the night was about, except that the host was DJ Sophie Morello, who also appeared to run a monthly lesbian night called 'Kidnapping'. The music clips posted on the event page were great, the venue intrigued me and was close by, admission was free and the hours were eight until twelve, which suited me better than the usual Paris thing of nothing happening until midnight. The new night looked like it was catering to a demographic similar to 'Kidnapping', so I sent Sophie a message. I didn't want to steam in and break some unwritten rule about straight men attending lesbian nights. She replied suggesting I find her and say hello when I arrived. The opening night was just a couple of days before Valentine's Day. I put it in my diary.

The inside of the venue was small, dark and intimate, all wood and mirrors, plus a mezzanine with a view over a balcony onto the ground floor. The bar didn't have a huge variety of drinks but five euros for gin and tonic up until 10 p.m. seemed reasonable. I ordered two, both for me, and, a little later, one for Sophie. I wish the four walls of Madame Arthur could talk; it wouldn't surprise me if they have witnessed some of the best profligate parties ever.

Sophie's DJ stuff was set up on a trestle table. Apart from a few coloured lights and a couple of microphone stands, the stage was empty. It was conspicuously a lesbian night, but it wasn't exclusively so. It wasn't even women-only – there were a few guys there. Although the crowd numbered less than a hundred people, it was enough to make it feel busy. Sophie was playing French pop, mixed with some lovely electro. She introduced me to her crew, including Laura who was a fantastic dancer, and the organiser of the onstage action. I didn't know this would happen, but every twenty minutes or so, a little cabaret turn happened, or Laura organised a game, some sort of blind date. The highlight was when one of the girls put on a gorilla suit and read nineteenth-century love poetry.

There was so much laughter, and even a girl on crutches recovering from a badly broken leg was dancing. Sophie got on the microphone occasionally welcoming people and intro-ing the onstage acts. I met a girl called Sandy who kept trying to initiate some kind of human pyramid, and several Maries and Marines. I also noticed one of the waitresses from Le Pain Quotidien there.

New friends, electronic dance music, a lesbian in a gorilla suit reading nineteenth-century love poetry; this was my kind of place. Naturally, I became a regular, attending every week, enjoying every moment, the music sounding brilliant, the laugh-ter washing through me.

A few weeks later, I arrived at Madame Arthur to find Sophie with a bottle of gin in a makeshift dressing room, a tiny space about the size of a hotel elevator, curtained off at the back of the stage. We had our first conversation that didn't involve shouting over the music.

'Why are you here?' Sophie asked, pouring me half a pint of gin.

'In Paris, or here at Madame Arthur?' I was hoping she just meant here because it was a shorter story and an easier answer.

'Here.'

'I like it,' I told Sophie. 'I feel at home. I always have a good time. I like the music because I don't know it but it sounds good. Because you are top. Because you and your friends are fantastic. You're the lesbians that saved my life.'

She poured more gin, and then the guest DJ played '*Laisse Tomber les Filles*' by France Gall, and we pushed aside the curtain, jumped off the stage, and I saw the girl with the crutch and she waved her crutch at me. Sophie got on the microphone and led a lesbian singalong, 'Laisse tomber les filles / Laisse tomber les filles / Un jour c'est toi qui pleureras'.

I fell into a routine, writing in the morning, walking in the afternoon, socialising in the evening. I found a great café to write in called Francis Labutte, just along rue Caulaincourt from Le Cépage, on the north (less touristy) side of Montmartre; a relaxed place with good background music, the kind of place I'd frequent if it was in Manchester. I went back a few times to Le Pain Quotidien too, especially after my Paris lives collided and I became friends with Soraya, the waitress who had attended Sophie's launch party.

The routines of my day created the rhythm of my life. The activities of the city around me became familiar; the kids taking their morning break in the schoolyard next to my apartment, the fishmongers at Pépone sweeping all their ice into the gutter at the end of the working day, the woman at the bottom of rue André Antoine asking me every time I passed her 'You want pussy?' (I would shake my head.)

True to the habits of a lifetime, I also began to seek out bands playing small venues. I felt porous in a way I'd forgotten how to be in Manchester; ready to absorb experiences, galleries, film screenings in old factories. I followed my passion for music and art and ideas effervescing under the surface or just breaking through.

I'd seen Joy Division playing to fewer than a hundred people in a mod club. I know that cultural significance can't be measured in big bucks, applause from the media or mass audiences. All good things start away from the spotlight, and sometimes remain that way. Why did Richey Edwards write to Big Flame? Because he understood that what they were doing was valuable, even though it was not something that you could sell to tens of thousands of people.

I spent two or three evenings every month at a venue hidden away near Porte de la Villette called Espace B. Four tables outside, a small bar in the front room, going through to where food is served – space for maybe twenty diners, although the chef clocked off by nine o'clock – and then through a corridor into the live room, holding a hundred and fifty people. At one end, a sound engineer and a tiny bar, at the other, a stage. The highlights of my visits to Espace B included seeing two Manchester-based bands, Pins and Horsebeach, and a brilliant solo set by one of my favourite French acts, La Féline.

It was illuminating but depressing to have two homes during

the Brexit campaign and the referendum vote. After Leave triumphed, it became clear that, like taking on the miners and the Iraq War, a divisive decision had been taken without a workable plan for the aftermath. Economic considerations were one thing, but the vote to Leave disappointed me on a symbolic, cultural and individual level.

The Brexit decision appeared to be part of a wider push away from the progressive causes I'd cherished when writing political polemics in *Debris* and marching with Rock Against Racism. And a world away from the communal spirit of the best dancefloors, and the sense of one nation under a groove. During the campaign, a few of my friends advanced reasons for voting Leave to do with democratic accountability, all very high-principled but, in effect, they'd lined up alongside xenophobes to create a less tolerant, more divided Britain fuelled by nostalgia and insularity.

The morning after the Leave vote, I was at Francis Labutte, as mums and dads walked the kids to school, traffic built up at the crossroads behind a bus, my diary full of music, lesbians and art-gallery openings. It was another morning sitting outside a café writing and watching the world go by, feeling embedded and content in the French capital.

One of the few times I left Paris in those months was when Ben Turner organised a meet up with Seth Troxler at Ibiza's electronic music business conference, the International Music Summit (IMS). Pete Tong was also at IMS. We talked about his record collection; some of it is stored in England, some of it is at his Los Angeles home. He asked me why I sold my records. I told him I wanted to 'resist the tyranny of things'. Pete said he'd been talking to Sasha about this (he lives in LA too).

'Does he want to resist the tyranny of things too?' I asked.

Tong said, 'No, I mean, about what to do with our record collections.'

I'd been invited by Ben to take part in an onstage event with Seth, discussing music, DJing and my collection (or, rather, *his* collection). We played 'On My Mind' by the Marine Girls as well as 'Flight' by A Certain Ratio. Seth was born the same year that I began my Haçienda residency but, when we talked about DJing, the age difference melted away; I adored his love for the music. Our conversation onstage got deep, too, which slightly freaked out the techno-boys in the audience who thought we'd be talking about Trax Records B-sides.

Later in the summer, I went to Paris for two more months, except this time on a smaller budget (I stayed in the far less posh Marcadet-Poissonniers area). By this time, Sophie's crew had got kicked out of their Thursday-night parties at Madame Arthur for taking their own bottles of gin instead of spending at the bar. We kept in touch, though – she addressed me as 'bitch' but in a voice that suggested it could be a term of endearment. She also booked me to play at a 'Kidnapping' event at a club called Wanderlust, my first set at a lesbian electro-disco party in Paris. Hundreds of exuberant people at a semi-open-air venue overlooking the river Seine. It was great being the token English heterosexual white man there.

Before my set, I was standing at the side of the stage just inside the crash barrier, and being older, taller and one of the only men there, I kept being mistaken for security. Girls kept asking me if they could dance on the stage and I smiled and allowed them up. This caused chaos and came back to bite me when it was my turn to DJ and I kept getting elbowed by the stage invaders, then someone had convulsions but they were OK. And talking of biting, I bit Sophie on the arm but she just laughed and then invited me to go to Nice with her for the weekend, by train, and meet her at the Gare de Lyon the next day at four. I was half tempted but fell asleep and missed the rendezvous. Being with the lesbians was perfect for someone who enjoys the company of women but who doesn't want pussy. Wanderlust had been a top night. I'd finished with 'I Feel Love', and it's true, I did, we all did.

32
The Bataclan,
One Year On

Soraya left Le Pain Quotidien, started DJing, and took me to see a couple of DJs called Acid Arab perform at a pop-up venue on an industrial estate somewhere at the end of a bus route. They were about to release their debut album on which the DJs – techno fans Guido Minisky and Hervé Carvalho – collaborate with Algerian and Turkish musicians, and an Israeli girl band called A-WA who combine Yemenite folk singing with electronic dance music. The Acid Arab album is called *Musique de France*.

This wasn't my last night out in Paris in 2016; I flew back there for a concert by Pete Doherty's band, a special show marking the reopening of the Bataclan. I'd been there before; it's always hot, and a bit cramped, the layout like a smaller version of the Apollo in Manchester. Soraya and I were right near the back on the ground floor, on a slightly raised area underneath the balcony behind the sound desk.

Given the circumstances, unsurprisingly, the atmosphere was highly charged and emotional. When the band took to the stage, the violin player began playing 'La Marseillaise' unaccompanied, although Pete started making attempts to join in, but it wasn't clear that he knew the words. Two showgirls arrived during 'Last of the English Roses', twisting and dancing like pissed auditionees at the Moulin Rouge. They accompanied the band for two and a half songs before being ushered off the stage.

It was chaotic; it reminded me a little of watching Happy Mondays in 1987, mesmerising, always on the edge of falling apart. But then the set leapt onto another level a minute or so into 'You're My Waterloo', when Pete's former bandmate in the Libertines, Carl Barat, bounded unannounced onto the stage to play his guitar solo. He got the biggest cheers of the night so far, and stayed onstage for another Libertines song ('Up the Bracket'). A French flag was passed to the front and unfurled; in the white middle section, someone had scrawled 'Fuck Terrorists Forever'.

Pete, wandering the stage, at one point looked at the setlist, studying it with the guitarist, but didn't seem to be able to focus his eyes enough to read the words. He seemed a little strung out; not slick nor sharp, but carefree and careless. Lyrics from a song on his most recent solo album took on extra resonance: 'The whole world is our playground / Take the night by the hand / And set it on fire again'.

He started throwing things into the audience, including a hat. He began one song and realised he didn't have a microphone because he'd just thrown that into the audience too; a roadie ran across the stage with another one. Then he chucked away his harmonica. Five minutes later he remembered he needed it.

'Can I have the harmonica back?' he asked and it came arcing out of the crowd and he caught it.

At the beginning of the second song in the encore, 'Time for Heroes', Pete threw his guitar into the crowd, and it was grabbed by someone about thirty feet from the stage. In some venues in some cities that guitar would have disappeared or been trashed, but a roadie ran out and implored the crowd to return it, and it was passed back to the stage.

I'm not head over heels in love with Pete Doherty and his slightly studied eccentricity, and it's frustrating that he loses his way in his career so often, but that night at the Bataclan was one of the best things I've attended.

Stephen Sondheim says, 'Art, in itself, is an attempt to bring order out of chaos.' I respectfully but totally disagree. That's not art; that's cutting a hedge. Pete Doherty's show at the Bataclan that evening, in all its chaotic glory, was great art that reflected what it's like to be human; often on the cusp of falling apart. Plus, in the context, an unhinged, flawed and uncontrollable performance was the perfect response to the mindset that produces ISIS or any other repressive and illiberal ideology.

The set closed with a totally brilliant 'Fuck Forever'. Sitting in a bar afterwards, on my last night in Paris for a while, Soraya thanked me for the Bataclan experience. 'A strong and beautiful night,' she called it. For everyone in the Bataclan at Pete Doherty's gig reflecting on the madness of what had happened on 13 November 2015, it was metempsychosis incarnate. You can repair, remake and reignite life. It's why I was in Paris, after all: to seek my personal rebirth. It's why there's always going to be extra depth to the work of New Order, who formed themselves out of the tragedy of Joy Division.

Joy Division and New Order were on my mind in those months, as I'd begun working with them on a project for the Manchester International Festival. It was thirty-seven years after I'd seen Joy Division at the mod club, and thirty years after I'd put words into the mouths of New Order in my first major *NME* feature. Christine Cort's colleague at MIF, the new artistic director John McGrath, had invited me to throw a few proposals at him, with a view to letting me loose on a big project. Among my ideas was a live-performance-with-a-difference by New Order.

I went to Stephen and Gillian's home and had half a conversation with the band, suggesting that quality remixers could reimagine some of the band's songs and then the band play a set of the remixes, no original versions, in an artistic, even challenging setting, not a straight music gig in a standard venue. It turned out that there was some synchronicity in the air; Manchester Art Gallery was already planning to stage an exhibition called *True Faith* exploring the enormous legacy of Joy Division and New Order visuals. The idea of including live shows would serve to emphasise that New Order were historic and iconic but still working, still creating and evolving.

I wrote notes on scraps of paper every time I met up with New Order and MIF. We looked at four potential venues; they all had merit. The band were very happy to experiment, to move away from a traditional gig. I kept calling it an 'art happening' but we didn't know what it was going to be. Art curator Mark Beasley was on board to advise on the visuals, and proposed that the conceptual artist Liam Gillick should design the staging and the overall presentation of the show, with Peter Saville a consultant on the project.

When I got back from the Pete Doherty concert, we were less than a year from the festival and, while all lines of communication were still open and a few ideas were flying around, John McGrath said that in order to progress with funding, we needed a concrete idea of what the New Order project was; preferably something that could be distilled into two sentences. He told me to chair an all-or-nothing meeting of the band, management and several MIF big cheeses. Er, OK. No pressure.

The band arrived. We dismissed all my ideas about the music and went with the one the band liked the most – to rework a load of their songs, then perform them with a synthesiser orchestra. We all agreed that the twelve synth players should be students from the Royal Northern College of Music. It was a perfect MIF thing to do – to provide a platform for young people to contribute their talent, learn about performance and have the time of their lives. It had already been decided that Joe Duddell – who had scored New Order songs for a string orchestra for some gigs in Australia – was easily the best choice to be the synth arranger and orchestra conductor.

We had a shortlist of venues, but I knew when we took the band into one of the big rooms at the old Granada TV studios they would immediately agree it was 100 per cent right, and so it turned out. The room, the size, the sightlines, the acoustics were all perfect. In addition, as Bernard pointed out, the first ever Joy Division television appearance was in one of the adjoining studios, when Tony Wilson put them on *Granada Reports*, months before Factory Records was up and running.

Plans with New Order had moved slowly but, with a deadline looming, we'd confirmed the final idea and venue. Liam Gillick began to develop the look of the stage based on some original ideas from Bernard. Then Liam and I wrote two paragraphs explaining the concept, and MIF went off and magicked up some funds, announced five shows and sold out all the tickets.

A great team was brought together and rehearsals began, and a few spin-off events discussed, including another trip to IMS. Ben Turner had been enthusiastic about me returning to Ibiza with Bernard, a year after my event with Seth, but although Bernard made the Ibiza trip I wasn't able to accompany him as it coincided with Liverpool Sound City where I was scheduled to host several onstage interviews, including one with John Cale of the Velvet Underground. But then, five weeks before the New Order shows, and just five days before Liverpool Sound City, the Manchester bombing took place at the Arena.

33

Hate Won't Tear Us Apart

I saw some social media reports of an incident at the Arena just as I was going to bed. In those first reports, nobody knew the cause of the loud bang, but the severity of the incident was clear, given the large number of ambulances and police cars in attendance.

After ninety minutes of reading speculation and guesses on Twitter and Facebook, a friend of mine posted what she'd heard from someone she knew working at the Arena that evening; a suicide bomber in the foyer of the venue had killed at least twelve people. She wouldn't have made it up. It was unbelievable, shocking and too much to 'share' or 'retweet'. I turned off my phone, but it took another two hours to fall asleep. The next day, it was the quietest school run ever. Parents holding their children's hands more tightly than usual, families walking in silence.

In the absence of any remote idea of how to process the event, or proceed with life, I stuck to my daily routine. I went out to my early morning café-bar, took some writing to do and continued my Liverpool Sound City research. I'm usually active on Facebook but I was too bewildered to know what to write. I posted some music, my favourite way of connecting, one to another. I posted Simon & Garfunkel 'The Sound of Silence' and, a few hours later, Marcel King 'Reach For Love'.

Being in the list of contacts the media gather in order to have talking heads on certain subjects, I was getting emails and phone calls asking for a reaction and to check my availability for radio and TV soundbites. This wasn't a standard music news story; the atrocity at the Arena was on another scale, something involving huge emotion. So, sitting in my favourite café-bar, I swerved almost all the invitations from broadcasters. I couldn't bring myself to do lots of talking about what had happened.

Martin Thomas used to get me DJ gigs in Dublin. His wife, Venetia, has a drive-time radio show in Ireland. I agreed to do a phone interview with her, and to do something for a fella from the BBC World Service because my son is friends with his girlfriend. To both, on air, I explained that the Arena was the softest of soft targets, that visits there are a rite of passage for young Mancunians. Raili had been there to see Beyoncé and Kylie Minogue. Jack had seen Soul II Soul and Kasabian. Those visits are often the beginning of a lifetime's love for music.

I also took a call from Tim Jonze from the *Guardian*. Tim talked about how Manchester music displays a strong sense of inclusivity. He mentioned the arms-around-shoulders singalongs shared at Oasis or Elbow gigs, and the diverse congregations that gathered on dancefloors during the late 1980s acid-house explosion. I agreed. 'Those of us from the Haçienda generation and beyond, we do have a very utopian sense of what music can do,' I said. 'We've been there and seen audiences full of people from all backgrounds. We've felt that connectivity and inclusivity.'

I told him about the time a New York DJ turned to me at the Boardwalk and said, 'You'd never get this mix of people in New York.' I explained that I didn't know what he meant at first. 'Then I looked out at the dancefloor, and there were black people, white people, students, dole-ites, fashionable types. For me that was regular. It was just what happens here.'

I'm not a spokesperson for anyone, I'm just a guy who believes the project of being human should be fuelled by talking, connecting, positivity and love. And music, of course. In fact, I was still mostly only responding to the attack by listening to music, and posting tunes on Facebook. Like 'Move On Up' by Curtis Mayfield.

The response of the people in the city was exemplary, including the emergency services, hotel staff who offered shelter to those injured and lost, and cab drivers taking distressed concert-goers across town free of charge. St Ann's Square became a sea of flowers, poems on scraps of paper and teddy bears. People of all ages were gathering there, clasping each other's hands. It was the site of a vigil three days after the attack, which included the crowd's spontaneous rendition of 'Don't Look Back in Anger'. In my neighbourhood, children, teachers and other staff from Cavendish school lined both sides of Burton Road and bowed their heads in silence.

My former 'Yellow' colleague Elliot Eastwick stepped up to begin organising a solidarity concert to raise funds for the victims. He worked with Joel Perry on this, and we all chipped in to try to secure DJs and bands; I asked DJ Mary Anne Hobbs and the band Pins, and they said 'Yes' without hesitation. Elliot's initiative was more evidence that Manchester was determined to create a collective push back against hate and division.

In the midst of all this solidarity and positivity, Morrissey waded into the situation with predictably Farage-like views. It was no surprise that he was divisive and unhelpful rather than gentle and kind. As someone once said, it takes guts to be gentle and kind.

Poet Tony Walsh had been a Haçienda regular in the mid- and late 1980s, and a Smiths fan like so many of the rest of us. He wasn't getting dragged into negativity. The poem 'This Is the Place', which he recited on the steps of the Town Hall at the official vigil following the attack, highlighted Manchester's radical politics, the city's inventiveness and resourcefulness, and the sense of unity among people; people 'born here' and also those 'drawn here'. As the newly appointed Mayor of Greater Manchester Andy Burnham said, 'I'll never forget that moment. Our darkest hour. Tony Walsh lifted people with a sense of belief. It was like a surge of electricity.'

Reporters from the radio station France Inter came to interview me. I pointed out to them that the ISIS statement following the Bataclan attack made clear their hatred of diversity and creativity, and I suggested that we should avoid exacerbating division and avoid feeding any sense of the West at war with Islam. ISIS want a world without ambiguity, a world of either/or and us/them binary choices. Their stated aim is to feed conflict and destroy the grey zone by driving the world towards polarity. An extreme response is exactly what ISIS want.

I explained that in the months after the Bataclan, I discovered alternative cultures still embedded in the Paris experience, along with joy in multiple-choice sexuality and the music of Acid Arab merging techno with sounds from Arab music traditions. In Paris, in Manchester, we should value and celebrate everything that expresses a permissive, radical, alternative spirit.

Elliot's event at the Deaf Institute sold out. I met Dan Hett there; his brother Martyn had been one of those who had died in the Arena attack. The same day, Ariane Grande hosted a huge 'One Love' concert at Old Trafford cricket ground where Liam Gallagher sang 'Live Forever'. A few days earlier Guy Garvey sang 'Wonderful World' at the Bridgewater Hall during a 'We Stand Together' concert featuring the Hallé Orchestra, the Manchester Camerata and BBC Philharmonic.

In the years of austerity, homelessness in Manchester has become a growing problem. Nineteen per cent of the adult population of the city have no qualifications, and more than a quarter of children are living in 'severe poverty'. The level of underage pregnancies is nearly twice the national average. Mental health is poor, and cuts to frontline mental health services are making a chaotic situation even worse. The riots in 2011 revealed the criminality of part of the community and the levels of alienation among some citizens.

In the response to the attack, though, Manchester was showing its best side, the best side of humanity, and its sense of positivity and community. The many of us who have had a part in the collective history of the music scene in Manchester had so many different motivations for participating. It's amazing to discover that all the efforts and entertainments and events over the last forty years have articulated so much – from joy to fear – which the rest of the world understands and connects with so deeply, but also created a reservoir of achievement and positivity the whole city can draw upon. Citizens born here, and those drawn here. ISIS picked the wrong city if they thought hate would tear us apart.

Four days after the Manchester attack, I was in Liverpool, back there to do onstage interviews with Jah Wobble, John Cale and others, but also with another task to perform. I had suggested to the Sound City organisers that during the conference I should invite delegates to observe a minute's silence. We decided to do it halfway through the day, when the conference would be at its busiest, and just before an onstage interview with the brilliant, provocative and creative Canadian electronic musician and performance artist Peaches.

So at three o'clock, Peaches and I walked on to the stage. I was intending to announce we would hold a minute's silence. I had words to say, words denouncing the attack and words honouring the victims, but I was too choked up to speak. When I wanted words, I got tears.

Peaches took the microphone from me and asked everyone to be quiet, including people at the back of the room who had just wandered in late. She thought I could get myself together.

'I can't do this,' I whispered to Peaches.

'You can,' she replied.

But I couldn't. I couldn't say all the words I had planned, all I could do was ask people to stand. Peaches put her arm around me, and we bowed our heads. Everyone in the audience stood, and was silent.

A few hours later, on the festival site, I was with Nathan and a few other friends and they all went off to find a bar without a long queue. I'm not much of a drinker, and even less of a queuer, so I just mooched about. I caught sight of Peaches wandering the site with a crew of five or six people. She saw me and came over and gave me another hug. Her friends went off to join the queue at the bar, leaving us talking, just ten yards from a stall selling various mezze including halloumi fries. I explained the appeal of halloumi fries to her, with great enthusiasm. I tried to describe the pleasures; crispy, soft, cheesy and squeaky. She seemed to like the sound of them.

'They're best squirted all over with yoghurt or harissa,' I said. 'Or maybe both?' I was amazing myself how long I could talk to Peaches about halloumi.

We wandered off together to the halloumi-fries food truck. She wanted the large portion (£8, hardly the best-value snack available, but that's festival food isn't it?). But she only had a bank card with her and her friends were some distance away in a barely moving beer queue. I told her I would treat her. Peaches ordered, got the large portion, and told the vendor, 'My sugar daddy has the cash,' and I stepped forward and paid. I had been designated Peaches's sugar daddy. I was honoured.

Then something extraordinary happened. I got this amazing message from a photographer who was at Sound City when I was onstage with Peaches. My vulnerability at the moment I had choked up had made a big impression. 'Fuck mate, if I haven't lived through that moment you had this afternoon a hundred times this week,' he told me. 'If I'd had to speak these words out loud, I'd have been exactly the same.'

He told me he thought he'd been desensitised from this type of thing. 'I almost pride myself on my emotional detachment,' he said.

He told me he'd wanted to catch me afterwards to say this: 'I've seen more than enough strong people stand up and deliver strong words this week. But I have never been more 100% with someone than I was with you on that stage. It mattered MORE to me that someone felt the same way. Big love mate.'

It's OK not to be perfect, it's OK to be flawed, it's enough just to stand up and be yourself.

34

New Order, My Heartbeat

New Order's live events at MIF were scheduled to begin five weeks after Sound City. There were rehearsals at the Royal Northern College of Music to attend and details to sort. At yet another meeting, I pointed out that, wanting the event to be different from a usual gig, we'd decided not to have a support act or a warm-up DJ; so, for an hour between the doors opening and the band performing there would be silence. I wondered; should we fill the silence with something?

All eyes on me. Someone said, 'What would you suggest, Dave?'

Words came tumbling out. 'An hour-long soundscape, just ambient weirdness, static maybe, doors opening and closing, disembodied voices, maybe the band's or Tony Wilson's. No synths, nothing to sabotage the impact of the New Order performance. Dark too, like you're in a womb, muffled sounds, a heartbeat. Yes, a heart beating.'

Someone else said, 'When can you do it by?'

'Me?'

So MIF flew me to Paris to work with Nadège; being a sound designer she knows how to layer, and give emotion and sonic depth to music. We decided to thread all the other sounds around a looped recording of my heartbeat. Bernard gave the nod to the piece – which Nadège and I called 'Breathless'.

Half an hour before the first show, the soundscape, complete with my heartbeat, was pulsing through the venue. On each of the five nights, the band played a different set, drawing from the seventeen or eighteen songs they'd nailed in rehearsals, with several featuring in all, and one or two only appearing once. Every night one of the highlights was 'Shellshock'. Bernard sings the chorus: 'The deeper you get, the sweeter the pain / Don't give up the game until your heart stops beating . . .'

I loved hearing 'Decades' and 'Vanishing Point'; the first time I heard them play 'Vanishing Point' in rehearsals took my breath away. But when they played 'Shellshock' on the opening night everything, especially the soundscape, made sense; 'Don't give up the game until your heart stops beating . . .'

I met up with Tony Wilson's son, Oli, at one of the Thursday shows; the same night Seth Troxler came too, with his mother (a big New Order fan). Seth and I had agreed we'd take the chance to DJ together, so after the MIF gig we played a benefit gig for two local mental health charities, CALM (the Campaign Against Living Miserably) and Manchester Mind. South nightclub gave us their venue for free, and we attracted a full house which included Seth's mother, my daughter, my son and Catherine. It was a family affair. Seth's mother is younger than me. She said I was her second favourite ever DJ.

The summer at MIF I finally got to meet the artist Scott

King, who had created a dot painting of the final Joy Division show, and in the aftermath of MIF, word was that there was a chance we could take the New Order show to Vienna and Turin. There was also interest in a performance of 'Breathless' live, in Berlin, and in Parma at Mauro's gallery. Plans were being laid for future involvement in Tim Peaks and Liverpool Sound City. Seth got in touch again, asking me if we could one day curate a festival together. I kept saying 'Yes' to stuff and my head was still buzzing with fanciful ideas.

Before I was due to share an evening with novelist Jay McInerney, interviewing him at Waterstones Deansgate, I sent Mr McInerney an invitation; I said that if he had time before our event, I would guide him to a couple of spots in the city that had a role to play in the Factory story.

We all have connections, but I knew we could have an especially intimate one. We shared a world. I knew he was interested in it all: Tony Wilson, Peter Saville, Factory Records. I recalled him writing about Joy Division, how he listened to their music while writing his book set in New York, *Bright Lights, Big City*. And I remember reading it at the time I'd just started DJing at the Haçienda.

We wandered around Manchester for an hour, I took him down Little Peter Street to a car park and challenged him to use his powers as a novelist to imagine there the semi-derelict warehouse where Joy Division used to rehearse, and to a block of apartments, the site of the Haçienda. At the back of the apartments, down by the canal, there's a timeline of key events in each year of the Haçienda's history.

After the Waterstones event we went for something to eat at the Italian restaurant San Carlo, which he enjoyed. He ate a plate of fancy ham, followed by lasagne and spinach ('I thought I might need something green'). We had bottles of red and half-bottles of white. He was somewhat agitated at the thought of getting up at 5.45 a.m. in the morning to get his plane to Dublin, so we agreed we'd call it a day and go get taxis sometime just after 11 o'clock.

I told him about Paris, about my attempts to rekindle my lust for life. I reminded him of a fabulous passage from his book *The Good Life*, which I'd read out earlier at the Waterstones event. He's describing people out after dark: 'Chasing through the night in their quest for the elusive heart of the city, which throbbed like a bass guitar line, just audible somewhere around the next corner, behind the next door, just ahead, down the next set of stairs.'

I like 'elusive', I told him. 'It's somewhere, the heart of the city, that late-night chase, hope . . .'

I asked him what replaces all that as you get older. He told me he eats in restaurants a lot; every night in fact, when he is in Manhattan. And there are gallery openings, dinner parties . . .

I interrupt: 'None of that is quite the same, is it?'

San Carlo was fun though. We agreed we were lucky, still on an adventure of some sort and still finding joy and inspiration in encounters with people, all kinds of people. We started talking about the Factory scene; not Wilson's Factory, this time, but Warhol's.

Jay told me he'd once had dinner with Lou Reed. It was during a literary festival in Venice. Jay recalled that just before their food was served, he'd reached for the basket of bread in the middle of the table but Lou grabbed his arm and pulled it away, shouting, 'It's poison!'

Jay was like 'What?!'

Lou pointed at the bread. 'Carbs are poison.'

Jay was laughing telling me this. He didn't mention to Lou how curious it was that after decades of alcohol destroying his liver, and cocaine abuse, and heroin, Lou finally drew the line at bread.

'The war on carbs will never be won,' I said to Jay.

He had a mouthful of lasagne. 'Indeed,' he replied, then swallowed. 'I think you're right, Dave.'

We had a funny, gossipy conversation about our mutual friend Jonathan Franzen. I talked about Morrissey (he said he was fascinated by him). We discussed my project with New Order. He'd chosen great wine. With a parting of the ways approaching, we looked at pictures of each other's kids on our phones. And declared them all beautiful.